CREATIVE WRITING

CREATIVE WRITING

Copyright © 1998, 2007 by Kimberley Nash
Published by RESURRECTION RESOURCES
Woodbury, Minnesota 55129
USA
sales@thefathersbooks.com
www.thefathersbooks.com

ISBN-13: 978-0-9792338-3-8
ISBN-10: 0-9792338-3-6

Writing and Graphics
   Kimberley Nash, B.A./B.S.
Editing
   Staff

Copyright Notice
Protected by International Copyright Treaties and United States copyright laws.
All rights reserved. No portion of this book may be copied or reproduced in any form. Electronic data retention and distribution are also prohibited. **Copyright infringement is a crime including infringement without monetary gain, such as making extra copies for your personal use or for additional students.** Criminal copyright infringement is investigated by the FBI and subject up to $250,000 in fines as well as 5 years in prison. Offenders will be prosecuted to the full extent of the law.
All pages in this book are registered under copyright law. **According to copyright law, this publication is protected for the life of the author plus 50 years after her death.** Please respect the author, editors, artists, and others, whose talents created this book for the education of your students, by obeying all copyright laws.

Scripture taken from THE SCRIPTURES, © 1998 by the Institute for Scripture Research (Pty) Ltd. Used by permission.

Printed in the United States of America.

CONTENTS
DAILY LESSON PLAN

TEACHER
    INTRODUCTION 1
    PREPARING, EDITING, CORRECTING, AND REVISING 1
    GRADING 3

STUDENT
    WORKBOOK INSTRUCTIONS 5

◆◆◆◆◆◆◆◆◆◆◆◆◆◆◆◆◆◆◆

UNIT 1: DESCRIPTION

CHAPTER
1. ETHICS SKILLS 7
    Creative Writing
    Writing Choices
    Scriptural Ethics
        Scripture Study

2. WRITING SKILLS 8
    The Art of Describing
    Mental Pictures Drawn with Words
    Descriptions with More Detail
    The Scene of a Story
    The Details of a Scene

WRITING CHART #1 16
WRITING ASSIGNMENT #1 17
WRITING WORKSHEET #1 18
WRITING PREPARATION 19

3. GRAMMAR SKILLS 20
    Grammar Rules
    Capital Letters
    Periods
    Exclamation Points
    Commas
    The Word "and"
    Verb Tense
    Sentence Length
    Paragraph Indention

WRITING CHART #2 27
WRITING ASSIGNMENT #2 28
WRITING WORKSHEET #2 29

UNIT 2: SCENE

4. ETHICS SKILLS 30
    Scriptural Ethics
        Scripture Study

5. WRITING SKILLS 31
    The Qualities of a Scene
    Development of a Scene
    Action in a Scene
    Style of Writing
WRITING CHART #3 36
WRITING ASSIGNMENT #3 37
WRITING WORKSHEET #3 38
WRITING PREPARATION 39
6. GRAMMAR SKILLS 40
    Grammar Rules
    Nouns
    Person Nouns
    Place Nouns
    Thing Nouns
    Idea Nouns
    Common and Proper Nouns
    Common and Proper Noun Pairs
    Nouns and Pronouns
WRITING CHART #4 47
WRITING ASSIGNMENT #4 48
WRITING WORKSHEET #4 49

UNIT 3: CHARACTERS

7. ETHICS SKILLS 50
    Scriptural Ethics
    Scripture Study
8. WRITING SKILLS 52
    Names for Characters
    Description of Characters' Features
    Description of Characters' Personalities and Behaviors
    Description of Characters' Clothing and Accessories
WRITING CHART #5 56
WRITING ASSIGNMENT #5 57
WRITING WORKSHEET #5 58
WRITING PREPARATION 59
9. GRAMMAR SKILLS 60
    Grammar Rules
    Adjectives
    Commas
    Verbs
    Subject/Verb Agreement in the Present Tense
    Helping Verbs
    Sentences and Fragments
    Homonyms
    Synonyms
WRITING CHART #6 68
WRITING ASSIGNMENT #6 69

WRITING WORKSHEET #6 70

UNIT 4: ACTION

10. ETHICS SKILLS 71
    Scriptural Ethics
        Scripture Study
11. WRITING SKILLS 74
    An Outdoor Event
    The Characters
    The Action
WRITING CHART #7 78
WRITING ASSIGNMENT #7 79
WRITING PREPARATION 80
12. GRAMMAR SKILLS 81
    Grammar Rules
    Subject/Verb Agreement in the Past Tense
    Past Tense Verbs with Spelling Changes
    Irregular Verbs in the Past Tense
    Similar Sentences
    Compound Subjects and Predicates
    Sentence Conjunctions
    Concise Sentences
WRITING CHART #8 88
WRITING ASSIGNMENT #8 89

UNIT 5: DIALOGUE

13. ETHICS SKILLS 90
    Scriptural Ethics
        Scripture Study
14. WRITING SKILLS 91
    Dialogue in a Story
    Creation of a Dialogue
WRITING CHART #9 93
WRITING ASSIGNMENT #9 93
WRITING PREPARATION 94
15. GRAMMAR SKILLS 95
    Grammar Rules
    Quotation Marks
    Names of Direct Address
    Interjections
WRITING CHART #10 98
WRITING ASSIGNMENT #10 99

UNIT 6: EXPLANATORY WORDS

16. ETHICS SKILLS 100
    Scriptural Ethics
        Scripture Study
17. WRITING SKILLS 102

    Creation of a Dialogue
    Explanatory Words
WRITING CHART #11 105
WRITING ASSIGNMENT #11 106
WRITING PREPARATION 107
18. GRAMMAR SKILLS 109
    Grammar Rules
    Apostrophes
    Verb Forms
    The Words "Lay" and "Lie"
    The Words "Set" and "Sit"
WRITING CHART #12 117
WRITING ASSIGNMENT #12 118

UNIT 7: PURPOSE

19. ETHICS SKILLS 119
    Scriptural Ethics
    Scripture Study
20. WRITING SKILLS 121
    Purpose in Dialogue
WRITING ASSIGNMENT #13 124
WRITING PREPARATION 125
21. GRAMMAR SKILLS 127
    Grammar Rules
    Appositives
    Colons
WRITING CHART #14 133
WRITING ASSIGNMENT #14 134
WRITING WORKSHEET #14 135

UNIT 8: PLOT

22. ETHICS SKILLS 136
    Scriptural Ethics
    Scripture Study
23. WRITING SKILLS 144
    Development of a Plot
    Realistic Action
    Development of the Action
WRITING ASSIGNMENT #15 148
24. GRAMMAR SKILLS 149
    Grammar Rules
    Hyphens
    Semicolons
    Paragraph Margins

GLOSSARY 153
INDEX 154
OTHER PRODUCTS 156

ANSWER KEY for PRACTICE EXERCISES 157
ANSWER KEY for TESTS 161
GRADING CHARTS 163
TESTS 165

DAILY LESSON PLAN

DAY 1	DAY 2	DAY 3	DAY 4	DAY 5
PP 5-6	U1/S1: C 1.1-1.2	C 1.3	C 2.1	C 2.2
C 2.3	C 2.4	C 2.5	WA #1	WA #1
WA #1	S2: PP 19	C 3.1-3.2	C 3.3-3.4	C 3.5-3.6
C 3.7-3.8	C 3.9	WA #2	WA #2	WA #2
Study for test	Test #1	U2/S3: C 4.1	C 5.1	C 5.2
C 5.3	C 5.4	WA #3	WA #3	WA #3
PP 39	C 6.1-6.2	C 6.3-6.4	C 6.5-6.6	C 6.7
C 6.8	C 6.9	WA #4	WA #4	WA #4
Study for test	Test #2	U3/S4: C 7.1	C 7.2	C 8.1
C 8.2	C 8.3	C 8.4	WA #5	WA #5
WA #5	PP 59	C 9.1-9.2	C 9.3	C 9.4
C 9.5	C 9.6	C 9.7	C 9.8-9.9	WA #6
WA #6	WA #6	Study for test	Test #3	U4/S5
C 10.1	C 10.2	C 11.1	C 11.2	C 11.3
WA #7	WA #7	WA #7	S6: PP 78	C 12.1-12.2
C 12.3-12.4	C 12.5	C 12.6	C 12.7-12.8	WA #8
WA #8	WA #8	Study for test	Test #4	U5/S7
C 13.1	C 14.1	C 14.2	WA #9	WA #9
WA #9	S8: PP 92	C 15.1-15.2	C 15.3-15.4	WA #10
WA #10	WA #10	Study for test	Test #5	U6/S9
C 16.1	C 17.1	C 17.2	WA #11	WA #11
WA #11	S10	PP 104-105	C 18.1-18.2	C 18.3
C 18.4	C 18.5	C 18.6	C 18.7	C 18.8
WA #12	WA #12	WA #12	Study for test	Test #6
U7/S11	C 19.1	C 20.1	WA #13	WA #13
WA #13	S12	PP 121-122	C 21.1-21.2	C 21.3
C 21.4	C 21.5	C 21.6	WA #14	WA #14
WA #14	Study for test	Test #7	U8/S13	C 22.1
C 22.2	C 22.3	C 23.1	C 23.2	Begin WA #15
Begin WA #15	C 24.1-24.2	C 24.3-24.4	C 24.5	C 24.6
C 24.7-24.8	Complete WA #15	Complete WA #15	Study for test	Test #8

LEGEND:
C = CHAPTER   PP = PAGES   S = SCRIPT (TEACHER'S)   U = UNIT
WA = WRITING ASSIGNMENT

INTRODUCTION
TEACHER

    This is a comprehensive, consumable textbook containing easy-to-understand graduated units that facilitate the learning of English writing and grammar. These units progress in a step-by-step learning and application process to promote the successful mastery of each basic skill studied. Each unit contains three chapters teaching ethics skills, writing skills, and grammar skills. The chapters contain multiple lessons that may be reinforced with scripture study, writing assignments, and/or **PRACTICE** exercises.

    A student who has mastered the prior educational steps of writing words, sentences, paragraphs, letters, e-mails, and book reports is ready to begin the study of creative writing compositions. The carefully written text of this book teaches the elements of this type of composition.

    Each unit encourages and guides a student to dwell on that which is good, lovely, and worthy of writing. Particular attention is given to developing healthful, scripture-honoring writing.

PREPARING, EDITING, CORRECTING, AND REVISING

HOW TO PREPARE
    The process of preparing a creative writing composition involves seven elements.

1. Deciding on a good, ethical story
2. Having good instructions to follow
3. Using a well-organized writing chart
4. Taking time to think about what will be written
5. Preparing a writing worksheet
6. Writing a carefully thought-out composition
7. Correcting and revising a composition until it not only meets the requirements of each assignment but also makes good grammatical sense

    When preparing to write and while writing, a student should work in a quiet place free of distractions. Regular homework periods will aid this fundamental part of writing. A cleared table or desk should be available with a supply of sharpened pencils, erasers, a dictionary, a thesaurus, and ample, clean paper.

HOW TO EDIT
    The best way to help the student begin learning how to edit is by showing him/her the correcting guidelines. Edit in a two-part process.

    1. Have the student check the paper to the correction guidelines without your help.

    2. Then sit next to the student and alternate editing paragraphs together. First, you read a paragraph **out loud** and, using a red pen, identify all the paragraph's mistakes. Second, have the student read the next paragraph out loud and, using a red pen, identify all of its mistakes. Continue in this manner until you have edited the complete paper.

    If you follow this process carefully, over time the student will be able to edit without your help. As you see the student progress in editing ability, you may release him/her a little at a time. To do this process, gradually have the student edit more paragraphs than you do until the student can edit completely on his/her own.

    Don't forget that reading out loud during editing is mandatory; this method is helpful because many mistakes are easier to hear than see. This fact is also why you are encouraged to read the Scriptures out loud in Deuteronomy/Debarim 31:11, "**When all Yisra'el comes to** appear before Yahweh your Elohim in the place which He chooses, read this Torah before all Yisra'el in their hearing."

HOW TO CORRECT

In the correcting phase, the teacher must be actively involved. In applying writing and grammar guidelines to a student's work, keep in mind that correction can at times be stressful and frustrating. When this situation occurs, slow down and take a break.

Many students do enjoy the learning/writing process to the extent that teacher frustrations may be minimal. Difficulties with students who are reluctant writers may be reduced by remembering that learning to write is a process that occurs through the writing of many compositions. Mistakes will gradually decrease if the teacher is patient and kind.

Each writing assignment in this book has a checklist and a grading chart. Some assignments include a writing chart and a writing worksheet. Normally, only the final composition is corrected and graded. However, when a student is first starting out in UNITS 1 and 2, you may choose to correct a first or second draft according to the grading chart guidelines. After correcting, discuss in a clear, positive process any misunderstandings or corrections pertaining to writing skills. Correcting procedures are located in the teacher's manual.

HOW TO DISCUSS CORRECTIONS

Your approach should always be kind and gentle so that a student's feelings are not hurt to the point that he/she feels too criticized and shuts down. Thinking of creative and encouraging ways to approach correction is always a challenge but worth the time spent as this process will help you grow in maturing wisdom. Here are a few examples of correction dialogue.

1. **When a student's writing is too simplistic**, try this approach. If a student turns in a composition with the simple sentence, "The day was nice," ask the student thinking questions like these: "This is an interesting sentence, Joey/Sally. I can understand from it that the day was nice. Why was it nice? What happened to make the day nice? What was the weather like?"

After he/she answers these questions, tell the student to go back and add these other interesting details to the sentence so that a reader can understand in more depth what made the day nice.

2. **When many errors in punctuation occur** throughout the composition, don't just point out errors. Try reading through the composition with the student to discover what correct punctuation is required.

♦If a period is missing, ask the student where the end of a particular sentence is located. By considering this question, a student will usually realize that the period is missing and will be able to correct the mistake. If, however, the student can show where the end of a sentence is, but he/she still does not know how to punctuate it, ask this question: "What kind of punctuation do you think should go at the end of this sentence? Does this sentence make a statement? What kind of punctuation is used at the end of a sentence that is a statement?"

♦If a sentence needs a question mark, read through the sentence together and help the student to recognize that the sentence is asking a question. Then ask this question: "What kind of punctuation mark belongs at the end of a sentence asking a question?"

♦For a missing exclamation mark, read the sentence together and ask the student if the sentence contains excitement or great enthusiasm. Then ask this question: "What kind of punctuation mark indicates excitement or enthusiasm?"

3. **With paragraph formation, if the paragraph contains unrelated sentences**, read through it with the student and talk about each sentence separately. Identify which sentences are written about the same thing and are related to one another. Label the sentences that belong together in the order they should be rewritten. When sentences that belong together in one paragraph are mixed with the sentences of another paragraph, use numbers (1, 2, 3,...)

for sentences that should occur in the first paragraph, and use letters (a, b, c,...) for sentences that should occur in the second paragraph.

    4. **Do not help a student with spelling errors**; instead, help him/her learn to navigate the dictionary. If you are not careful in this respect, you will become the student's dictionary. Simply ask the student to take a look in the dictionary to see if there is a difference between his/her spelling and the dictionary spelling.

    5. **If the variety in sentences is not adequate**, the best approach is to write on the chalkboard several examples of a variety of sentences that you have created. Make sure they are related in subject but different in both length and content. Here are some examples.

- The day was nice.
- The sky was blue, and the weather was warm.
- Overhead the clouds looked like soft, floating pillows.
- My friends and I were going to ride our bikes to the old Bernard farm.
- We had been looking forward to visiting Tommy Bernard all week.

HOW TO REVISE

Revising a corrected paper is always necessary to learn good writing. Rewriting reinforces correct writing while helping a student to recognize his/her mistakes and break any pattern of mistakes. Explain that this process is very important for preparing a well-done composition. Require a student to rewrite and resubmit the composition to you for further review and/or correction as many times as necessary to achieve a well-written paper. If the composition has to be rewritten several times while the student is learning to be a careful writer, be patient.

FINAL NOTES

    1. After a student edits and revises, but before he/she submits the final composition, you should encourage him/her to read it out loud to a parent. This task will help the student hear whether the composition makes sense--and maybe even receive some well-deserved praise.

    2. This book includes original Hebrew names, such as the one for God (Yahweh), Jesus (Yahshua), and the Holy Spirit (Ruach Hakodesh).

PRONUNCIATION

Yahweh	say	YAH way	**Yahshua**	say	Yah SHOE uh
Ruach	say	RUE ahch	**Hakodesh**	say	ha KO (as in "go") desh

GRADING

The **GRADING CHARTS** are located at the back of this book to assist in the process of grading a student's compositions. Cut out these pages, write the student's name on the first page, and then staple all of the charts for that student together.

For each composition, review the applicable **GRADING CHART**; then follow the chart to determine a percentage for each grading item. Next, total all of the percentages and divide by the number noted on the **TOTAL** line. A percentage scale and grading guide are offered in the notes below each grading chart.

Do not push a student to get high grades just for the sake of pride. Grades should be viewed by both teacher and pupil as an important measure in helping a student desire to try harder and in seeing his/her progress. A teacher who has had a bad experience with grades in his/her own school years should seek Jesus/Yahshua for healing over that experience. This healing will free the teacher to make grading a positive experience for his/her students. In a classroom with a totally different environment and a different teacher or parent, grades can be a positive, helpful, and motivational tool when employed with the right attitude.

Please note the **CREATIVITY** boxes on the **GRADING CHART** as they deal with the imagination and reality of the composition. A good creative writing project involves imagination, reality, and inventiveness. Reality, however, must be the first thing considered when writing a story. While a story can be made up, it must be realistic. When a student makes up a story, imagination and inventiveness can be employed as long as what is created is realistic. The student should consider whether what is written is truly something that could or has happened in reality. A student should absolutely not write about stories, characters, and settings that are fantasies. The scriptures are very clear about the types of thinking that are healthy for a student and others. These are the scriptures about which a student will be learning in the **Scriptural Ethics** sections of this book. For believing Christians, these sections should not only cause a student to be careful about what types of writing to read, but also should translate into what a student presents to others in writing.

Fantasy is a mode of thinking that is not truthful. Many in today's society have succumbed to mental illness, distorted/sinful behavior, and irrational thinking as a result of fantasy writing, fantasy role-playing, fantasy movies, and other forms of fantasy entertainment. Fantasy is especially dangerous when it is presented to children (ages 0-12) who are in the concrete-only phase of their minds' development. While these children can role play or make believe about something that they have experienced in reality, such as a friend, they cannot process what is not a concrete reality in their everyday life. From exposure to fantasy stories, these children often develop nightmares, especially when the characters are evil, sinful, or destructive.

In this book, a student will learn scriptural wisdom and ethical values that will not only benefit and train him/her in creating healthy writing, but also help with other healthy life choices. What is learned will also aid in guarding one's mind from sinful values, sinful characters, sinful behaviors, and sinful beliefs.

When writing, a student must remember the reader. Stories with sinful behavior will confuse the reader and lead that person away from Jesus/Yahshua. Stories with sinful behavior expose a reader to wrong role-models and teach that person incorrect ways of interacting with others. Writing stories filled with sin is not healthy. God/Yahweh dislikes this type of writing.

Contrary to what many may think, too much writing and reading about evil does not cause a person to turn from that evil, but actually causes the reverse. Too much writing or reading about sin erodes a person's goodness and places thoughts in that person's mind, thereby causing him/her to give in to evil. If a person's mind becomes filled with sin in this way, that person will spend a lifetime struggling against evil thoughts, which may even become evil actions (a truly pitiful way to live).

Any story a student writes that contains even the smallest amount of sin **should clearly explain that the sin is wrong** and **should clearly correct the sin** somewhere in its contents. Do not allow the writing of stories that contain sin for the purpose of **entertaining, thrilling,** and **convincing others that to participate in sin is permissible**.

Help a student to be careful in story choices and remember that even in Christian circles, there are stories that contain large amounts of sin. These stories may even be presented as "good to read" by people who do not honor scriptural truth, do not know scriptural truth, or desire to profit from the buying of their writing. Please help a student learn from this book about what Jesus/Yahshua truly wants Christians to write. What is learned may cause some serious soul-searching. A student may need to learn to reject story ideas, values, and topics that he/she previously learned were good or fun, but their teaching really wasn't according to scripture.

As long as sin sells, publishers will continue to fill bookstores with such writing. When this cycle continues, there often occurs a shortage of good, clean, wholesome, scriptural stories for everyone to read.

TEXTBOOK INSTRUCTIONS   STUDENT

WORKBOOK FORMAT

A workbook format is the best way to learn writing and grammar skills. The "hands-on" format causes you to actively participate in the learning process, which increases your ability to learn and remember what you have learned. Our special step-by-step approach, along with writing assignments and **PRACTICE** exercises, help you to master each writing skill and grammar skill you will use in your creative writing compositions. Using these skills will reinforce what you have learned.

A workbook format not only provides a complete record of your learning progress but also has many other benefits. The workbook format is a treasure of all your hard work and progress. The completed workbook may also be helpful for home school/private school credits or in reviews when samples of your work or course of study must be provided to an official agency. Finally, this workbook will be most helpful for any higher grade level, including college, to review when writing your more creative writing compositions assigned in another class.

STUDENT INSTRUCTIONS

This textbook is **only** helpful when it is completed in order and through the last page. Completing **all** the chapters in each unit is also important. Do not skip around in this textbook, or you will not master the course nor obtain the desired results.

Each unit in this textbook contains two writing assignments. By completing multiple writing assignments of the same type, you will be able to remember how to write a creative writing composition better. This repetition is important because when the time between repeating a task is too long, the memory of how to perform that task can be forgotten. The result of forgetting is that your time is wasted and the task will need to be learned again.

Additionally, the writing assignments in each unit build your story writing skills in a step-by-step process. You will first learn describing and then dialogue before you learn how to put them together in a story. By using this method, when you come to your final compositions you will be able to write them with a good degree of success.

SCRIPTURAL ETHICS

Each unit begins with a chapter titled **ETHICS SKILLS**. This chapter contains scriptures you must look up, write out, or study. These scriptures will help you decide how to prepare a composition that will honor and please the Messiah.

Use what you learn to create each of your compositions so that they contain the healthy family values in the scriptures. This study will help you remember scriptural wisdom and ethics that will not only benefit and train you in making healthy writing choices, but also help you in other healthy life choices. What you learn will also aid you to guard your mind from sinful values, sinful characters, sinful behaviors, and sinful beliefs.

As you grow older, you will continue to learn about sin, but there is always harm in writing or reading about sin because it will confuse you, lead you away from the Messiah, expose you to wrong role models, and teach incorrect ways for you to interact with others. Continuing on a regular basis to write compositions filled with sin, or allowing your writing to tempt you into sin, is not healthy, nor does your Heavenly Father desire this activity for you.

Contrary to what many may think, writing evil compositions does not cause you to turn from that evil, but actually causes the reverse. Writing sinful compositions causes giving in to evil by eroding your goodness and placing thoughts in your mind that cannot be removed. If you mind becomes filled with sin in this way, you will spend a lifetime struggling against evil thoughts, which may even become evil actions (a truly pitiful way to live).

We suggest that any composition containing even the smallest amount of sin **should**

clearly explain that the sin is wrong and clearly correct the sin somewhere in its contents. We also suggest that you should learn about sin only in books such as a dictionary that defines a word, a ministry book that teaches about right and wrong, or The Scriptures. **Avoid** writing sinful compositions for the purpose of **entertaining, thrilling,** and **convincing others that to participate in sin is permissible**.

Be careful in your writing choices and remember that even in Christian circles, there are writings that contain large amounts of sin. These writings may even be presented to you as "good to read" by people who do not honor scriptural truth, do not know scriptural truth, or desire to profit from your buying their writing. Please be willing to learn from this textbook what the Messiah truly wants you to write. What you learn may cause you to do some serious soul-searching. You may need to learn to reject ideas, values, and topics for writing that you learned were good or fun, but their teaching really wasn't according to scripture. As long as sin sells, publishers will continue to fill bookstores with such writing. When this cycle continues, there often occurs a shortage of good, clean, wholesome, scriptural writing for you to read.

WRITING TOPICS

Each unit contains specific topics about which to write. Do not change the topics to write about something else. These topics were chosen to guide you in developing healthy writing.

PLAGIARISM

When writing the paragraphs of a composition, you must always try to write **in your own words**. You must never copy the exact words from a sentence, phrase, or paragraph from someone else's writing. When you do this copying, you are committing the sin of stealing. This sin is also named **plagiarism**. It means that you have taken the exact words that someone else wrote and have used them as your own in your writing. Never do this sin in any writing; always write using your own words.

In this textbook, examples of writing are sometimes given before a writing assignment to help you understand the type of writing that is required. Do not copy the style of the writing or the type of story, either. Each person has their own unique style for writing. Instead of mimicking someone else's writing, work on developing your own individual style. This will help you to have a voice in writing that is all your own.

GRADES

When your teacher grades your compositions, he/she will use a standard grading chart. For each unit you are provided with a check-off list on the **WRITING ASSIGNMENT** pages. Use this list to check and correct your work before giving your compositions to your teacher.

FUTURE BENEFITS

This textbook is a keepsake of your education and development in writing creative compositions. Your textbook will be helpful for you to review when, in any higher grade level, you are required to write a creative writing composition.

SYMBOLS AND NAMES

When the text of this textbook instructs you to do written work on another page, the instructions will begin with a "pencil symbol" as a visual clue. The pencil will be located to the left of those instructions. Follow the instructions next to each pencil carefully.

This textbook includes the Hebrew names for God (Yahweh), Jesus (Yahshua), and the Holy Spirit (Ruach Hakodesh) because they are their true names.

PRONUNCIATION

Yahweh	say	YAH way	**Yahshua**	say	Yah SHOE uh
Ruach	say	RUE ahch	**Hakodesh**	say	ha KO (as in "go") desh

DESCRIPTION: ETHICS SKILLS

UNIT 1
SUPPLIES

BIBLE
COLORED PENCILS
green
brown
blue
DICTIONARY
HIGHLIGHTER
PENCIL
WRITING PAPER

1.1 Creative Writing

Creative writing is fun! The art of creative writing uses many different English skills to create something that is good to read. In this textbook, each skill is taught very carefully one at a time. For each skill, different types of written exercises are required to reinforce this teaching. As you work through these exercises, you will record information that will help you plan a good composition.

This textbook will teach you good grammar and how to write a good story. To learn how to write a story, you must learn how to describe, how to write dialogue, and how to put these two elements together into a story with a purpose. Two writing compositions will be assigned during the course of each unit. The amount of writing required will at first be simple but will increase as you learn more about how to write the different elements of a story.

1.2 Writing Choices

A good creative writing project involves imagination, reality, and inventiveness. Reality, however, must be the first thing you think about when writing a story. While a story can be made up, it must be realistic. When you make up a story, you can use your imagination and inventiveness as long as what you create is realistic. Ask yourself if what you have written is truly something that could happen or has happened in reality. What you should absolutely not write about are stories, characters, and scenes that are fantasies. The Bible is very clear about the types of thinking that are healthy for yourself and others. It contains scriptures that you will be learning about in the **ETHICS SKILLS** chapters of this textbook. As a believing Christian, these scriptures not only should cause you to be careful about what types of writing you read but also should translate into what you present to others in writing.

Fantasy is a mode of thinking that is not truthful. As a result of fantasy writing, fantasy role-playing, fantasy movies, and other forms of fantasy entertainment, many in today's society have succumbed to mental illness, distorted and sinful behavior, and irrational thinking. Fantasy is especially dangerous when it is presented to children (ages 0-12), who are in the concrete-only phase of their minds' development. These children can role-play or make-believe about something with which they have had experience in reality, such as a friend; however, they cannot process what is not a concrete reality in their everyday lives. From exposure to fantasy stories, these children often develop nightmares - especially when the characters are evil, sinful, and destructive.

1.3 Scriptural Ethics

Each unit in this textbook begins with a chapter titled **ETHICS SKILLS**. This chapter contains scriptures you must look up, write out, or study. These scriptures will help you decide how to prepare a composition that will honor and please Jesus/Yahshua. You will learn scriptural wisdom and ethical values that will not only benefit and train you in creating healthy writing but also help you in other healthy life choices. What you learn will aid you to guard your mind from sinful values, sinful characters, sinful behaviors, and sinful beliefs.

As you write, you must remember your reader. Stories with sinful behavior will confuse your reader and lead that person away from Jesus. Stories with sinful behavior expose a reader to wrong role models and teach that person incorrect ways to interact with others. Writing stories filled with sin is not healthy, nor does God/Yahweh desire this type of writing.

Contrary to what many may think, writing evil compositions does not cause a person to turn from that evil but actually causes the reverse. Writing sinful compositions causes giving in to evil by eroding a student's goodness and placing thoughts in his/her mind that cannot be removed. When a mind becomes filled with sin in this way, a lifetime can be spent struggling against evil thoughts, which may even become evil actions (a truly pitiful way to live).

Any story you write containing even the smallest amount of sin **should clearly explain that the sin is wrong** and **clearly correct the sin** somewhere in its contents. Do not write stories that contain sin for the purpose of **entertaining, thrilling,** and **convincing others that to participate in sin is permissible**.

Be careful in your story choices and remember that even in Christian circles, there are stories that contain large amounts of sin. These stories may even be presented to you as "good to read" by people who do not honor scriptural truth, do not know scriptural truth, or desire to profit from your buying their writing. Please be willing to learn from this textbook about what Jesus/Yahshua truly wants you to write. What you learn may cause you to do some serious soul-searching. You may need to learn to reject story ideas, values, and topics that you learned were good or fun, but their teaching really wasn't according to scripture.

As long as sin sells, publishers will continue to fill bookstores with such writing. When this cycle continues, there often occurs a shortage of good, clean, wholesome, scriptural stories for everyone to read.

Scripture Study

Find the following verse in a Bible. Write it on the lines provided. It will help you learn **good** things about which to write.

YOUR WRITING SHOULD **PROMOTE** THESE VALUES.

Philippians 4:8 _____
_____
_____
_____

This scripture tells you eight values that are good topics about which to think and write. Thinking about those eight values will help you with writing your first two compositions in this unit. Write the eight values on the following lines. The first one is done for you.

1. <u>true</u>
2. _____
3. _____
4. _____

5. _____
6. _____
7. _____
8. _____

CHAPTER 2

DESCRIPTION: WRITING SKILLS

2.1 The Art of Describing

The first English writing skill about which you will learn is how to **describe**. Describing is very important to creative writing. Your ability to describe can make a composition fun and interesting or dull and boring. In this chapter, you will learn how to describe a water scene. There are many places where water can be found. Additionally, there are many types of bodies of water that you could name. There are also many objects that can be described in and around a body of water. To write about a water scene, you need to be able to describe the water and whatever objects surround the water. To try to describe the body of water and all of the objects that might surround it can seem like a large, overwhelming project. However, by working on one description at a time, a large project can be simplified and made manageable.

In this textbook, you will learn how to develop each description a little at a time so that the work of writing does not become too much for you. The work of describing will be manageable, and your descriptive writing will improve if you start by asking yourself questions about the things that you want to describe. When beginning to write about a water scene, the easiest way to begin is to ask yourself the question: "In what types of places might water be found?" Think through this question's answers for a minute or two; then list at least six of those water places in this box. Write one water place after each diamond.

```
┌─────────────────────────────────────────────────────┐
│           PLACES WHERE WATER IS FOUND               │
│  ◆ lake                                             │
│  ◆ _____    ◆ _____       │
│  ◆ _____    ◆ _____       │
│  ◆ _____    ◆ _____       │
└─────────────────────────────────────────────────────┘
```

Which one of the places in the box is your favorite body of water? Mark your favorite body of water with your highlighter.

Next, turn to page 16. Notice that it contains several empty boxes and spaces. At various times during this lesson, you will be instructed to write information in these boxes and spaces that will help you write your composition. Each time you are to write on this page, you will be instructed in the text of this lesson. The instructions will begin with a pencil symbol as a visual clue. The following is your first set of instructions of this type. Notice that the instructions have the pencil symbol located along the left-hand margin. Please follow the instructions next to the pencil carefully; then return to this page and continue with the lesson.

✎ Turn to page 16 and write the word **LAKE** in the box under the words **WRITING CHART #1**.

In this chapter, the word **description** has been used many times. Do you know what the word description means? Find the word **description** in the dictionary and write several of the definitions on the following lines.

Description:_____

_____

Did you find from your dictionary search that a description is the "art of using words to draw a mental picture"? Have you ever used words to draw a mental picture before? Do you think that drawing a mental picture simply by the use of words is possible?

2.2 Mental Pictures Drawn with Words

You live in a world of visual stimuli. Everywhere around you are things to see, pictures to view, signs to read, and movies and television programs to watch. In fact, because your world is so visual, most people are better at understanding a visual representation of something than at interpreting any other form of presentation. These forms of visual stimuli were not created with just words, but mainly with pen, pencil, paint, computer graphics, and other forms of tangible mediums. How then can a mental picture be drawn using just words?

Words are powerful! They can be used to describe something so that a person can see in his/her mind a picture of the thing described, just by hearing or reading those words. How is this "word picture-making" done? Can anyone draw a picture in someone else's mind? Is this picture-making hard to do? The answer to all of these questions is that word pictures are so easy to create, anyone can come up with at least one simple word picture because word picture association is the first and simplest way everyone learns vocabulary.

Have you ever tried to teach a toddler a new word by pointing at something like a bike and saying the word **bike** as you did this? What happened? Did the toddler look at the bike and hear the word bike? If he/she did, almost instantaneously the toddler's mind was seeing a picture of the bike sent there by his/her eyes and was processing the word bike that was heard by his/her ears. If this method of teaching was repeated several times, the toddler's mind would begin regularly to associate the word bike with the picture of the bike seen in his/her mind. From then on, these two pieces of information would be linked together and stored in the toddler's mind so that whenever someone mentioned the word bike, the toddler would be able to recall the picture of the bike in his/her mind.

By pointing at something and stating its name, a person learns. When beginning to learn about describing, you can use the results of this simple form of learning to make word pictures. How is this process done?

Everything on earth that man has encountered has been given a name. In the beginning, God brought all of the livestock, beasts, and birds to Adam, "**to see what he would call them and whatever the man called each living creature, that was its name.**" (Bereshith/Genesis 2:19-20) Later, other things were given names by other people, but all of those names have something in common in that they represent the simplest way to identify and describe. Names of things are words that help to describe.

Look at the picture on the right. What do you see in the picture? On the following lines, write the names of the objects you see in the picture next to their corresponding number.

1._____
2._____
3._____

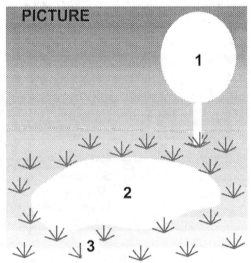

Congratulations! By using identifying names for what you saw in the picture, you created three descriptions. Wasn't that easy?

Now look at the name you wrote on line #1. Did you write the word **tree**? If the word tree was used in writing a phrase or a sentence, would you see a picture of a tree in your mind when you read that word?

Read this sentence: **I like that tree.**

When you read the sentence, did you see a picture of a tree in your mind, or could you easily make your mind see a picture of a tree? Tree is a name for an **object**; it is also a word that names an object so that you can see it in your mind. An object is a person or material thing that can be seen or touched. With creative writing, the gap between seeing an object in the world and seeing that object in your mind is bridged by **using words that name**. The sentence **I like that tree** uses the name word tree, which is also a word that helps a description. Because this sentence uses a naming word, it is a good basic describing sentence.

Turn to page 16; find the three boxes below the **DESCRIPTION WORDS** box. From the above picture, write one object name in each of the these boxes in this order: **tree, lake, grass**.

Each one of the names tree, lake, and grass is a description word for an object. The word tree helps you to see a tree in your mind because you know what at least one tree looks like. If you have ever seen a lake in real life or in a picture, your mind can recall what it looked like. Similarly, the word grass causes your mind to remember what it looks like, too. Each one of the words tree, lake, and grass is capable of helping you see a simple picture in your mind. Each word is simple but useful in creative writing because each word can create a simple word picture. Now that you understand simple word pictures, try to create six more. First, think of the names of objects that create the most visual pictures in your mind; then write those names on the following lines.

1._____ 4._____
2._____ 5._____
3._____ 6._____

2.3 Descriptions with More Detail

Whenever you are attempting to write creatively, simple word pictures are the first descriptions on which to work. However, creative writing is most often about describing in more detail. For instance, there are many kinds of trees in the world that come in all types of sizes, shapes, colors, and textures. By using just the word tree in a sentence (I like trees.), a reader will not necessarily know all that he/she needs to know to see a complete picture of that tree.

If you look at the black and white objects in the picture box on page 10, you might notice that there is something not quite realistic about the picture. In fact, it seems to be missing something. What might it be missing that could make the objects in it look more real? How about color? Would the picture look better if it had colors? Answer the following questions by writing your responses on the lines provided.

1. What color would you use to describe the wood of the **tree** in the picture?_____
2. What color would you use to describe the **lake** in the picture?_____
3. What color would you use to describe the **grass** in the picture?_____

You may have answered the three questions above by using the **color** words **brown**, **blue**, and **green** respectively, or you may have chosen other color words. Whatever you chose, turn to page 16, and write your color words in the color column under each object word. Your chart is correct if you wrote your color for the tree in the correct color column under the box with the word tree, your color for the lake in the color column under the box with the word lake, etc.

Now that you have written your color words under each column, ask yourself this question: "Do the color words brown, blue, and green help you to see each object better in your mind?" Color words are describing words. They help to define what an object looks like in more detail so that you can draw a better picture of that object in the mind of someone who reads your writing.

Lesson 2.2 began by identifying the names for objects in a picture. One of those names was the word tree. Next, the lesson identified a good, simple sentence that described, as being the sentence: I like that tree. This sentence contains the object tree that makes a word picture. If a color word is added to that sentence, it would improve the descriptive quality of the sentence. The sentence **I like that brown tree** is more descriptive because the word brown adds more detail. The word brown also makes the tree more realistic. Thus, the color brown gives more detail about a tree so that the sentence draws a better picture in your reader's mind.

There are other types of words that can be used to describe a tree. To determine these words, you need to think about what a tree looks like. Think about the different parts of a tree. One of the most noticeable parts you may think of first is the leaves. The leaves of a tree are something that you can readily imagine in your mind. You have seen them in your daily life at various times of the year. They appear in many colors during different seasons. The word leaves, however, is not a color word, is it? The word leaves is an object word.

You have learned that object words help a description. If the word leaves is added to the sentence I like that brown tree, you will be helped to see that tree in your mind better. The sentence "I like that brown tree with **leaves**" gives you more information about the tree so that you can see it better in your mind. If you can "see" the tree better, so can someone who reads your writing. More object words add more detail to your writing.

 Turn to page 16 and find the **OBJECT** column that contains the word tree. Write the word leaves under the word tree. In the picture on page 10, use your pencil to draw several leaves on the tree.

Object words and color words are words that add more detail to your writing. Now that you have added more detail to your writing by using the object word leaves, turn to the picture on page 10. What color might you add to the leaves to make that picture seem more realistic? If the season is spring or summer, you would color them green. If you added the word green to the sentence I like that brown tree with leaves, where would you add the word green? A good place to insert the word green would be before the word leaves. This sentence would be written as shown here.

I like that brown tree with **green** leaves.

Does this sentence help you to see a better picture of the tree in your mind? Try to memorize the sentence and say it to yourself out loud with your eyes closed. See if you can visualize in your mind the tree and the leaves on the tree when you are repeating the sentence. Can you also see the color of the leaves and the color of the tree? If you have difficulty memorizing, have someone read the sentence to you while your eyes are closed.

On page 10, color the leaves on the tree green. How does your tree look now? Does it look more realistic? Next, turn to page 16 and write the word green in the **COLOR** column next to the word **leaves.**

Each object word that names something, like leaves and tree, draws a picture. Color words, like green and brown, also add to a picture. All of these words improve a mental picture description because they help you to see a picture not with your eyes, but in your mind. This mental picture is a goal of descriptive writing.

On page 10, look at the picture of the water scene. Are there other types of words that might help you describe the objects in the picture? Do **size** words like **big, little, tiny, small,** and **huge** describe objects better? Are there any other size words that you could add to this list?

Which size words would you use to describe the tree in the picture? Are there any special size words you would use to describe the lake or the grass in the picture? What size words would you use to describe the leaves in the picture? Write your answer to each of these three questions on the lines provided here.

1. Tree:_____
2. Lake:_____
3. Grass:_____

4. Leaves:_____

Turn to page 16. Locate the word tree and write #1's size words in the column titled **SIZE**. Then locate the words for lake and grass, and write your size words in their **SIZE** columns. Finally, locate the word leaves and write your size words in its column for **SIZE**.

You can continue to add more details to your writing by describing more of an object with words about its color and size. Every object is either a small or large part of a scene. When a writer writes, he/she must choose what objects to describe and what ones are not necessary to describe. Thus, a scene may only have a few objects in it that a writer can describe in great detail or many objects that are described only briefly.

2.4 The Scene of a Story

The next important element about which you will learn in descriptive writing is named the **scene**. The **scene** of a story is the setting of the story and often a place of action. A story may contain one scene or a series of scenes. Each scene of a story, unlike a flat picture on a wall, has the third dimension of depth. A scene may also contain moving and non-moving objects. A flat scene is what you encountered in the picture on page 10 and described as you worked your way through the past three lessons.

A scene is the setting of a story. When you describe a scene, you want to create one that has depth and possibly action. You describe your scene so that a reader can picture it in his/her mind. How you write this description is not really very hard; the process just takes several steps. First, close your eyes and turn around in your chair; then open your eyes. What do you see? A scene very simply is what you see when you open your eyes. A three-dimensional scene is what you are looking at now; it has depth, and it is not flat. Depth is sometimes hard to describe, but moving objects within a scene are not.

In a story, you want to create three-dimensional scenes for your reader because they depict reality. A black-and-white picture of a lake, tree, and grass is a flat picture, but when leaves and color are added, depth is created. For your first composition, the scene on which you will work will have depth. For your second composition, you will learn how to make that scene have not only depth but also action. Your assignment for both compositions will be to write a description of a scene about your favorite body of water.

Now is the time to begin your first composition. You will write about a scene in which nothing is moving. This scene will not be like a picture on a wall; there will be depth. To help you know how to create depth, you learned to develop the description of a scene with a lake, tree, and grass. Now you will begin to work on writing about the body of water that you chose as your favorite place on page 9.

If a scene only contained a lake, would it be interesting? Would a picture be interesting if it contained a lake and nothing else? The answer to both of these questions is **no**. A scene, like a well-painted picture on a wall, often contains many more objects. When describing a scene, if you include more of those objects, then your writing will be more interesting because you will be helping your reader to visualize that scene better in his/her mind.

Remember the picture on page 10? With that picture, you learned to describe the tree, the lake, and the grass. There are many other objects that you might describe that could be in a lake scene. Some other ideas might be to describe the sky with its weather, people with their children, a road with its cars, or a house with a barn. The possibilities of what might appear in a scene are many. However, to create a really good scene, a description must make sense by being realistic. To be realistic, a scene must be created that looks like what you might see any day of the week when you live your daily life.

Once you have decided about which realistic water scene you would like to write, you must decide what other objects you will have in your water scene. Perhaps you will decide to have a lake, trees, flowers, and clouds in your scene. On the other hand, maybe you will have a river, a bridge, and snow in your scene. Other ideas would be to have a road, rocks, cars, and the sun in your scene. Whatever you decide to include, you must first think about your scene and write down some of the objects that you think might make your scene interesting.

On the following lines, write some of your ideas about what objects might be interesting in your water scene.

1._____ 5._____
2._____ 6._____
3._____ 7._____
4._____ 8._____

Now is the time to create a new chart for your first creative writing composition. Turn to page 16. Look at the bottom half of the page. In the box above the **DESCRIPTION WORDS** box, write the **name of your favorite body of water** that you marked with your highlighter on page 9. From your list above, choose your three favorite objects you think might make your scene interesting. Below the **DESCRIPTION WORDS** box are three smaller boxes. Write one name in each box for your three favorite objects.

2.5 The Details of a Scene

You are almost ready to write your first creative writing composition. In Lesson 2.4, you identified your favorite water scene and identified three of the objects that you want to write about in your water scene. Today, you must give more information about the objects you recorded in the boxes on page 16.

What describing words can you use to tell about each object so that your reader will be able to see a better picture in his/her mind of your favorite water scene? Remember that you have learned about how color and size words help to make a good mental picture. Take a few minutes to think about your objects. Think about what might be the colors or sizes of those objects. Then write those colors and sizes in the correct columns under the object boxes.

The objects that you wrote in your boxes may have more objects that go with them, just like our tree had leaves in Lesson 2.3. For new objects that go with one of your box's objects, write their names in the **OBJECT** column under the box to which they belong. Next, take some time to think about the colors and sizes of those new objects. Once you have decided on the colors and sizes of the new objects, write them in the **COLOR** and **SIZE** columns next to the names of the new objects.

You may also want to add some objects to your water scene that are not in your boxes or related to your boxes. These types of objects might include a road, a car, a house, a barn, an animal, or other items. For all of these types of non-related objects, write their names in the three columns that appear below the horizontal dotted line. Take some time to think about the colors and sizes of these non-related objects. Once you have decided on the colors and sizes, write them in the **COLOR** and **SIZE** columns next to the names of the objects.

Look at your chart. It contains a lot of good object words and describing words. Using these words, you are going to write sentences that describe the objects in your favorite water scene. To help you get started, suppose you are writing about a lake. The lake scene has flowers. Some of the flowers are tall, and some are short. The flowers are also colored purple or white. Here are two examples of sentences that could be written about the flowers and the lake.

Many tall and short, purple and white, wildflowers surround a large lake.
A clump of slender, tall, white daisies can be seen on the grassy shore of the lake.

Now is the time for you to try to write some sentences about the objects in your water scene. Use the writing worksheet on page 18. Try to write six to eight sentences about the objects in your picture.

After you have written your sentences, you will need to group them together into paragraphs. A paragraph is a grouping of sentences that make sense and have some logical relationship to one another. Sentences in a paragraph should either relate by topic or follow a logical sequence.

The **topic** of a paragraph is the one idea or subject about which all of the sentences in the paragraph are written. For instance, a one-topic paragraph about dolphins would focus only on dolphins and could explain their size, shape, color, and eating habits. However, this paragraph would not include boats on the sea nearby or birds flying overhead.

A paragraph that has sentences that follow a logical sequence **can** have boats and birds along with dolphins if you are describing how they are all located with respect to one another. You could also describe what all of these things are doing together.

When you write paragraphs for this lesson, you will first write all of the sentences you want to write about your water scene. Next, choose the sentences you like the most; group all of the related sentences together carefully. Your paragraphs should contain sentences that are about only one topic, or the sentences must relate to each other in a logical order.

To help you get started on your first composition, here are two short descriptions of water scenes where nothing is moving. These descriptions are examples of good writing.

1. A big, yellow boat is on the long, green river. It has four tall, blue sails. There are two people standing on the boat and two sitting. From a distance, they look very small.
On the side of the river, there are many tall evergreen trees and small, yellow shrubs. There are areas of rocks along the river banks that alternate with areas of short, brown grass and tan, sandy dirt. Perching on some of the rocks are tall, white egrets.

2. The pool at the clubhouse is shaped like a large rectangle. It is full of water that looks blue. There are also long, black stripes painted on the bottom of the pool.
Around the pool are many large and small, blue chairs. They are all lined up in long, straight rows. Some people with blue, yellow, red, and orange bathing suits are sitting in the chairs.

Turn to **WRITING ASSIGNMENT #1** on page 17. Read the entire assignment carefully. If you have any questions about what you are to do, ask your teacher. When writing about your water scene, use the words you chose and recorded on **WRITING CHART #1**, page 16. While working on your writing, you may also use new words for objects and new describing words as you like. Do not copy the examples of water scenes above. Write your own water scene with your own words.

WRITING CHART #1

DESCRIPTION WORDS

COLOR	SIZE		COLOR	SIZE		COLOR	SIZE	
OBJECT	COLOR	SIZE	OBJECT	COLOR	SIZE	OBJECT	COLOR	SIZE

DESCRIPTION WORDS

COLOR	SIZE		COLOR	SIZE		COLOR	SIZE	
OBJECT	COLOR	SIZE	OBJECT	COLOR	SIZE	OBJECT	COLOR	SIZE

WRITING ASSIGNMENT #1

Your assignment is to write a description of your favorite **water scene**, using lots of words that will help a reader see a picture in his/her mind when he/she reads your writing. Everything in the scene must be completely still, like a picture on the wall. As you work, use the checklist boxes below to mark each item you have completed.

Compose your sentences and paragraphs on the writing worksheet that follows these instructions. Complete your final paper on a fresh sheet of writing paper. If your teacher allows, you may type your paper on the computer.

1. **Format**
   - ☐ Write a title in capital letters at the top of the page.
   - ☐ Write your name under the title.
   - ☐ Begin the first paragraph on the **second** line below your name.
2. **Construction**
   - ☐ Your description must have **two** paragraphs.
   - ☐ Each paragraph must have **three** sentences that have **more than seven** words in them.
   - ☐ Choose **objects** for your scene that would normally be found together.
   - ☐ Choose **color** words that are realistic for each object.
   - ☐ Choose **size** words that are realistic for each object.
3. **Grammar**
   - ☐ Capitalize the first letter of the word beginning each sentence.
   - ☐ Make some of your sentences long and some short.
   - ☐ Indent your paragraphs.
   - ☐ Make sure each paragraph contains unity, flows logically, and relates to the others.
4. **Polish**
   - ☐ You may have to write your description several times.
   - ☐ Only turn in a final copy of your composition that has been written neatly and clearly with no smudge marks.
   - ☐ Make sure you have spelled all of your words correctly.
   - ☐ Use the dictionary to check the spelling of difficult words.
5. **Ethics**
   - ☐ Work on your own and make your description original.
   - ☐ Do not copy a description from any other writing.
   - ☐ Make sure the language of your composition conforms to Philippians 4:8.
6. **Creativity**
   - ☐ Make sure your composition creates an interesting mental picture for your reader.

TRY TO DESCRIBE A WATER SCENE THAT IS TRULY BEAUTIFUL!

WRITING WORKSHEET #1
COMPOSE YOUR SENTENCES ON THE FOLLOWING LINES.

1. _____
2. _____
3. _____
4. _____
5. _____
6. _____
7. _____
8. _____

ORGANIZE YOUR PARAGRAPHS ON THE FOLLOWING LINES.

_____
_____
_____
_____
_____
_____
_____
_____
_____
_____
_____
_____
_____
_____
_____
_____
_____
_____

WRITING PREPARATION

You have written about a water scene in which everything is still. Now you will try writing about a water scene where there is action. First, you must choose a new water scene. Take a few minutes to think of a new water scene about which you would like to write. Turn to page 27 and write your choice in the box below the words **WRITING CHART #2**.

Decide on six main objects that will be in your water scene. Write those objects in the six blank boxes. What colors and sizes do you want for your main objects? Write their colors and sizes in the correct columns under each box. Do your main objects have any related objects, like a tree has leaves? If so, write those related objects in the correct columns. Decide the colors and sizes of your related objects and write them in the columns next to each object's name.

For your first water scene, you used the names of objects, colors, and sizes in your descriptions. The objects in your scene did not move. In this composition, you will use words that show movement or action. Action words are different than object words. **Action words** tell about what an object is doing. For instance, the following sentences tell about the action of some flowers by a lake.

The big, red tulips by the lake **swayed** in the gentle breeze.
The yellow pansies and the tall, blue catmint **blossomed** near the lake.

The words **swayed** and **blossomed** show action. Action makes a scene come alive. Action words change a scene like a picture on a wall into a movie, a television show, or a play on a stage. To add action to your writing, you must think about each object in your picture and decide how it might move in some way that you can realistically describe.

Now think about each one of your objects on page 27. Ask yourself if you have ever seen each object move in real life? How did it move? For each object that you have seen move, write a few action words in its column below the dashed line.

Your chart should now be full of lots of object words, action words, color words, and size words. You are ready to begin your next creative writing composition. To help you get started on your second composition, read the following two short descriptions of water scenes with action. They are examples of good writing. See if you can identify the action words.

1. Today the sea is full of big boats with white sails. The wind is blowing each sail, puffing them out like big, fat pillows, and making each boat move farther out to sea. There are even huge, white clouds in the sky that seem to be moving as fast as the sailboats.
Overhead, the sun is bright, and the water sparkles in the warm light. Nearby, the waves of the sea lap softy upon a pebbly beach. Some children are throwing stones at the waves, and several sea gulls are looking for food.

2. I know where there is a small pond with shiny, blue water that sparkles like diamonds. Sometimes when the sun shines just right, the pebbles on the bottom of the pond look like topaz, beryl, agates, and rubies. The trees growing around the pond are very tall and have moss growing up their sides. Their bark is soft, and their leaves are bright green.
On top of this pond is a favorite place for ducks to swim. Often, you can see small yellow ducks swimming in little groups with their mothers. Once, I found a tree with a low branch on which I could climb. From there, I was able to watch the ducks sitting on the island in the middle of the pond.

Turn to page 28, read **WRITING ASSIGNMENT #2**, and begin your writing.

DESCRIPTION: GRAMMAR SKILLS

CHAPTER 3

3.1 Grammar Rules

Grammar is the study of the rules of English writing. When you learn grammar, you learn how to write so that other people can understand what you are telling them. The rules of grammar are important to learn. When you learn them and practice them, they will become easy to remember. They also make writing enjoyable!

In this chapter, you will review several basic rules about punctuation, word usage, sentence construction, and paragraph formatting. Read each grammar rule and do the **PRACTICE** exercises. When working on your writing assignments, remember to follow these rules. Part of your grade will be determined by how well you follow **all** of the rules you learn.

3.2 Capital Letters

In the English language, every letter in our alphabet can be represented by a capital letter and a small letter. In sentences and certain words, capital letters are used in special ways. This section reviews two rules about capital letters. The first rule is about the first word of a sentence. Review it and then complete the **PRACTICE** exercise.

> **RULE #1**
> Always **capitalize** the **first** letter of the **first** word of a sentence.

EXAMPLE: **A**ll of the boats on the water were blue.

PRACTICE: Write each sentence and **capitalize** the **first** letter of the **first** word.

A. that flower is red._____
B. the tree is big._____
C. water was everywhere._____
D. swimming is fun._____
E. sailing is swell._____
F. fishing requires patience._____

The second rule about capital letters has to do with respecting the name of each person on earth. To show respect for a person's name, you always write it in a special way.

> **RULE #2**
> Always **capitalize** the **first** letter of a person's name.

EXAMPLE: **J**essica

PRACTICE: Rewrite these names and **capitalize** the **first** letter of each one.

A. ralph_____   E. jenny_____
B. alex_____   F. peter_____
C. mark_____   G. sarah_____
D. cindy_____   H. moses_____

Review your writing worksheet, page 29. Have you forgotten to capitalize the first word of each sentence and any names for people? Correct your writing at this time.

3.3 Periods

There are two types of sentences that end with a period. A **declarative** sentence declares something or makes a statement. The information in a declarative sentence may be either true or false. A declarative sentence must end with a special type of punctuation.

RULE #1
Always draw a **period** at the end of a **declarative** sentence that declares something or makes a statement.

EXAMPLES:
The grocery store is across the street. (True)
The moon is made of cheese. (False)

PRACTICE: Draw a **period** after each of the 4 sentences that are **declarative** sentences.

A. That seagull is big
B. The barn is red
C. Can I play with you
D. Are there any apples left to eat
E. There are two chairs on the patio
F. Michael caught several fish

The second type of sentence that ends with a period is named an imperative sentence. An **imperative sentence** gives a command. Every imperative sentence has the same subject; that subject is the pronoun **you**. In most imperative sentences, the pronoun **you** does not always appear in the text of the sentence. When the pronoun **you** does not appear in the text, it is always implied within the command or request.

RULE #2
A **period** is placed at the end of an **imperative** sentence that **gives a command or request**.

EXAMPLES:
Please sweep the dirt outside.
Break the eggs into a clean bowl.

PRACTICE: Draw a **period** after each of the 4 sentences that are **imperative** sentences.

A. Help me put the pickles in the jars
B. Who made the sandwiches today
C. Ride your bike to the end of the street
D. Drink all of the milk in the glass
E. Can we take a hike out to the lake
F. Please help me carry the packages

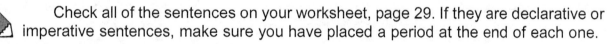

Check all of the sentences on your worksheet, page 29. If they are declarative or imperative sentences, make sure you have placed a period at the end of each one.

3.4 Exclamation Points

In any type of writing, the **exclamation point** (!) is used to identify an exclamatory sentence which shows that the writer feels strongly about his/her comment.

RULE #1
An **exclamation point** is placed at the end of an **exclamatory** sentence that shows **excitement, exaggerated/strong emotion, surprise, enthusiasm, or determination**.

EXAMPLE: Look at that huge, hot air balloon!

PRACTICE: Place an **exclamation point** at the **end** of each sentence that requires one. (HINT: There are only **four exclamation points**.)

A. That's the most beautiful color I've ever seen
B. The students were doing their homework
C. What a great surprise
D. Last night's music concert was spectacular
E. The children helped their parents weed the garden
F. The stars are extremely bright tonight

Read your water scene worksheet to see if you have any sentences that show excitement, exaggerated/strong emotion, surprise, enthusiasm, or determination. These types of sentences should end with an exclamation point. To any sentences that need exclamation points, add them.

3.5 Commas

Today you will learn about two rules for commas that are important to good grammar. A **comma** is a type of punctuation that looks like a hook (,).

RULE #1
Always use **commas** when you have **more than two** names in a series within a sentence. (Draw one comma after each of the names except the last.)

EXAMPLE: The main characters of the story were **Sue, Brian,** and **Phil**.

PRACTICE: Draw **two commas** at the correct places in each of these sentences.

A. Ellen Rita and Jeff went sledding with their fathers.
B. Jenna Joleen and Jasmine planned a party for their new friend.
C. I went to the play with Rebecca Amy and Joanna.
D. I sang in the choir with Arnold Hal and Kevin.
E. Sonia Gerald and Louise went to visit their grandparents across the street.
F. I will call Eric Alice and Tom to dinner.

RULE #2
Always use **commas** when you have **more than two** thing words or describing words in a series within a sentence. (Draw one comma after each of the thing words or describing words except the last one that appears in a row within a sentence.)

EXAMPLES:
The **book,** the **lamp,** and the **pencil** are on the shelf. (THREE THING WORDS)
The water in the pool looks **cool, wet,** and **refreshing**. (THREE DESCRIBING WORDS)

PRACTICE: Draw **two commas** at the correct places in each of these sentences.

A. My bike skates and sled are all blue.
B. A goose duck and frog were sitting beside the lake.

C. The coral reef was shades of pink orange and yellow.
D. The new sweater was soft white and pretty.
E. Those bananas are long yellow and ripe.
F. His face was familiar friendly and kind.

Review your writing worksheet. Does it contain **more than two** name words, thing words, or describing words in a series within a sentence? If so, draw one comma after each of the name words, thing words, or describing words (except the last one) that appear in a series within that sentence.

3.6 The Word "and"

Do you know what **too many ands** do to a sentence? They confuse a reader. A reader also loses track of what you are trying to say in your writing.

The word **and** is helpful in a sentence when you need to connect more than one idea, person, place, or thing together. However, did you know that you should use **ands** sparingly? Many people use the word **and** so often that they don't even notice what they are doing. Do you use too many **ands** in a sentence? To find out whether your sentences have too many **ands**, follow these instructions.

Count the number of **ands** in your sentences. If there is more than one **and** in one sentence, the sentence probably has too many. A sentence with too many **ands** in it should be rewritten into two or more sentences.

EXAMPLE:
The basket was full of fruit **and** sitting on the table, **and** the fruit looked very fresh.

This sentence has too many **ands**! A sentence with too many **ands** needs to be rewritten into two or three sentences because it goes on and on without a reasonable end. To make a new sentence, you may also have to add some extra words or change some words. Carefully read the following sentences of how the **EXAMPLE** sentence can be rewritten. They will show you how to write better sentences without using too many **ands**.

Two sentences:
The basket was full of fruit and sitting on the table.
The fruit looked very fresh.

or

Three sentences:
The basket was full of fruit.
It was sitting on the table.
The fruit looked very fresh.

PRACTICE: The following sentences have **too many ands**. Rewrite each sentence as **two** or **three separate sentences**.

A. The grocery store was crowded, and the people were shopping, and they were buying food.
_____
_____
_____

B. The sun was bright, and the desert was dry, and the sand was hot.

_____
_____

C. The hikers were walking uphill, and they were talking to each other, and they were telling funny stories.

_____
_____

D. For lunch I ate a hamburger and some french fries and a vanilla shake.

_____
_____

 Review your water scene worksheet. Does it contain a sentence with more than one **and**? If so, rewrite that sentence into two or three sentences.

3.7 Verb Tense

Tense is about time. The time of a sentence may be past, present, or future. The **verb** or **verbs** in each sentence are the words that show the reader what tense the writer is using when writing that sentence. The tense could be **past**, **present**, or **future**. The following verbs are shown in their different tense forms.

PAST	PRESENT	FUTURE
liked	like	will like
jumped	jump	will jump
stopped	stop	will stop
talked	talk	will talk

In this part of the textbook, the verb tense you use in your creative writing compositions must be the same from the first sentence to the last sentence. In your first paragraph, you must decide the verb tense for the whole composition. If you decide to write in the past tense, then the composition must continue in the past tense. If you decide to write in the present tense, then the composition must continue in the present tense.

Be careful when you are writing to make sure that every verb you write is written in the same tense for the whole composition. If you are not careful, you will write a confusing composition that indicates you are also confused. You may end up with a verb in one sentence that is in the past tense and a verb in another sentence that is in the present tense. This change is named **tense shifting** and should be avoided. Later, you will learn how to use different verb tenses in a story when you begin to write dialogue.

 Review your worksheet and take the extra time needed to write your sentences carefully. When your composition is done, check every sentence to make sure each one uses the same verb tense.

3.8 Sentence Length

Good writing has a **variety of sentences**. Today's lesson is about how a writer writes well by preparing a variety of sentences with different lengths. **Varying sentence length** is accomplished by writing a mixture of long sentences and short sentences.

Have you ever been a passenger in a car on a long trip? At first, the scenery outside your window may have been very interesting. However, if the scenery didn't change once in a while, you soon became bored looking at the same thing over and over.

When all of the sentences in a paragraph are the same length, the important information you write does not seem very interesting after a while. A reader needs to have a little change of sentence length in a story once in a while. In varying the length of your sentences by making some short and some long, you add vitality and renewed interest to your writing so that a reader can enjoy all of your story.

The following group of sentences becomes more and more uninteresting as you read through it because the sentences are all the same length.

The building was big. The windows were small. The doors were open. The entrance was empty.

These sentences can be improved and made interesting from the first sentence to the last when rewritten like this example.

REWRITTEN:

The new Franklin Building in our city was very big. It had hundreds of small windows. On this special grand opening day, the doors were open, but the entrance was still empty.

PRACTICE: Rewrite the following sentences into new sentences. Make some **long** and some **short**. You can add any words you need to create **variety**.

A. We went camping in a tent for our vacation last year. We stayed in a hotel for our vacation two years ago.

_____
_____

B. The night was dark. The air was warm. The birds were quiet.

_____
_____

C. Mosheh/Moses was a prophet. Mosheh/Moses was a leader. Mosheh/Moses was a husband. Mosheh/Moses was a father.

_____
_____

D. Tommy played with sand. Tommy built a castle. Tommy dug a canal. Tommy filled the canal.

_____
_____
_____

Review your worksheet. Read the sentences to see if you have created sentence variety. If you have too many sentences written one after the other that are all the same length, rewrite them to make some long and some short.

3.9 Paragraph Indention

A **paragraph** is a grouping of sentences that are related to each other. The sentences present information about one topic or information and are arranged in a logical order. When a writer wants to present new information, the writer begins a new paragraph. If all of these sentences were written one right after another, it would sometimes be difficult to know where one paragraph ended and another began. For this reason, a method for identifying new paragraphs was created. How does a reader know when a writer has written a new paragraph? A new paragraph is identified by the indenting of the beginning of that paragraph. **Indenting** a paragraph means that you are to start the first word of the first sentence of a paragraph five spaces in from the left hand margin of your composition.

RULE #1
Every paragraph must be **indented**.

EXAMPLE:

➡ **The little boy sat on the beach by the ocean. He watched the waves come in and go out as he played with his new, red shovel. After a little while, he began to dig a small hole in the sand. When his hole was finished, he went out to the edge of the water and dug a canal that stretched all the way to his new hole. When his canal was complete, he sat down next to the hole and waited. The next wave of ocean water brought what he wanted. Slowly, little by little, the canal filled with water that flowed into the small hole. The little boy watched the success of his work and smiled with delight!**

PRACTICE: The following paragraphs have not been **indented**. Rewrite each paragraph and start the first word **five spaces** in from the left.

Joseph/Yoseph wanted to obey God. He wanted to protect his family and give his family a good life. When the angel of God told him to leave Bethlehem/Beth Lehem, he listened and did what he was told. Joseph took his small family to Israel/Yisrael.

_____
_____
_____
_____

The janitor at the Philpod's Company worked late at night after all of the employees had gone home. He liked the quiet of the evening hours because he could complete his work faster. Every night he remembered the employees of the day hours and how hard they had worked. Knowing that he personally could make their daytime hours more comfortable and pleasant, he tried earnestly to clean each employee's office as if it were his own.

_____
_____
_____
_____
_____

Now is the time to complete your composition. Rewrite or type it neatly on a fresh piece of paper and turn it in to your teacher. Don't forget to indent your paragraphs.

WRITING CHART #2

DESCRIPTION WORDS

	COLOR	SIZE		COLOR	SIZE		COLOR	SIZE
OBJECT	COLOR	SIZE	OBJECT	COLOR	SIZE	OBJECT	COLOR	SIZE

DESCRIPTION WORDS

	COLOR	SIZE		COLOR	SIZE		COLOR	SIZE
OBJECT	COLOR	SIZE	OBJECT	COLOR	SIZE	OBJECT	COLOR	SIZE

WRITING ASSIGNMENT #2

Your assignment is to write a description of another favorite **water scene**, using lots of words that will help your reader see a picture in his/her mind when he/she reads your writing. This time, however, you must add action to your scene. As you work, use the checklist boxes below to mark each item you have completed.

Compose your sentences and paragraphs on the writing worksheet that follows these instructions. Work through the grammar chapter; it will instruct you when to complete your composition.

1. **Format**
   - [ ] Write a title in capital letters at the top of the page.
   - [ ] Write your name under the title.
   - [ ] Begin the first paragraph on the **second** line below your name.
2. **Construction**
   - [ ] Your description must have **two** paragraphs.
   - [ ] Each paragraph must have **three** sentences that have **more than seven** words in them.
   - [ ] Choose **objects** for your scene that would normally be found together.
   - [ ] Choose **color** words that are realistic for each object.
   - [ ] Choose **size** words that are realistic for each object.
3. **Grammar**
   - [ ] End each sentence with a **period, exclamation point,** or **question mark**.
   - [ ] Draw **commas** between multiple describing words.
   - [ ] Begin each sentence with a **capital letter.**
   - [ ] Indent the beginning of each paragraph.
   - [ ] Be careful to use proper word tenses.
   - [ ] Make some of your sentences long and some short.
   - [ ] Make sure each paragraph contains unity, flows logically, and relates to the others.
4. **Polish**
   - [ ] You may have to write your description several times.
   - [ ] Only turn in a final copy of your composition that has been written neatly and clearly with no smudge marks.
   - [ ] Make sure you have spelled all of your words correctly.
   - [ ] Use the dictionary to check the spelling of difficult words.
5. **Ethics**
   - [ ] Work on your own and make your description original.
   - [ ] Do not copy a description from any other writing.
   - [ ] Make sure the language of your composition conforms to Philippians 4:8.
6. **Creativity**
   - [ ] Make sure your composition creates an interesting mental picture for your reader.

TRY TO DESCRIBE A WATER SCENE THAT HAS LOVELY MOVEMENT!

WRITING WORKSHEET #2
COMPOSE YOUR SENTENCES ON THE FOLLOWING LINES.

1. _____
2. _____
3. _____
4. _____
5. _____
6. _____
7. _____
8. _____

ORGANIZE YOUR PARAGRAPHS ON THE FOLLOWING LINES.

_____
_____
_____
_____
_____
_____
_____
_____
_____
_____
_____
_____
_____
_____
_____
_____
_____
_____
_____
_____

SCENE: ETHICS SKILLS

UNIT 2
SUPPLIES

BIBLE
DICTIONARY
PENCIL
THESAURUS
WRITING PAPER

4.1 Scriptural Ethics

You are learning scriptural wisdom and ethical values that will benefit and train you in creating healthy writing. As you write, remember your reader; stories with sinful information will confuse your reader. Writing and reading about evil will lead a person away from Jesus/Yahshua. If a person's mind becomes filled with sin in this way, that person will spend a lifetime struggling against evil thoughts, which may even become evil actions. Do not write a composition that contains sin for the purpose of **entertaining**, **thrilling**, and **convincing others that to participate in sin is permissible**.

Scripture Study

The following scripture, Tehillim/Psalms 23, is a lovely pastoral description. It tells about who God is and what He does for us. Read the verses carefully. After the scripture, there are several numbered lines. Each number corresponds to a key word. To find the key words, begin with the first word and count until you find the word that corresponds to the numbers on the lines. When you have found each correct key word, write it on the line to which it belongs.

Yahweh is my shepherd;
I do not lack.
He makes me to lie down in green pastures;
He leads me beside still waters.
He turns back my being;
He leads me in paths of righteousness
For His Name's sake.
When I walk through the valley of the shadow of death,
I fear no evil.
For You are with me;
Your rod and Your staff, they comfort me.
You spread before me a table in the face of my enemies;
You have anointed my head with oil;
My cup runs over.
Only goodness and kindness follow me
All the days of my life;
And I shall dwell in the House of Yahweh,
To the length of days!

KEY WORDS

OBJECTS
4. shepherd
17. _____
23. _____
33. _____
45. _____
48. _____

COLORS
16. _____

QUALITIES
35. _____
53+54. _____
92. _____
94. _____

ACTIONS
10. _____
19. _____

25. _____
30. _____
42. _____
66. _____
69. _____
89. _____
95. _____
106. _____

The Bible contains many beautiful writings. The text may contain simple to complex descriptions. These descriptions may use object words, color words, size words, or action words. In Tehillim/Psalms 23 you also encountered **quality words** that you wrote on the key word lines. Quality words tell you about the ethics of someone or something. The quality words that were used to describe the pastoral scene were righteousness, no evil, goodness, and kindness. These are qualities that represent good, ethical writing. Look up the following words in your dictionary. Write a correct definition for each word or phrase on the lines provided.

Righteousness:_____
_____
(No) evil:_____
_____
Goodness:_____
_____
Kindness:_____
_____

When you prepare a creative writing composition, an important goal is to think about the qualities that you want your reader to find in your writing. Qualities that honor Jesus/Yahshua are the best to use in your writing. They help your reader to learn about how to be a better person or how to think well of the world in which you live.

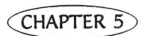

SCENE: WRITING SKILLS

5.1 The Qualities of a Scene

The English writing skill of **describing** is a very important part of creative writing. Your ability to describe can make a composition realistic and believable. You have learned how to describe a water scene using object words, color words, size words, and action words. In this chapter, you will learn how to describe a pastoral scene using these kinds of words and more. You will learn to write about the **qualities of a scene**.

Writing about the qualities of a scene is important so that your reader will not only be able to see the scene in his/her mind but will also be able to feel the scene. Quality words that are used to describe a scene impart a personality to the scene. These words are the same kind of words you would use to describe a person's character.

Before you can write about the qualities of a scene, first you must understand what a pastoral scene is. What do you think pastoral means? **Pastoral** has to do with places you might find in the country, especially places where shepherds work. These places are simple, natural, beautiful, and peaceful. These places are not in the city.

Can you name a few pastoral places? Think about this question for a minute or two; then list at least four pastoral places in this box. Write one place after each diamond.

PASTORAL PLACES	
♦ _____	♦ _____
♦ _____	♦ _____

There are many types of pastoral places. Did you name gardens, forests, and valleys in your list of pastoral places? Why do you think of the places you listed as pastoral? Do they meet any of the qualities that you learned about in chapter 4: righteousness, no evil, goodness, and kindness? Are they places that are simple, natural, beautiful, and peaceful? Perhaps there are other qualities you think of when hearing the name of a pastoral place. To begin learning how to describe a pastoral place, you need to start by setting up your writing chart. (From now on, a pastoral place will be named a **pastoral scene**.)

Turn to page 36 and write the words **PASTORAL SCENES** in the empty box under the box with the words **WRITING CHART #3**. Under the box with the words **DESCRIPTION WORDS** are three more boxes to write the names of three pastoral scenes. In the first box, write the word **GARDEN**; in the second box, write the word **FOREST**; in the third box, write the word **VALLEY**.

A garden, a forest, and a valley each make you think of different places. Each of these places may have a quality about it that makes you feel good. The quality may be one that you read about in Tehillim/Psalms 23, or it may be another, like quietness, refreshment, happiness, etc. Thinking of and deciding upon the quality of which a pastoral scene reminds you will help you to begin writing about that place.

Take a few minutes to think about each of the pastoral scenes on the writing chart. About what qualities does each place make you think? These qualities will give each scene a personality, so be careful that the qualities you pick are realistic for the type of pastoral scene of which you are thinking. For instance, a garden might be a happy or cheerful place, but it might not be a still or meek place. In the column directly under the name of each pastoral scene, write the qualities which you have decided to use.

5.2 Development of a Scene

In Lesson 5.1, you learned how to give a scene a personality by identifying the most realistic qualities that come to mind when you think of a particular pastoral scene. The information that you recorded on the writing chart was a good start for a composition about a pastoral scene. Now is the time to fill in those scenes a little more by thinking about what might be found in them that you would want to describe for your reader.

In UNIT 1, you learned to think about what objects might be in a scene. The objects in a pastoral scene may be similar to or different from those found in a water scene. The objects in a pastoral scene may be living or nonliving. For this lesson, you must think about only non-living objects by trying to imagine that you are sitting in front of the scene. If you looked around, what would you see?

Take a few minutes to mentally sit in front of each scene listed on the writing chart. What nonliving objects might there be that would be realistic to that scene? What kind of nonliving objects would you find in a garden, a forest, or a valley? Write your answers in the **OBJECT** column under each type of pastoral scene.

There are many kinds of describing words, including color words. You live in a visual world that is rich with many colors. In addition, colors have many different names, depending upon their different shades and hues. What would you do if you couldn't remember the name of a particular color? What would you do if, when describing, you couldn't think of the right word to use? How could you get help in these situations?

The answers to these questions can be found in a very helpful book that contains all kinds of describing words. This book is a thesaurus. A **thesaurus** is a reference book of words in alphabetical order. The thesaurus is a tool for a writer to use to find additional describing words of which he/she hasn't already thought when trying to describe something. The thesaurus can also help a writer to find a more exact word to use in a description.

For instance, if a writer wanted to find other describing words for the color red, first he/she would look in the thesaurus for the word **red** by finding it alphabetically. Then the writer would be able to read all of the words listed after the word red. Some of the words that would be found are **crimson**, **ruby**, **scarlet**, and **cardinal**.

Can you find all the words for red by looking in a thesaurus? Start by finding the word red alphabetically in the thesaurus. Read the words following the entry for red and write what you find on the following lines.

Red:_____

_____

Are you surprised at how many words there are for the color red? Did you learn some new ones of which you had never heard before? The words you found can be used in a description in one (or more) of three ways: to replace the word **red**, to add a fun touch in writing, or to improve the accuracy of the color when it is described.

The thesaurus is truly a handy book to help you when working on any creative writing composition. Keep it next to your dictionary, and you will have two important books that can help you become a better writer.

Now that you have learned how to find different variations of a color, take time to think about what colors might be in the pastoral scenes listed on the writing chart. What colors might you realistically find in a garden, a forest, or a valley? Take a few minutes to think about this question by trying to imagine that you are sitting in front of each pastoral scene and looking around you. What colors would your objects be? If you need help with a name for a color, don't forget to look in the thesaurus. Write your color selections in the **COLOR** columns next to each object.

This lesson would not be complete unless you decided what sizes you think might realistically be depicted in each of the pastoral scenes. Could the garden be big or small? Might the forest be huge or the valley long? Try to think of the words you might use to describe each pastoral scene if you were assigned to write a paper about it for tomorrow. Then write your word choices for each pastoral scene under the columns titled **SIZE**.

Each object you listed in the writing chart will also have a size. Decide on those sizes and list your word choices for each object in its **SIZE** column. Remember to make your size choices realistic. For instance, a car could not be larger than a barn, or grass would not be taller than a tree. Pick size words that do not distort how objects might really exist in relation to one another.

5.3 Action in a Scene

Describing action in a scene gives it the quality of being like a play, movie, or television show, as opposed to a picture on a wall. **Action words** are also description words that tell about what an object is doing. To add action to a scene, you must think about the objects that are in a scene. Do they move in reality? How do they move? How would they move in relation to one another? For instance, if the weather were windy, trees in a scene would be swaying; they would not be standing still. If water in a river were moving, so would a boat in its midst. On the other hand, if a day were hot and still, people and animals in the scene would probably be moving slowly, lazily, or even not at all!

Action makes a scene come alive. There are two ways to describe action in a scene. To understand the two ways to describe action, think of a party. At a party you can either be a spectator watching the guests/activities or a participant interacting with the guests/activities. If you are a spectator, you will spend the whole time watching the actions of others. If you are a participant, you will experience the action as you move and as others move around you.

For your first composition in this unit, you will write about the action in a scene as though you were a spectator. You will create your scene so that your reader can not only see the objects in the scene but can also see and feel the action. To add action to your scene, you must think about the things that move. Most things that move are living objects. Two types of living objects that move are plants and animals. While the movement of growth for a plant is not usually described in a scene, a plant may move when an outside object acts upon it, like the wind blowing or an animal scurrying past. An animal, however, can easily move on its own.

A pastoral scene is a place where both plants and animals are normally found. These living objects are important to describe in your scene to fill it in further. On your writing chart, page 36, there are columns for plants and animals under each type of pastoral scene. Take a few moments to decide what plants and animals would be present naturally in each pastoral scene. Then write the names of those plants and animals in the correct columns.

Have you ever viewed a picture with cloudy, rainy weather and a storm-tossed sea? Do flowers look prettier in the sunshine or on a cloudy day? Are animals more likely to frolic and play on a sunny day or a stormy day? The weather is an important part of an outdoor scene. Whether it is sunny, cloudy, or stormy determines what might be happening in nature. The weather is something you must consider when you are writing a scene about the outdoors.

Look at your writing chart. For each pastoral scene, choose a type of weather about which you might like to write; record that weather type in the columns titled **WEATHER**. Each weather type you choose will have certain conditions that are characteristic to it. For instance, a stormy day might have rain, wind, and dark clouds. The clouds may be moving fast or slow. A sunny day might have sunshine, a clear blue sky, and maybe a slight breeze. Take a few moments to decide what weather conditions are characteristic to the type of weather you chose for each a pastoral scene. Below the dashed line in each column titled **WEATHER**, write these weather conditions and any action words that go with those conditions.

To make a pastoral scene more than just a picture on a wall, you need to add action. The animals and plants on the writing chart are capable of movement. What kind of movement might they exhibit? How might they move in relation to one another? What effect might the weather have on their movement? Take a few moments to think about the animals, plants, and weather that you chose for each pastoral scene on the writing chart. How might the weather affect the movements of the animals and the plants? Below the dashed line, write your answers as action words for the plants and animals.

5.4 Style of Writing

Style is the unique manner in which a writer uses words, phrases, and sentences in writing. Each writer's style is uniquely his/her own because it comes from his/her personality and opinions. For instance, some writers use many words to describe, while others use only a few. Some writers describe a lot of little details while others describe only big details. Some writers are able to write in different styles depending upon the type of composition they are writing; others prefer to stick with only one style for all of their writing.

Your style in writing is what makes your compositions different from another person's. You should never try to copy or imitate the writing style of other people. Their style belongs uniquely to them. When you use your own style, your writing is more honest and readable. When you write, think of your reader. If your writing style is dull and boring, your reader will be bored. When your words, sentences, and paragraphs are confusing, your reader will be confused. If your writing does not come from your experiences and the reality of your life, the believability will diminish for your reader. The best thing to do is to write like you think or talk; then correct your grammar and make sure you have conveyed yourself as clearly as possible, being honest, accurate, and realistic.

You are now ready to write your third creative writing composition. Return to Lesson 5.1 and choose your favorite pastoral place by marking it with a highlighter. Write its name on the writing chart, page 36, in the first blank box half way down the page. Decide on what qualities and size you might use to describe your pastoral scene. If you need help, review Lesson 5.1. On page 36, write the qualities and size in the columns under the box containing the name of your favorite pastoral place.

Next, think of three objects that would naturally occur in your scene. write the names of these objects in the three blank boxes under the **DESCRIPTION WORDS** box. What color and size words can you use to tell about each object so that your reader will see a picture of it in his/her mind? Write those colors and sizes in the correct columns under the boxes.

Plants, animals, and weather are natural things that are found in pastoral places. What ones would you like to include in your scene and make it interesting? In the columns provided, write the names of the plants and the animals that you like. Next, in their columns write what types of weather you would like your scene to have. What are the conditions of your weather types? Below the dashed line in the **WEATHER** columns, write those conditions and their action words.

Finally, think about how your plants and your animals might move in your scene. How might the weather affect their movements? Below the dashed line, write your answers as action words for the plants and the animals.

Your chart should now be full of lots of object words, quality words, action words, color words, size words, and words telling weather types and conditions. You are ready to begin writing your next creative writing composition. For this composition you will be writing as though you were a spectator watching the action in a pastoral scene. To help you get started, read the following short description of a scene with action. Can you visualize the scene and action in your mind?

The gray sky was still and quiet. No animals were in sight. Nearby, endless volleys of water came tumbling over the cliff and formed a waterfall, flowing into a shallow basin below. From the basin, made completely of rock, the water spilled out over huge shelves of smooth, worn rock to become smaller cascading waterfalls until a stream formed amongst many broken rocks and pebbles.

A bridge and an observation area spanned the top of the waterfall. Cliffs with profusely growing, green vegetation flanked the waterfall. A narrow path leading down to the shelves of smooth rock invited tourists to get a closer look at the splendor of this majestic sight.

Turn to your homework assignment on page 37 and read it. If you have any questions, ask your teacher. Do not copy the example of the pastoral scene above. Write your own pastoral scene with your own words. This reminder will help you develop your own unique style of writing.

WRITING CHART #3

DESCRIPTION WORDS

QUALITY	SIZE		QUALITY	SIZE		QUALITY	SIZE	
OBJECT	COLOR	SIZE	OBJECT	COLOR	SIZE	OBJECT	COLOR	SIZE
PLANT	ANIMAL	WEATHER	PLANT	ANIMAL	WEATHER	PLANT	ANIMAL	WEATHER

QUALITIES   SIZE

DESCRIPTION WORDS

COLOR	SIZE		COLOR	SIZE		COLOR	SIZE	
PLANT	ANIMAL	WEATHER	PLANT	ANIMAL	WEATHER	PLANT	ANIMAL	WEATHER

WRITING ASSIGNMENT #3

Your assignment is to write a description of your favorite **pastoral scene**, using lots of words that will help a reader see your scene in his/her mind when he/she reads your writing. You will write about your scene as a **spectator**. Do not describe any people, but you may use the words **I**, **he**, **she**, **we**, or **they**. As you work, use the checklist boxes below to mark each item you have completed.

Compose your sentences and paragraphs on the writing worksheet that follows these instructions. Complete your final paper on a fresh sheet of writing paper. If your teacher allows, you may type your paper on the computer.

1. **Format**
   - [ ] Write a title in capital letters at the top of the page.
   - [ ] Write your name under the title.
   - [ ] Begin the first paragraph on the **second** line below your name.
2. **Construction**
   - [ ] Your description must have **three** paragraphs.
   - [ ] Each paragraph must have **three** sentences that have **more than seven** words in them.
   - [ ] Choose **objects** for your scene that would normally be found together.
   - [ ] Choose **quality**, **color**, and **size** words that are realistic for each object.
   - [ ] Choose the **weather** and its **conditions** that are realistic for your scene.
3. **Grammar**
   - [ ] End each sentence with a **period, exclamation point,** or **question mark**.
   - [ ] Draw **commas** between multiple describing words.
   - [ ] Begin each sentence with a **capital letter.**
   - [ ] Indent the beginning of each paragraph.
   - [ ] Be careful to use proper word tenses.
   - [ ] Make some of your sentences long and some short.
   - [ ] Make sure each paragraph contains unity, flows logically, and relates to the others.
4. **Polish**
   - [ ] You may have to write your description several times.
   - [ ] Only turn in a final copy of your paper that has been written neatly and clearly with no smudge marks.
   - [ ] Make sure you have spelled all of your words correctly.
   - [ ] Use the dictionary to check the spelling of difficult words.
   - [ ] Do not forget to use your thesaurus if you need help finding a word.
5. **Ethics**
   - [ ] Work on your own and make your description original.
   - [ ] Do not copy a description from any other writing.
   - [ ] Make sure the language of your paper conforms to Philippians 4:8.
6. **Creativity**
   - [ ] Make sure your composition creates an interesting mental picture for your reader.

WRITING WORKSHEET #3
COMPOSE YOUR SENTENCES ON THE FOLLOWING LINES.

1. _____
2. _____
3. _____
4. _____
5. _____
6. _____
7. _____
8. _____
9. _____

ORGANIZE YOUR PARAGRAPHS ON THE FOLLOWING LINES.

_____
_____
_____
_____
_____
_____
_____
_____
_____
_____
_____
_____
_____
_____
_____
_____
_____
_____

WRITING PREPARATION

Have you ever been a team member in a sports game? Perhaps you have attended a party. What about church? How many times have you stood or sat in church and looked around at all of the things that occurred during a Sabbath service? When you participate in an activity, you have a different experience than just watching the activity. You have the experience of being able to interact with all of the elements of that activity. You can observe objects from different angles, see their colors and sizes up close, and be a part of the action of the activity.

You have written about a pastoral scene as a spectator looking at that scene. Now you will try writing about a pastoral scene as a participant. Being able to write about a scene as though you were a participant will help you later when you learn to write stories with characters in them. Characters interact with their environment, the weather, and other characters. Being able to describe those interactions is important to making a story realistic and believable.

To write as though you were a participant in a pastoral scene, you must choose a new scene. Take a few minutes to think about a new pastoral scene in which you would like to participate. Then turn to page 47 and write your choice in the box below the words **WRITING CHART #4**.

What qualities and size might you use to describe your pastoral scene? If you need help, review Lesson 5.1. On page 47, write the qualities and size in the columns under the box containing the name of your favorite pastoral place.

Decide on three main objects that will be in your pastoral scene. Write those objects in the blank boxes below the **DESCRIPTION WORDS** box. What colors and sizes do you want for your main objects? Write their colors and sizes in the correct columns under each box.

Plants, animals, and weather are natural things that are found in pastoral places. What ones would you like to include in your scene that will make it interesting? In the columns provided, write the names of the plants and animals that you like. Then write what type of weather you would like your scene to have in the **WEATHER** column. What are the conditions of your weather type? Below the dashed line in the **WEATHER** column, write those conditions and any action words that go with those conditions.

Finally, think about how your plants and your animals might move in the scene. How might the weather affect their movements? How might the plants and animals affect each other's movement? Write your answers as action words below the dashed line in the plant and the animal columns.

Your chart should now be full of lots of object words, quality words, action words, color words, size words, and weather words. You are ready to begin writing your creative writing composition. For this composition you will be writing as though you were a participant in the action of your pastoral scene. To help you get started, read the following short description of a scene with action. Can you visualize the scene and action in your mind?

As we walked down the path on a gray, cool day, a brown rabbit nibbled on a hosta plant next to the trail. Most of the path was lined with dense, green vegetation, but eventually we could see a clearing up ahead. We continued down several stairs and onward until the path ended on a large shelf of smooth rock.

Once on the shelf, we were able to walk upwards again towards a magnificent waterfall. Endless volleys of water came tumbling over a cliff into a shallow basin below our feet. We followed the journey of the water as it flowed over the smooth rock under our feet until it once again fell in a succession of smaller waterfalls. After climbing down each waterfall, we found the beginning of a stream forming.

Turn to page 48, read **WRITING ASSIGNMENT #4**, and begin your writing on page 49.

SCENE: GRAMMAR SKILLS

CHAPTER 6

6.1 Grammar Rules

The study of grammar helps you to learn how to write so that other people can understand what you are telling them. The rules of grammar are important to learn. When you learn them and practice them, they will become easy to remember. They also make writing enjoyable!

In this chapter, you will review some rules about nouns and pronouns, both common and proper. You will also learn about when to capitalize them. Read each grammar rule and do the **PRACTICE** exercises. When working on your writing assignments, remember to follow these rules. Part of your grade will be determined by how well you follow **all** of the rules you learn.

6.2 Nouns

To communicate with others, you talk or write in sentences. Each word in a sentence has a grammar name. One of the most important words in a sentence is the noun. A **noun** is a type of word. It is also an important part of communication in the English language. Many words used in descriptions are nouns. All nouns have a rule to help you identify them by **type**.

> **RULE #1**
> A **noun** is a word for a **person, place, thing,** or **idea.**

In the next lessons, you will learn about each type of noun in this rule. Just to see how much you already know, try writing two words that are nouns for each type listed below.

PRACTICE: Write **two words** that you think are correct for each of these **types**.

PERSON	PLACE	THING	IDEA
_____	_____	_____	_____
_____	_____	_____	_____

PRACTICE: Circle the words in the following list that are **nouns**.

car	walnut	stopping	damaged
doctor	electrical	book	teacher
building	think	eat	compose
skates	banana	write	hide

6.3 Person Nouns

A **person** is a human being. A person is not an animal or an object. In communication, a person is also the part of grammar named the noun.

> **RULE #1**
> A **noun** is a word for a **person**, place, thing, or idea.

EXAMPLES:
boy   girl   man   woman

PRACTICE: After these nouns, can you write six **person** nouns that are in a family?

mother _____   _____   _____

father _____ _____ _____

People that work are persons, too. They may make financial decisions as an **accountant**, work with plants as a **gardener**, or study the ocean as an **oceanographer**. All of these people that work are persons. The words that represent these working persons are nouns.

PRACTICE: Under the nouns listed below, can you write six **nouns** for persons that work?

accountant	**gardener**	**oceanographer**
_____	_____	_____
_____	_____	_____

The words that identify persons in a family and persons that work are all **nouns**. There are also other words that name persons that are nouns, such as the following.

neighbor	friend	child	mentor
woman	wife	husband	enemy

PRACTICE: Can you identify these three **person** nouns by solving their word puzzles?

    f__llow   h__man   m__n

6.4 Place Nouns

A **place** is a location that you can go visit, like a city, town, state, carnival, or park. In communication, a place is the part of grammar named the noun.

> **RULE #1**
> A **noun** is a word for a person, **place**, thing, or idea.

EXAMPLES:

pasture	town	state	city	park

PRACTICE: A **place** noun is somewhere you can visit. After the following examples, can you write four nouns that are wet places you might visit on a vacation?

    ocean _____ _____
    beach _____ _____

PRACTICE: After the following noun, can you write two nouns that are low **places** you might visit on a vacation?

    desert _____ _____

PRACTICE: The words that identify places you might go on a vacation, on a field trip, or on any kind of outing are all nouns. Can you identify these **place** nouns by solving these word puzzles?

    zo__   vol__ano   ca__p   __heater   __ountain

6.5 Thing Nouns

A **thing** is an object that occupies space and has mass. In communication, a thing is the part of grammar named the noun.

> **RULE #1**
> A **noun** is a word for a person, place, **thing**, or idea.

EXAMPLES:

cloud   lake   wind   pool   road   grass

PRACTICE: After the nouns listed below, write six **thing** nouns that are related to a garden.

flower _____ _____ _____
rake _____ _____ _____

PRACTICE: Buildings, vehicles, animals, plants, tools, decorations, and many more objects are things. The words that represent these things are all nouns. Can you write three nouns for **things** that are objects under each of the categories listed below?

Buildings	Vehicles	Animals	Plants	Tools
_____	_____	_____	_____	_____
_____	_____	_____	_____	_____
_____	_____	_____	_____	_____

PRACTICE: Can you identify these **thing** nouns by solving their word puzzles?

po__ch   r_ver   t_ee   bro_k

6.6 Idea Nouns

An idea does not occupy space or have mass. An idea is something that comes from the mind. It is something that can be known or thought about, but cannot be touched physically. An **idea** noun may be the name for a feeling or behavior.

> **RULE #1**
> A **noun** is a word for a person, place, thing, or **idea**.

EXAMPLES:

love   joy   happiness   greed

PRACTICE: Words that name **feelings** are ideas. The words that represent feelings are nouns. Write four nouns for feelings after the nouns listed below.

love _____ _____
joy _____ _____

PRACTICE: Words that name **kinds of behavior** are also ideas. The words that represent behaviors are also nouns. After the following nouns, write four nouns for kinds of behavior.

goodness _____ _____ _____ _____

PRACTICE: Can you identify four **behavior** nouns by solving these word puzzles?

t__ntrum   f__t   kin__ness   char__ty

6.7 Common and Proper Nouns

In addition to classification by type, nouns are also classified according to whether they are common or proper. All nouns, no matter what type, must fall into one of these two categories: common or proper. A **common noun** is a general word or name for a person, place, thing, or idea. A common noun is a noun that is not capitalized except when it appears at the beginning of a sentence. Up to this lesson, most of the nouns that have been presented to you have been common nouns. Here are some examples for you to review.

chemist	lake	niece	town	country	beach
magazine	building	ladder	sea	cow	door

Now it is time to learn about proper nouns. Proper nouns are words that are always capitalized whether they are at the beginning of a sentence or somewhere else within a sentence. Furthermore, a **proper noun** is a specific name. This rule will help you identify a proper noun.

> **RULE #2**
> A proper **noun** is a **specific** name for
> a person, place, thing, or idea that is capitalized.

For a person, a proper noun is the name of that person, such as these.

| Flora | Sally | Jenny | Harry | Adam | Sam |

For a place, a proper noun is the specific name of that place, such as these.

| Sahara | Pacific | Australia | Europe | Alabama |

For a thing, a proper noun is the specific name of that thing, such as these.

| Petunia | Earth | Apollo 10 | Congress | Kleenex |

For an idea, a proper noun is a specific name or title, such as these.

| Christianity | Victorianism | Reaganomics | Judaism |

PRACTICE: If you looked at a list of nouns, you would be able to identify proper and common nouns by looking for the words with capital letters. Can you circle the four proper nouns in the following list?

Kim	police	Antarctica	light
kindness	Venus	forest	life
neighbor	greed	Texas	toy

Identifying proper nouns in a list is easy, but identifying them is not as easy in sentences. This difficulty occurs because even common nouns are capitalized when they are found at the beginning of a sentence. In order to identify proper nouns in a sentence, you must look at the capitalized words and ask yourself if they are specific names for a person, place, thing, or idea. Look at the examples on the next page. The proper nouns are underlined, and the type of noun is identified after each sentence.

Helen went to the store to buy some flour to make bread. (person)
Baseball was what Rick and Nick played in their back yard. (person)
The tallest mountain in the world is Everest. (place)
California and Florida are known as the sunshine states. (place)
Bottle after bottle of Ketchup sat lined up on the table. (thing)
Wheaties are a wonderful cold cereal. (thing)
Judaism is the foundation for Christianity. (idea)
In their chambers, legislators voted for a balanced budget using Reaganomics. (idea)

Now look at these sentences again with the common nouns identified in bold black ink.

Helen went to the **store** to buy some **flour** to make **bread**.
Baseball was what Rick and Nick played in their back **yard**.
The tallest **mountain** in the **world** is Everest.
California and Florida are known as the sunshine **states**.
Bottle after **bottle** of Ketchup sat lined up on the **table**.
Wheaties are a wonderful cold **cereal**.
Judaism is the **foundation** for Christianity.
In their **chambers**, **legislators** voted for a balanced **budget** using Reaganomics.

Notice how some common nouns were capitalized, like **baseball** and **bottle**, but only because they were at the beginning of a sentence. Furthermore, **baseball** and **bottle** are not specific names, like Rick, Nick, Ketchup, and California. So how could you tell the proper nouns from the common nouns? Here are three good steps to follow.

1. First, look at each capitalized noun you find in a sentence.
2. Second, ask yourself if the capitalized noun is a specific name for something.
3. Third, if the capitalized noun is a specific name for something, then it is a proper noun; if not, then it is a common noun.

PRACTICE: Here are a few sentences for you to practice identifying proper nouns from common nouns. Underline all of the proper nouns in each sentence below.

1. The postal route was out of the way for Bob Stewart.
2. Flora pruned the roses in her garden in February.
3. My sister likes to look for seashells at the beach near Oceanside.
4. Money is not to waste but to use with care.
5. When winter is over, we will happily travel to Iowa and Minnesota to visit friends.

PRACTICE: Now look at the above sentences again. Circle all of the common nouns in each sentence. Are you getting better at distinguishing proper nouns from common nouns?

 Look at your writing worksheet on page 49. Did you write any nouns that are proper nouns in your sentences? Did you capitalize those nouns? If not, do so now.

6.8 Common and Proper Noun Pairs

Capital letters are special markers in good writing. They show where sentences begin, what should be respected, and what is important to people who speak the English language. When a proper noun names a specific place, it is capitalized. The names for countries and states, such as Canada, America, Minnesota, and Iowa, are proper nouns that are capitalized because they name a specific place. Words like **street**, **river**, **lake**, and **mountain** may also be a part of a name for a specific place. These words are common nouns which are not normally capitalized. When they are paired together with a proper noun naming a place, however, a new rule of grammar applies.

> **RULE #3**
> A **common noun** that is paired with a **proper noun** which names a specific place, must be capitalized.

EXAMPLES:

Baltimore **S**treet Mississippi **R**iver
Lake **M**ichigan Cascade **M**ountains

PRACTICE: Rewrite the following names of places; capitalize all of the **common** nouns that are **paired with a proper noun**.

A. mount Baldy_____
B. Suez canal_____
C. Ohio drive_____
D. Missouri river_____
E. lake Erie_____
F. Niagara falls_____

 Look at your writing worksheet. Did you write any common nouns that are paired with a proper noun? Did you capitalize both nouns? If not, do so now.

6.9 Nouns and Pronouns

Capital letters are special markers in good writing. A noun that names a specific person, place, thing, or idea is capitalized. A common noun that is paired with a proper noun which names a specific place, must be capitalized.

There is one more rule to learn. This rule will help you when writing your compositions. It will also help you to know what should be important and respected in your everyday life. This rule is about nouns and pronouns. The word **pronoun** is composed of two separate parts: pro and noun. The word part **pro** means to be for something. You already know that a **noun** is a word that names a person, place, thing, or idea. A **pronoun** is a word that is **a replacement for** a noun. Pronouns are words like **I**, **he**, **she**, **it**, **you**, **we**, **they**, **them**, etc.

You have learned to capitalize a person's name. This capitalization is done not only out of respect but also because a person's name is a specific title for someone. A person's name is a proper noun. A person's name is more specific. It cannot be applied to every male or female on earth because not every person on earth has the same name. A person's name names only a limited number of persons who were given that name in some official or culturally recognized way.

We love and honor one Elohim/God who has been made know to us in three different identities. These three are sometimes referred to by the group-word **Trinity**, which means three are one. These three are very important and worthy of our utmost respect. Each One has a real, proper name that must always be capitalized. Their real names are not English names; they are Hebrew names. Our Heavenly Father has a real name (Yahweh), as does Jesus (Yahshua) and the Holy Spirit (Ruach Hakodesh).

When these three are named by other nouns and pronouns, such as **father, son, spirit, he, him, elohim, trinity,** or **the word**, a new rule of English grammar is necessary. Without this rule, these words are not normally capitalized because they are common nouns and common pronouns. However, when using these words in reference to God/Yahweh, Jesus/Yahshua, and the Holy Spirit/Ruach Hakodesh, out of respect we treat them as proper nouns and proper pronouns, which must be capitalized.

> **RULE #4**
> Always **capitalize** a **noun** or **pronoun** that refers to God/Yahweh, Jesus/Yahshua, or the Holy Spirit/Ruach Hakodesh.

EXAMPLES:

1. "For **Elohim** so loved the world that **He** gave **His** only brought-forth **Son**, so that everyone who believes in **Him** should not perish but possess everlasting life." (John/Yohanan 3:16)
2. Yahshua answered, "Truly, truly, I say to you, unless one is born of water and the **Spirit**, he is unable to enter into the reign of **Elohim**." (John/Yohanan 3:5)
3. "Set them apart in **Your** truth - **Your Word** is truth." (John/Yohanan 17:17)

PRACTICE: Rewrite the following scriptures and **capitalize** all of the **nouns** and **pronouns** that refer to God/Yahweh, Jesus/Yahshua, or the Holy Spirit/Ruach Hakodesh.

A. Show me your ways, O yahweh; teach me your paths. (From Proverbs/Mishle)

_____

B. And he said, "abba, father, all is possible for you. Make this cup pass from me. Yet not what I desire, but what you desire." (Yahshua praying to Yahweh)

_____

_____

C. And turning around and seeing his taught ones, he rebuked Kepha/Steven, saying, "Get behind me, Satan! For your thoughts are not those of elohim, but those of men."
(Yahshua speaking to Steven/Kepha)

_____

_____

_____

Look at your writing worksheet on page 49. Did you write any nouns or pronouns that represent a person of the Trinity? Did you capitalize those nouns and pronouns? If not, do so now. Now is the time to complete your composition. Rewrite or type it neatly on a fresh piece of paper and turn it in to your teacher. Don't forget to indent your paragraphs.

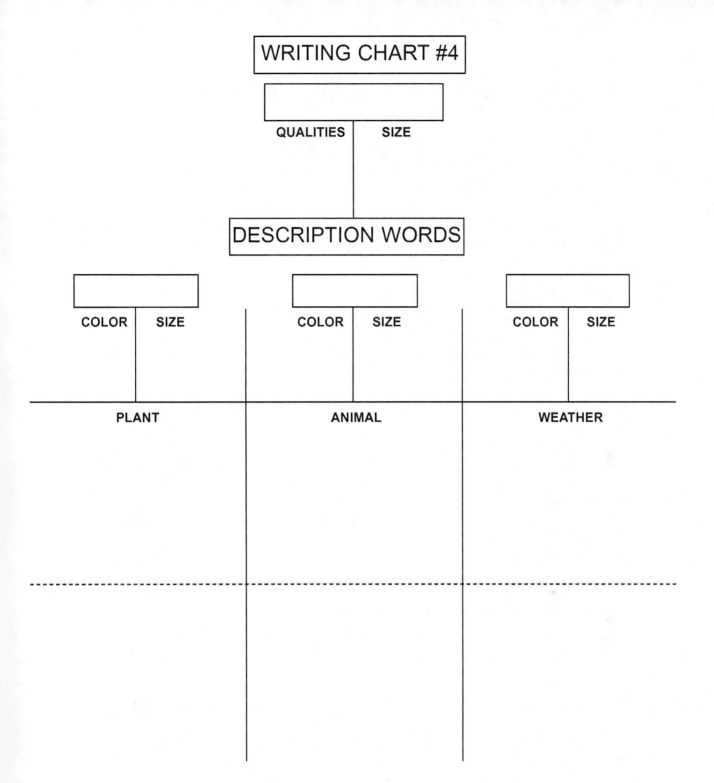

WRITING ASSIGNMENT #4

Your assignment is to write a description of your favorite **pastoral scene**, using lots of words that will help a reader see your scene in his/her mind when he/she reads your writing. You will write about your scene as a **participant**. Do not describe any people, but you may use the words **I**, **he**, **she**, **we**, or **they**. As you work, use the checklist boxes below to mark each item you have completed.

Compose your sentences and paragraphs on the writing worksheet that follows these instructions. Work through the grammar chapter; it will instruct you when to compete your composition.

1. **Format**
   - [ ] Write a title in capital letters at the top of the page.
   - [ ] Write your name under the title.
   - [ ] Begin the first paragraph on the **second** line below your name.
2. **Construction**
   - [ ] Your description must have **three** paragraphs.
   - [ ] Each paragraph must have **three** sentences that have **more than seven** words in them.
   - [ ] Choose **objects** for your scene that would normally be found together.
   - [ ] Choose **quality**, **color**, and **size** words that are realistic for each object.
   - [ ] Choose the **weather** and its **conditions** that are realistic for your scene.
3. **Grammar**
   - [ ] End each sentence with a **period, exclamation point,** or **question mark**.
   - [ ] Draw **commas** between multiple describing words.
   - [ ] **Capitalize** all words properly.
   - [ ] Indent the beginning of each paragraph.
   - [ ] Be careful to use proper word tenses.
   - [ ] Make some of your sentences long and some short.
   - [ ] Make sure each paragraph contains unity, flows logically, and relates to the others.
4. **Polish**
   - [ ] You may have to write your description several times.
   - [ ] Only turn in a final copy of your paper that has been written neatly and clearly with no smudge marks.
   - [ ] Make sure you have spelled all of your words correctly.
   - [ ] Use the dictionary to check the spelling of difficult words.
   - [ ] Do not forget to use your thesaurus if you need help finding a word.
5. **Ethics**
   - [ ] Work on your own and make your description original.
   - [ ] Do not copy a description from any other writing.
   - [ ] Make sure the language of your paper conforms to Philippians 4:8.
6. **Creativity**
   - [ ] Make sure your composition creates an interesting mental picture for your reader.

WRITING WORKSHEET #4
COMPOSE YOUR SENTENCES ON THE FOLLOWING LINES.

1. _____
2. _____
3. _____
4. _____
5. _____
6. _____
7. _____
8. _____
9. _____

ORGANIZE YOUR PARAGRAPHS ON THE FOLLOWING LINES.

CHARACTERS: ETHICS SKILLS

UNIT 3 SUPPLIES

BIBLE
DICTIONARY
PENCIL
THESAURUS
WRITING PAPER

7.1 Scriptural Ethics

You have learned that to write well, you need to keep your mind focused on good things that are of good report. This advice means that you are to work to push bad thoughts out of your mind and stay away from evil. When studying about pastoral scenes, you learned that they contain the qualities of goodness and kindness. Kindness is a good quality to use in your writing.

Another word you found in studying the scriptures was the word **righteousness**. Righteousness is a big word that has a lot of powerful meaning. It is often spoken about in the scriptures because righteousness is very important to understand in the walk of a Christian. Righteousness involves doing what is right, doing what is fair, and doing what is morally correct. Christians must behave well and do what is right. In their relations with others, they must be fair and not selfish. Christians must also have moral values that they live by so that they do not fall into sin.

In writing, the best type of compositions focus on that which is good and right, fair and morally correct. Writing of these things helps and teaches others how to behave well. They also fill another person's mind with good things about which to think. The good values you share with others will help them to know what is a good value. You may help those persons to stay strong in their good values or to begin to have good values.

To share good values with others, however, you must have good values yourself. They must be values by which you live. Otherwise, your sharing with others will not be helpful. If you do not live by the values you share, others will not believe that they are good values. Also, when you do not live by the good values that you share, you make Jesus/Yahshua meaningless and worthless to others. To make Yahshua and His death on the cross meaningless brings shame upon Him and all good Christians. This behavior is a very bad sin. Therefore, studying the scriptures is important to make sure that you know good values and live by them.

Scripture Study

A hard thing to learn and understand is how to interact with others in the best ways possible. When you think of an unkind or crabby person, sometimes knowing how to deal with them is difficult. When you meet new types of people with whom you have not had any prior experience, you may not be aware of things that offend them. The Bible teaches about different types of problems that may occur in your life and how to deal with them. They also teach about universal types of behavior that will not offend anybody.

For most people, dealing with people who are nice and good is easier that dealing with those who are mean and sinful. While mean and sinful people sometimes need to be dealt with in a firm manner which protects you from harm, sometimes all they need is a little wisdom from Heaven that you can share with them. Wisdom from Heaven can be shared with others in your writing. To learn about wisdom from Heaven, locate the following scripture verse and write it on the lines provided.

YOUR WRITING SHOULD **PROMOTE** THIS TYPE OF WISDOM.

James 3:17-18 _____

_____

_____

_____

The scripture you just looked up has many describing words in about wisdom that comes from Heaven. This wisdom is very important and helpful when you are having a problem. Have you ever had a problem about which you either prayed to Jesus for a solution or asked another human being for a solution? If you received a solution, were you sure it came from Heaven? This scripture is a guide to help you decide whether a solution you might like to try for a problem is from Heaven. By carefully reviewing what the scripture tells you and comparing it to the solution you have received, you can determine whether Heaven is blessing you or not.

The first thing to notice that the scripture tells you is that wisdom from Heaven is clean. Being clean means that something does not contain sin. So, when one needs to solve a problem, if the solution to that problem involves doing something sinful, then that solution is not from Heaven. If the wisdom you use to solve a problem is clean, the solution must then also be peaceable and gentle. If it is not peaceable and gentle, the solution is not from Heaven. A good solution from Heaven will also cause the people involved in a problem to be ready to obey what is right.

Many problems in life involve either someone being wrongly hurt or something being wrongly destroyed. That fact is why the scripture next tells you that wisdom from Heaven will offer that person or situation compassion. That wisdom will also cause good fruit or a good result.

In solving a problem, wisdom will not favor unfairly the wrong over the right, the rich over the poor, or the smart over the challenged person, etc. Have you ever felt that someone you knew pretended to care about you when he/she really did not care about you? Have you ever had someone tell you how to behave well when they did not themselves behave well? This type of fake behavior is named **hypocrisy**. The wisdom from Heaven truly cares to set a bad problem right and is never fake. The wisdom from Heaven also knows exactly how to set a situation right without failing to accomplish the goal of goodness. When a problem is set right, the result is named **the fruit of righteousness**. This result means that the problem will be corrected in a way that the right person or right situation will prevail, and peace will result.

When you write stories that might have a problem in them, a most helpful favor to others is to write about things that have happened in your life where you have found a Heavenly solution. When you do this sharing, you may help another person to solve a problem.

7.2 Scriptural Ethics

The Bible teaches about different types of problems that may occur in your life and how to deal with them. When you are seeking a solution to a problem, pray to Jesus for His answer. Next, to test the answer that you think you received, make sure that it obeys James 3:17-18. If it does, try solving the problem with that answer and see what happens. Good solutions to problems always seem like wonderful miracles. As you learn to find Heavenly solutions to all of your problems, you will get better at recognizing the right solution as well as become a better person yourself.

In your communications with others and especially people with whom you have not had any prior experience, the Bible can teach you how to be a pleasant person who does not offend. Find the following verses in a Bible and write their teachings on the lines provided.

YOUR WRITING SHOULD **PROMOTE** THIS TYPE OF WISDOM.

Proverbs 22:11 _____

Proverbs 27:9 _____

The verses you looked up tell about how to be friendly. First, you must love cleanness of heart. This love means that when you think of another person or meet another person, you must try to think well of them and not have any feeling in your heart that is unkind towards that person or mankind in general.

Mattithyahu/Matthew 12:34 tells you, "**For the mouth speaks from the overflow of the heart**." If your heart is sad, you will speak sad words, but if your heart is happy, you will speak happy words. This truth is why you must guard your heart to keep it clean. If you have any sin against another in your heart or any general sin, like pride, that may hurt another person, you will surely say something that is unkind. Then you will not be a friendly person. However, when your heart is clean, your speech will be pleasant and even a king will want to be your friend!

The second way to be friendly is to make sure that anything you share with others that tells them how to do something should always be sweet. To be sweet means to be pleasant, kind, and gentle. This type of behavior will not offend anybody.

When you write about people or to people, if you follow what you have learned in these verses, you will write good things that others will like to read. You will also make friends even with readers you do not know!

CHAPTER 8

CHARACTERS: WRITING SKILLS

8.1 Names for Characters

You have learned how to write a scene with no action and a scene with action. Describing the elements of a scene takes time but is well worth the work to make a story interesting and realistic. Sometimes the actions of one element of a scene affect the actions of other elements. You have learned to think about when this effect might happen and how to describe that interaction. Now is the time to learn about adding people to a scene.

The people in a story are named the **characters**. The characters often talk and move about in a story. These characters and their actions must be carefully planned and thought out to make them fit well in a story and be believable. In order to tell about the characters in a story, you must be able to identify and describe them.

To learn about how to write realistically about characters, you will learn to write about people that you know. These people will be your friends. Write the word **FRIENDS** in the box under the words **WRITING CHART #5** on page 56. What kind of friends do you have: male or female?

Think of three of your friends. How would you begin to identify them? Would their names help to identify them? Does a name identify? If you and your mother were at a party in a room full of your friends, and you wanted your mother to find one of your friends, would telling her that friend's name be helpful? Would the name help her find that person? Would the name help her in the future to be able to identify that friend from other people in the world?

A person's name identifies that individual person from other people you know. When you write about a friend, would mentioning the name of that person help a reader remember what you wrote about the friend? The name of a person helps a reader to remember about whom you have written. In order to help a reader remember the characters in a story, the best method is to give them names. When you assign names to characters, not only can they be easily identified, but also they can keep your reader from being confused.

 To write about your friends, a helpful step is to first start by writing their names in the three boxes below the **DESCRIPTION WORDS** box on page 56. Now you have the names of three characters for a story.

8.2 Description of Characters' Features

When you described objects in a scene, first you identified their names; then, you decided what colors and sizes they were. When describing characters, you will not only describe colors and sizes but other physical features of those characters as well. Think about the many different parts of the body, which may include a head, torso, legs, and arms. These parts of the body have other parts, like eyes, a nose, or even toes. Characters also have hair that they arrange in many different styles. They wear clothes and accessories that come in all kinds of shapes, styles, and sizes. Characters may also exhibit different varieties of expressions, like happiness and sadness. These qualities may be expressed through laughing or crying.

There are many parts to each character, and describing them can seem to be a very big task. In **UNIT 1** you learned that when a task is big, the best approach is to break it down into little pieces and work on those pieces one at a time. When describing a character, the best method is to choose just a few features so that you are not overwhelmed trying to write about them. Certain features about a character are more important to describe than others. These features are the ones that are not usually changed in a story, such as nationality, size, hair color, eye color, or skin color. When you describe a character, if you keep these types of features unchanged throughout the story, your reader will be better able to keep tract of that character in the story.

Once you have chosen the features of a character, how do you decide what those features will look like? This decision is another place where writing about reality is a good idea. A lot of good stories are written about real life and real people. A special friend, neighbor, worker, or relative you know might have the perfect features for a character of a story. When you design a character like someone you know, deciding what his/her features will look like is easier.

On your writing chart, you have three characters that are your friends. To describe these people, you will need to ask yourself many questions. You can ask a question about each of the categories listed in the **WRITING CHART** on page 56. Start by asking yourself what nationality your friends are; then write your answer for each friend under each word **NATION**.

People and characters come in many different sizes and shapes. Are your three friends tall, short, skinny, plump, or somewhere in between? Think about each friend and try to come up with one or two words that describe each one's size and shape. Write those words under the **SIZE** columns on the writing chart.

The hair, eyes, and skin of a character may also be important to describe in a story. What color of hair do your friends have? Is their hair brown, blond, red, black, or some shades of these colors? What color are their eyes? Are they blue, brown, green, or hazel? Write your answers to these questions under the **HAIR** and **EYES** columns of the writing chart. What is the color and texture of their skin? Do your friends have freckles, moles, porcelain skin, or smooth skin? Write the answers to this question under the **SKIN** column for each of your friends.

Now look at your chart and see how much information you have about each friend. All of the description words you have on your chart can be used in your writing. Wasn't asking questions about your friends helpful? Remember this helpful step in your future writing about anything, whether a person, scenery, an animal, or an object, such as a spaceship or a house.

Ask yourself as many questions as you can about what you want to describe; then write your answers down and see how many description words you have for your writing.

8.3 Description of Characters' Personalities and Behaviors

You have filled your writing chart with many good words telling about what the features of your friends look like. Describing how a friend looks is also like a paint-by-number painting. In this type of painting, the outline is already drawn for you, and all you have to do is paint colors inside the lines. Just like in one of these paintings, in a description of a friend, you do not have to describe the outline of their features unless they are very different than standard. We all know what an eye, ear, or arm looks like. This fact makes your description job a little easier so that you only have to fill in the features with words. As with the colors in a painting, you can identify each feature in more detail by writing words such as **blue eyes** or **long, straight nose**.

The features of a character that don't usually change in a story are nationality, size, hair, eyes, skin color, and skin texture. These are helpful things to describe about a character when you are first introducing your reader to that character. Another feature of a character that is helpful to describe is his/her personality. Describing personality helps your reader get to know your character a little better. If you were writing a story with conversation, personality could also be an important part of that conversation. What do you think personality is? Can you explain it?

Personality is about a person's patterns of habit. Personality is also about physical or mental types of behavior that make a person unique or identify him/her. How can you describe personality? Words like **happy**, **sad**, **bubbly**, and **shy** all describe personality. Words like **funny**, **awkward**, **quick-witted**, and **polite** also describe personality.

How can you see evidence of personality in a character's behavior? You can describe the evidence of that personality when writing words and phrases like **smiles a lot**, **bounces**, or **waves his/her arms when he/she talks**. Personality behaviors may also be described by telling that a character always walks fast or slow. Telling jokes, whistling, laughing, or singing a lot are also personality behaviors.

Have you known your friends for a long time? If you have, you have seen how they behave in many different situations. When you see the behavior of a person over a period of time, you will see a pattern. That pattern will tell you about their personality. When writing about the personalities of your friends, you tell about what behaviors make them unique or identify them as individuals. To do this describing, you must think about their moods and habits; then try to describe their moods and habits in words. Take a few moments now to think about each of your three friends. Write some words that tell about their personalities in the columns for each friend under the **PERSONALITY** boxes. Make sure that you include words and phrases that also describe the behavior of their personalities.

8.4 Description of Characters' Clothing and Accessories

In today's world, many people are able to dress according to their personality. Others choose the way they dress because of finances, trends in fashion, or dependence on someone else to pick their clothes for them. No matter why a person wears the clothes they do, clothes cover a large part of a person's body. Telling about those clothes helps to describe a character in a story. Some writers also try to match the personality of a character with the type of clothes he/she wears. This technique helps to strengthen the understanding of a character's personality and also helps to make a character predictable and memorable.

Your friends may dress according to their personalities, or they may not. However they dress, try to remember the last time you saw them. Next, try to answer each of the following questions about each friend. Write all of your answers for each friend in the columns under the **CLOTHES AND ACCESSORIES** box on page 56.

GIRLS
1. What objects of clothing and accessories do the girls wear?
   For example, do they wear dresses, or do they wear pants with shirts or blouses? Do they wear necklaces or barrettes in their hair?
2. Are their clothes fancy or plain?
3. What colors are the clothing and accessories the girls wear?
4. What size of clothing or accessories do they wear? Are these items large or small?

BOYS
1. What objects of clothing and accessories do the boys wear? For example, do they wear pants and shirts--or sweat suits? Do they wear watches or rings?
2. Are their clothes fancy or plain?
3. What colors are the clothing and accessories the boys wear?
4. What size of clothing or accessories do they wear? Are these items large or small?

Now you have a lot of description words to use when writing about your friends. You should not describe every feature for each friend as that describing will take too long. You will have to decide what features you want to include in your writing assignment so that a reader can form a good picture of that person in his/her mind. You can start with any of your friend's features: eyes, nose, hair, height, body size, or clothes.

This lesson's assignment is to write descriptions of your three friends. You will write those descriptions including features and personality. What description words will you use to write about your friends so that a reader will be helped to see them as you do? Look at the lists you have made on the writing chart. Circle the best words that describe each friend. Do you need to add any more description words? Also, think about what action words you might use to describe each friend's personality behaviors. Circle the best action words on your lists.

Here are two examples of descriptions of people that are examples of good writing. The first example has description and action; the second example contains description, action, and personality.

1. Jessica has braided, shining, blonde hair that reaches all the way down her back to the belt on her blue jeans. Her face is pretty and sweet. The skin of her complexion is a soft, smooth, brown color.

When Jessica plays jump rope, her braids fly up and down just like the pink and green bracelets on her wrists. Jumping rope is easy for Jessica because she is not very tall but not very short either. Some would describe her height as just about average.

2. Sam is a strong, tall man. He is so tall that often his head is well above a crowd. Sometimes he has to duck when going through doorways.

His eyes are light blue like the sky on a partly cloudy day. His hair is brown and always neatly combed. When he smiles, his white teeth flash brightly and sincerely. His smile and laughter can cheer up a whole room of people.

Turn to the writing assignment on page 57 and read it. If you have any questions, please ask your teacher. On the **WRITING WORKSHEET**, page 58, prepare your sentences and paragraphs for the first friend.

WRITING CHART #5

DESCRIPTION WORDS

NATION	SIZE		NATION	SIZE		NATION	SIZE	
HAIR	EYES	SKIN	HAIR	EYES	SKIN	HAIR	EYES	SKIN

PERSONALITY

CLOTHES AND ACCESSORIES

OBJECT	COLOR	SIZE	OBJECT	COLOR	SIZE	OBJECT	COLOR	SIZE

WRITING ASSIGNMENT #5

Your assignment is to write **three descriptions, each of a different friend**. Write each description, using features, personality and/or behavior, and clothes and/or accessories. Use lots of words that help a reader see a picture of your friends in his/her mind when he/she reads your writing. Prepare your sentences and paragraphs about the first friend by writing them on the **WRITING WORKSHEET** (p. 58). Use some fresh writing paper to prepare your sentences and paragraphs about the other two friends.

1. **Format**
   - ☐ You will prepare three separate papers.
   - ☐ Write the name of one friend in capital letters at the top of each page.
   - ☐ Write your name under the title.
   - ☐ Begin the first paragraph on the **second** line below your name.
2. **Construction**
   - ☐ You must describe **three** friends. Write **one or two** paragraphs about each friend.
   - ☐ Each paragraph must have **seven or more** sentences.
   - ☐ Choose the features of your friends that are the most interesting and most memorable.
   - ☐ Choose words and phrases that apply to their personalities and behaviors.
   - ☐ Choose words and phrases that apply to their clothes and accessories.
3. **Grammar**
   - ☐ Capitalize your words properly.
   - ☐ Use periods, exclamation points, question marks, and commas properly.
   - ☐ Indent the beginning of each paragraph.
   - ☐ Make some of your sentences long and some short.
   - ☐ Be careful to use proper word tenses.
   - ☐ Make sure each paragraph contains unity, flows logically, and relates to one another.
4. **Polish**
   - ☐ You may have to write your description several times.
   - ☐ Only turn in a final copy of each paper if it has been written neatly.
   - ☐ Make sure you have spelled all of your words correctly.
   - ☐ Use the dictionary and the thesaurus to find better words.
5. **Ethics**
   - ☐ Work on your own and make your descriptions original.
   - ☐ Do not copy a description from any other writing.
   - ☐ Do not write what you would not want a friend to write about you.
   - ☐ Make sure the language of your paper conforms to Philippians 4:8.
6. **Creativity**
   - ☐ Write your composition to create an interesting mental picture for your reader.

WRITING WORKSHEET #5
COMPOSE YOUR SENTENCES ON THE FOLLOWING LINES.

1. _____
2. _____
3. _____
4. _____
5. _____
6. _____
7. _____
8. _____

ORGANIZE YOUR PARAGRAPHS ON THE FOLLOWING LINES.

WRITING PREPARATION

Did you have a lot of fun writing about your friends? Was writing about someone you know easier than creating a whole new person? In most stories, the characters are very important. For this reason, an equally important goal is to describe the characters very well. To learn how to describe characters well just takes practice. When you start with people you know, you make this work a little easier. You are also assured that your characters will be realistic and believable.

To gain more practice at describing characters, you will write in your next assignment about family members. Think of three family members (or relatives) whom you know well so that you can easily write about them. In the blank box below the **WRITING CHART #6** box on page 68, write the word **FAMILY**.

For the descriptions of your friends, you used their names. A name helps to identify someone. A title such as father, mother, sister, or brother also helps to identify someone, though not as uniquely as a name. In a story, however, you may only want to use the title of a person throughout your writing. For this reason, you will practice using only titles in the descriptions of your family. In the three blank boxes under the **DESCRIPTION WORDS** box, write the titles of your three family members, such as mother, father, sister, brother, etc.

Now you have a lot of description words to choose for each family member. To think of those words, carefully work through the following list for each person. Write your answers to each question in the correct columns on **WRITING CHART #6**.

1. What nationality is each of your family members?
2. Are your family members tall, short, skinny, plump, or somewhere in between? Try to think of one or two words that describe each one's size and shape.
3. What color of hair does each of your family members have?
4. What color are their eyes?
5. What is the color and texture of each family member's skin?
6. What one word would you use to describe each family member's personality?
7. What behavior does each personality exhibit?

GIRLS

8. What objects of clothing and accessories do the girls wear? For example, do they wear dresses, or do they wear pants with shirts or blouses? Do they wear necklaces or barrettes in their hair?
9. Are their clothes fancy or plain?
10. What colors are the clothing and accessories the girls wear?
11. What size of clothing or accessories do they wear? Are these items large or small?

BOYS

12. What objects of clothing and accessories do the boys wear? For example, do they wear pants and shirts--or sweat suits? Do they wear watches or rings?
13. Are their clothes fancy or plain?
14. What colors are the clothing and accessories the boys wear?
15. What size of clothing or accessories do they wear? Are these items large or small?

Now you have a lot of description words to use when writing about your family members. Decide on the best words you want to use in your writing, and circle those words. Next, review the writing examples on the bottom of page 55.

Read **WRITING ASSIGNMENT #6** on page 69 and begin your writing. Prepare your sentences and paragraphs on the **WRITING WORKSHEET**, page 70, for the first family member.

CHAPTER 9
CHARACTERS: GRAMMAR SKILLS

9.1 Grammar Rules

The study of grammar teaches you how to write better so that other people can understand what you are telling them. The rules of grammar are important to learn. When you learn them and practice them, they will become easy to remember. They also make writing enjoyable!

In this chapter, you will review rules about adjectives, nouns, verbs, sentence structure, commas, homonyms, and synonyms. Read each grammar rule and do the **PRACTICE** exercises. When working on your writing assignments, remember to follow these rules. Part of your grade will be determined by how well you follow **all** of the rules you learn.

9.2 Adjectives

You have learned that description words help your reader to see a picture of something in his/her mind. Description words make your writing more interesting. There are many kinds of description words. Words that **name things** are named **nouns**. A noun can name a person, place, thing, or idea. Describing words that **give more information about a noun** are named **adjectives**. Adjectives can be size words, such as **big**, **small**, **tall**, or **little**. They can also be color words, such as **red**, **yellow**, **black**, or **blue**. Texture words like **soft**, **rough**, **smooth**, or **abrasive** are also adjectives.

> **RULE #1**
> An **adjective** describes a noun by **giving more information** about that noun.

Using adjectives to help your reader see something better in his/her mind makes for better writing and better reading. Suppose you were describing a character in a story, and you wrote this sentence.

> John is a man with hair and skin.

If there were more information in your writing about John, you could write a better sentence. You could add the adjectives **tall**, **red**, and **smooth** to give more information about John.

> John is a **tall** man with **red** hair and **smooth** skin.

This sentence is more interesting because more information is given about John. A complete list of the types of adjectives would include words that tell about behaviors, color, shape, size, sound, taste, and touch. In your writing before this chapter, you only used adjectives that describe behavior, color, shape, and size.

PRACTICE: In each of these sentences, circle the **adjectives**.

A. The gold medal was won by a great athlete.
B. She had a big umbrella.
C. The slow elephant walked down the road.
D. The sky turned pink and purple just before sunset.
E. Inside the building, a round fountain made a musical sound.
F. Bananas are sweet and soft when they are ripe.

Many of the words you wrote on **WRITING CHART #6** are adjectives. The sentences on your worksheets contain many of these words. How many adjectives did you use? Could your sentences be improved by adding more adjectives? If so, make those changes now.

9.3 Commas

You are learning to use a variety of description words in your sentences. They may be nouns or adjectives. Often when you use adjectives in writing, they appear right before the noun about which they are giving more information. If you use more than one adjective in a series, your sentence might look like this one.

The **lazy, black** dog was sitting under the cool shade of the tree.

When using several adjectives in a series, pay special attention to the use of commas to separate the adjectives from one another. There are three simple rules about commas.

1. The first rule of commas applies when you use only one adjective before a noun in a sentence; there is no need for any commas.

> **RULE #1**
> When **one adjective** is written before a noun, there is no **comma**.

EXAMPLE: She has **beautiful** hair.

The second rule of commas is the most difficult. When you use two adjectives in a row before a noun, you must place a comma after the first adjective if the adjectives could be written in reverse order or be joined by the word **and**, and the sentence still makes sense.

> **RULE #2**
> Where **two adjectives** are written in a series before a noun, a comma must be placed after the first adjective if the sentence still makes sense (1) when the adjectives are written in reverse order, and (2) when the adjectives are joined by the word **and**.

EXAMPLES: She has **thick, brown** hair. (She has **thick**/brown and **brown**/thick hair.)
She has **autumn brown** hair. (This sentence has no commas
because **She has autumn and brown hair** does not make sense;
neither does **She has brown and autumn hair**.)

The third rule of commas covers when you use three or more adjectives in a row before a noun; you must place commas after all but the last adjective.

> **RULE #3**
> When **three adjectives** are written in a series before a noun, place a comma after all but the last adjective.

EXAMPLES: Her **blue, pink,** and **yellow** dress was pretty.
She has **beautiful, thick, brown** hair.

PRACTICE: In these sentences, place **commas** after the adjectives where they are needed.

A. The huge brick house was built on a hill.

B. The soft green grass was wet with dew.
C. The winter white paint was perfect for the kitchen pantry.
D. The long tall fence surrounded a small garden house.
E. Father added a log to the hot flamy fire.
F. The large Monday brunch started before all of the guests arrived.

Review the adjectives that you have used in your writing. Did you write more than one adjective in a series before a noun in any of your sentences? If so, did you insert commas properly where they belong? When you are not sure whether to use a comma, read your sentence out loud and insert the word **and** in between the adjectives. Does it make sense? Insert a comma. If it doesn't make sense, omit the comma.

9.4 Verbs

Another type of word that is important in a sentence is the verb. The **verb** of a sentence tells what the subject or character is **doing** or **being**. Verbs help your reader see what is happening in the scenes of your stories. An **action verb** uses an **action** (doing) word. Examples of action verbs are words like **wash**, **bounce**, **swim**, or **drive**.

RULE #1
The **verb** of a sentence tells what the subject or character is **doing** or **being**.

PRACTICE: In each sentence circle the **action verb** that tells what the subject is **doing**.

A. My dog likes the rain and its puddles.
B. Jesse closed the window.
C. The ballerina twirled on her toes.
D. The band marched around the block.
E. Lisa braided her long hair.

A **verb** that tells what the subject or character is **being** is usually some form of the verb "to be." Examples of being verbs are words such as **is**, **was**, **am**, and **are**.

PRACTICE: Circle the **being verbs** in these sentences.

A. Tony was a basketball player.
B. The pasture is green.
C. I am very cold.
D. Doughnuts are yummy!
E. There are four grandparents with homes on my street.

Review your worksheets to make sure that all of your sentences contain a verb.

9.5 Subject/Verb Agreement in the Present Tense

Every sentence contains at least one subject (noun or pronoun) and one verb. Subjects and verbs usually appear as pairs in a sentence. No matter where they appear in a sentence, any subject and verb that are paired must follow **RULE #1**.

RULE #1
In every sentence written in the **present tense**, any **subject** and **verb** that are paired must **agree** with one another.

This sentence has a **SUBJECT** (**father**) and a **VERB** (**talks**) that agree.
EXAMPLE: The **father talks** very fast!

Subject and verb pairs agree in the present tense when they follow these rules about being singular or plural.

RULE #2
When a **subject** is **singular**, the **verb** must also be **singular**.

Most singular verbs end with the letter **s**.
EXAMPLE: The toddler **likes** to eat ice cream!

EXCEPTION TO RULE #2
When the **subject** is **I** or **you**, the **verb** must be **plural**.

Plural verbs **do not** end with the letter **s**.
EXAMPLE: I **like** to eat ice cream!

PRACTICE: Write the correct **singular verb** for each **singular subject** on the line.

A. **She** _____ to make quilts. (like, likes)
B. **He** _____ a rock in a pond. (throw, throws)
C. **It** _____ time to build a house. (take, takes)
D. The **frog** _____ from rock to rock in the little stream. (jump, jumps)
E. The **girl** _____ her pencil. (sharpen, sharpens)
F. **Mother** _____ the milk this time. (buy, buys)

RULE #3
When a **subject** is **plural**, the **verb** must also be **plural**.

EXAMPLE: They **like** to eat ice cream!

PRACTICE: Write the correct **plural verb** for each **plural subject** on the line.

A. **They** _____ clothes to the poor. (give, gives)
B. **We** _____ strawberries in the summer. (pick, picks)
C. The **sisters** _____ the baby to sleep with a lullaby. (sing, sings)
D. The **uncles** _____ change the flat tire. (help, helps)
E. The **neighbors** _____ their gardens each week. (weed, weeds)

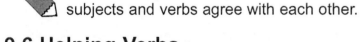

Review your worksheets to make sure that in all of your sentences, the paired subjects and verbs agree with each other.

9.6 Helping Verbs

The **verb** of a sentence tells what the subject or character is doing or being. An action verb uses an action (doing) word. A verb that tells what a subject or character is being is usually some form of the verb "to be."

Many simple sentences contain only one verb, as in this sentence: He **sat** on the chair. In this sentence, the verb **sat** is named the **main** verb. More complex sentences often contain more than one main verb, as in this sentence: He **sat** on a chair while she **sang** a pretty song.

Each verb in this sentence is still named a main verb even though there are two verbs in the sentence. This fact is because each verb stands alone as the only word telling what the subject of each part of the sentence is being or doing.

Sometimes a main verb does not stand alone. In some sentences, there may be more than one verb written together in a phrase. When this happens, the group of verbs is named a verb phrase. A **verb phrase** consists of a main verb and one or more helping verbs that are written before a main verb. A **helping verb** supports a main verb by adding more meaning to the action or state of being of that main verb.

RULE #1
A helping verb may only occur in a verb phrase. A **helping verb** is an extra verb (or verbs) that is written **before a main verb** in a sentence.

The helping verbs in these examples are printed in bold. There is **one** helping verb in each verb phrase. The helping verb appears **before** the main verb (a form of the verb **go**).

EXAMPLES:

she **was** going   he **can** go
they **have** gone   they **should** go
he **did** go   she **will** go
you **may** go   I **am** going

The helping verbs in the following examples are printed in bold. There are **two** helping verbs in each verb phrase. Notice how the helping verbs appear **before** the main verb (a form of the verb **sleep**).

EXAMPLES:

she **may be** sleeping   he **has been** sleeping
they **have been** sleeping   they **should be** sleeping
he **must have** slept   she **will be** sleeping
you **could have** slept   I **can be** sleeping

To decide whether a sentence has a verb phrase containing one or two helping verbs, first you must find the main verb. The main verb will tell what the subject is doing or being, while a helping verb or verbs will support the main verb by adding more meaning to its action or state of being.

Helping verbs may be (1) forms of words that are normally "being" verbs, like **are** and **was**; (2) the action verbs **do** and **will**; (3) the action verb that shows possession (has); or (4) words that give permission, like **may** and **can**. The following is a list of common helping verbs and the various forms in which they may be written.

HELPING VERB FORMS

be: be, is, am, was, were, are, been, being
do: do, does, did
has: has, have, had
may: may, might, must
can: can, could
shall: shall, should
will: will, would

PRACTICE: In these sentences, circle the main verb.

A. The ball rolled across the pavement.
B. The plane flew over the houses.
C. A balloon floated into the clouds.
D. The store light blinked red and green.
E. The sprinklers watered the lawn.

PRACTICE: In these sentences, circle the main verb or verbs.

A. The girls giggled when the boys told funny stories.
B. The grass is green.
C. My dog slept while my cat played.
D. Each person ate one sandwich.
E. The batter hit the ball, and the crowd shouted for joy.

PRACTICE: In each sentence, circle the **helping verb**.

A. The sun was setting in the west.
B. The skates should stay in the closet.
C. Samuel can bring the lantern.
D. The dresses would look pretty in pink.
E. Each person may bring a toy.

PRACTICE: In these sentences, circle the helping verbs.
(HINT: There are ten.)

A. She would have liked to play outside.
B. They might have gone to the park.
C. Everyone had been swimming before lunch.
D. Tom should have listened to the instructions.
E. You have been traveling for twenty hours.

Review your worksheets. Are there any sentences that contain verb phrases with helping verbs? Are there any sentences you could rewrite to contain verb phrases with helping verbs? If so, make these changes at this time, but remember your sentences must still make sense in the context of what you are writing.

9.7 Sentences and Fragments

A sentence is a part of speech that presents to the reader a complete thought. Every sentence must have a subject-noun (or pronoun) and a verb. Sometimes a sentence may have a subject-noun and a verb, but still not be a complete sentence. A sentence may be missing a subject-noun, a verb, supporting words, or a helping verb. When a sentence is missing important words, it may not be complete. Sentences that are not complete are named **fragments**.

For a sentence to be complete, it must have two parts: a **subject** and a **predicate**. The **subject** of a sentence must tell about **who** or **what** the sentence is written. The **subject** of a sentence will contain a **noun** and other **words that support** that noun.

The **predicate** of a sentence contains the **verb**, **helping verbs**, and **supporting words** that all together tell what the subject **does** or **is**.

Writing complete sentences makes for good grammar, but the process takes time and practice. How can you tell if a sentence is complete? Use the following list of rules each time you write a sentence to prepare that sentence correctly. Read these rules a few times until you are sure you completely understand them; then try to do the **PRACTICE** exercise.

RULES FOR COMPLETE SENTENCES
1. A sentence must have both a subject (with a noun or pronoun) and a predicate (with a verb).
2. The subject must be a noun/pronoun that is a person, place, thing, or idea.
3. The subject must tell the "who" or "what" of the sentence.
4. The noun/pronoun of the subject may or may not have supporting words that help give more information about the noun.
5. The subject and verb must agree in number (singular or plural) and tense.
6. All paired subjects and verbs within the sentence must also agree.
7. The predicate must tell what the subject is or is doing.
8. The predicate of a sentence must have a verb.
9. The predicate can contain other supporting words with the verb.

PRACTICE: Draw a **line** through the following groups of words that are **fragment sentences**.

A. The stories in the Scriptures help us to understand Yahweh's friendship.
B. Titus is the good servant.
C. King Shaul/Saul the first.
D. Shall not want.
E. A friend loves at all times.
F. Golyath/Goliath was taller than.

Check all of your sentences for your current writing assignment. Does each sentence have a subject and a predicate? Review the rules for complete sentences if you are unsure. Then correct any sentences that are fragments by adding to them whatever is missing.

9.8 Homonyms

Some words sound alike but are spelled differently because they mean different things. These words are named **homonyms**. When you are writing, you must be careful to use the **correct spelling** of words that sound alike.

> **RULE #1**
> If you do not know the **correct spelling** of a word you use, look up its definition in the dictionary.

Look at this list of paired words that sound alike. Say them out loud. Then tell what each word means.

sum--some	one--won	bee--be	meat--meet
new--knew	sea--see	road--rode	eight--ate

PRACTICE: For each sentence, write the **correct spelling** for the **sound-alike word** in the blank space. Use the dictionary if you need help.

A. I like the _____ flowers. (blew/blue)
B. The _____ houses were ready to paint. (for/four)
C. He is _____ in the kitchen. (hear/here)
D. Can you see _____ the dark? (in/inn)
E. How can you _____ for sure that you are right? (no/know)
F. Those two gloves are a _____. (pair/pear)
G. Will you _____ us a quilt? (so/sew)
H. She watched_____ children until they came home. (there/their)
I. _____ are you going? (Wear/Where)
J. Seven days complete one _____. (week/weak)

Review all of your sentences for your current writing assignment. Do they contain any homonyms? If so, make sure you have used the correct spelling. Check your dictionary if you are unsure.

9.9 Synonyms

A description must give enough information so that a reader can form the best picture in his/her mind about what you are describing. When you first try to describe something, the best method is to make notes of the first words that come to your mind. Sometimes the words you have written down are either not specific enough or not descriptive enough to give the best picture to a reader of what you are describing. Where can you find more words that give a better description than what you have initially written down?

There are two helpful books that you can use to do an investigation. In the last unit, you learned about the thesaurus. The **thesaurus** helps in finding other words that mean almost the same thing as a word you are investigating. Often, that slight difference in words leads to the exact word that is best for the description you are trying to make. When you are looking in the thesaurus, remember that the words are presented in alphabetical order.

When you cannot think of the right word, try to think of a similar word and investigate that similar word in the thesaurus. You may take the word you cannot find and look it up in the second helpful book: the dictionary. The **dictionary** is an alphabetical listing of words containing information about those words. You can use the dictionary to help you find similar describing words by finding the word you are investigating, reading the text about it, and noting if any synonyms are given at the end of the definition section for that word.

A **synonym** is a word with the same meaning, or nearly the same meaning, as another word. To learn how synonyms help, get out your dictionary and find the word **recover**. Write what you find on the following line.

Recover:_____

A synonym may help you to describe something better for your reader. The dictionary is a very helpful book when trying to find a synonym. Look at the sentences in your writing assignment. Could you improve your descriptions by using one or more synonyms? If so, make those changes now; then complete your composition. Rewrite or type it neatly on a fresh piece of paper and turn it in to your teacher.

WRITING CHART #6

DESCRIPTION WORDS

NATION	SIZE		NATION	SIZE		NATION	SIZE	
HAIR	EYES	SKIN	HAIR	EYES	SKIN	HAIR	EYES	SKIN

PERSONALITY

CLOTHES AND ACCESSORIES

OBJECT	COLOR	SIZE	OBJECT	COLOR	SIZE	OBJECT	COLOR	SIZE

WRITING ASSIGNMENT #6

Your assignment is to write **three descriptions, each of a different family member**. Write each description, using features, personality and/or behavior, and clothes and/or accessories. Use lots of words that help a reader see a picture of your family members in his/her mind when he/she reads your writing. Prepare your sentences and paragraphs about the first family member by writing them on the **WRITING WORKSHEET** (p. 70). Use fresh writing paper to prepare your sentences and paragraphs about the other two family members.

1. **Format**
   - [ ] You will prepare three separate papers.
   - [ ] Write the name of one family member in capital letters at the top of each page.
   - [ ] Write your name under the title.
   - [ ] Begin the first paragraph on the **second** line below your name.
2. **Construction**
   - [ ] You must describe **three** family members.
   - [ ] Write **one or two** paragraphs about each family member.
   - [ ] Each paragraph must have **seven or more** sentences.
   - [ ] Choose the features that are the most interesting and most memorable.
   - [ ] Choose words and phrases that apply to their personalities and behaviors.
   - [ ] Choose words and phrases that apply to their clothes and accessories.
3. **Grammar**
   - [ ] Capitalize your words properly.
   - [ ] Use periods, exclamation points, question marks, and commas properly.
       Multiple comma rules:
       1. **One** describing word: no commas
       2. **Two** describing words: one comma if the describing words can be joined by the word **and**
       3. **Three** or more describing words: commas after all but the last describing word
   - [ ] Indent the beginning of each paragraph.
   - [ ] Each paragraph must contain unity, flow logically, and relate to one another.
   - [ ] Make some of your sentences long and some short.
   - [ ] Be careful to use proper word tenses.
4. **Polish**
   - [ ] You may have to write your description several times.
   - [ ] Only turn in a final copy of each paper if it has been written neatly.
   - [ ] Make sure you have spelled all of your words correctly.
   - [ ] Use the dictionary and the thesaurus to find better words.
5. **Ethics**
   - [ ] Work on your own and make your descriptions original.
   - [ ] Do not copy a description from any other writing.
   - [ ] Do not write what you would not want a family member to write about you.
   - [ ] Make sure the language of your paper conforms to Philippians 4:8.
6. **Creativity**
   - [ ] Write your composition to create an interesting mental picture for your reader.

WRITING WORKSHEET #6
COMPOSE YOUR SENTENCES ON THE FOLLOWING LINES.

1. _____
2. _____
3. _____
4. _____
5. _____
6. _____
7. _____
8. _____

ORGANIZE YOUR PARAGRAPHS ON THE FOLLOWING LINES.

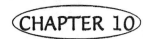

ACTION: ETHICS SKILLS

UNIT 4
SUPPLIES

BIBLE
DICTIONARY
PENCIL
THESAURUS
WRITING PAPER

10.1 Scriptural Ethics

To write well, you must fill your mind with good thoughts and live by good values. When you do these actions, you will naturally be able to write good things. Goodness, kindness, righteousness, fairness, peacefulness, gentleness, and pleasantness are all behavior qualities that you have studied in this textbook. They are behaviors that are Christian. They bring forth good fruit in your life and in the lives of other people. To have these behavior qualities, you must practice them in your daily life. Many of these behaviors are named the **fruit of the Spirit**. They are behaviors of a born-again Christian. If you are not a born-again Christian, these behaviors will be hard for you to master.

To be able to have these good behaviors, you must become a born-again Christian. To become a born-again Christian, you must realize that you are not perfect, that you make mistakes or behave badly sometimes, and that these mistakes and bad behaviors are named **sin**. Did you know that the Creator of all things, God/Yahweh, is perfect and does not sin? When He made all things, He made them according to His perfect will. When you do not behave as He does or according to His will, you sin. Sin is something that you cannot remove from your life. You can apologize for your sins and try to change your behavior, but you cannot wipe out the memory of those sins in God's mind.

God did not want sin to enter into His creation, so He made the payment for sin to be death. This truth means that every time you behave badly, you deserve death as the only way to remove that sin. God is also so perfect and good, that every time you sin, you separate yourself from Him. This separation is forever, as is death. However, God loves you very deeply and does not want to be separated from you. He does not want you to have to die every time you sin, so He came up with a way to be able to forgive you for your sins and to wipe them away from His memory. The way involved someone else taking your sins upon Himself and dying as a substitute for you. Could you suffer in that way? Could you die for another person to let them live? Most people could not, but God had someone who could and did die for you. That someone was God's Son, Jesus/Yahshua. Jesus died on the cross so that you could be forgiven of your sins, and they would be forgotten from God's memory. He died so that you would not have to be separated from God. He also died so that you could inherit eternal life with Him and His Father.

However, you do not get forgiveness just because of what Jesus did. You do not automatically inherit eternal life either. In order to receive these things from God, you must do something. What you must do is know that you are a sinner, know that Jesus died on the cross for you, and know that He is Elohim and King of everything. You must also know that on your own, changing your sinful behavior is pretty hard, so you need someone to help you. You must pray to Jesus and ask Him to forgive you of your sins. You must tell Him that you believe in Him alone. You then tell Him that you want Him to become the Elohim/Lord of your life, and you must ask the Ruach Hakodesh/Holy Spirit to come into your being.

The Ruach Hakodesh is the Spirit of God, our Elohim. When the Holy Spirit comes into your life, He helps you to change your behavior, but you must let Him lead you. Romans 8:14 teaches you, "**For as many as are led by the Spirit of Elohim, these are the sons of Elohim.**" When you let the Holy Spirit lead you, then you are walking with Him. Galatians 5:25 further explains to you, "**If we live in the Spirit, let us also walk in the Spirit.**" When you walk in the Spirit, the fruit of the Spirit will begin to become your behavior. The Holy Spirit in you, a born-again Christian, will help you do good things, fill your mind with good things, help you be a good writer, and help you write about good things that others will be blessed to read.

Scripture Study

Find the following verses in a Bible to find out what they have to say about the fruit of the Spirit. Write the verses on these lines.

YOUR WRITING AND LIFE SHOULD **PROMOTE** THESE TYPES OF BEHAVIORS.

Galatians 5:22-23 _____
_____
_____
_____
_____

These verses contain several more words that you have not yet studied. The words love, joy, patience, trustworthiness, and self-control are behaviors that are the fruit of the Spirit. Look these words up in the dictionary and write their definitions on the following lines.

Love: _____
_____

Joy: _____
_____

Patience: _____
_____

Trustworthiness: _____
_____

Self-control: _____
_____

Which one of the words above is your favorite behavior to find in a friend or in a story? Which behavior do you understand the best and could therefore describe most easily? Behaviors that you already exhibit are behaviors that you can describe most easily. Remember this fact when you are writing your papers for this unit.

10.2 Scriptural Ethics

Writing about your own life is the easiest type of writing to tackle. This easiness is because you already know a good story to tell. The things that happen in your life are good stories. In fact, they are the best stories and the most believable to tell. When you write about your life, you can tell about the good things that happened when you behaved well. If bad things happened when you behaved badly, only write about those things if you can tell how you changed your behavior for good.

In UNIT 3, you learned how to solve problems using the wisdom that comes from God. You learned that the wisdom from Him gives the right result when something has gone wrong. This truth means that the problem will be corrected in such a way that the right person or the right situation will prevail, and that peace will once again occur.

When you write stories that might have a problem in them, a good help to others is to write about things that have happened in your life when you have found a Heavenly solution. When you do this type of writing, you will help another person see how to solve a problem.

There is another way to prevent things from going wrong. The way to prevent things from going wrong is to avoid bad situations where sin is often found. Since sin is caused by people, and all people are sinful, how do you avoid bad situations without entirely shutting yourself off from the rest of the world? The Bible has much to say on how to avoid trouble.

Scripture Study

Find the following verses in a Bible and read what they teach you about avoiding sinful situations. Take your time writing out the verses carefully on these lines.

YOUR WRITING AND LIFE SHOULD **PROMOTE** THIS TYPE OF BEHAVIOR.
2 Corinthians 6:14-18 _____

_____
_____
_____
_____
_____
_____
_____
_____
_____
_____
_____
_____
_____
_____

God knows where sin is lurking. He also knows that even Christians can be tempted to be sinful when they are around too much sin. Those who are not born-again believers are more sinful because they do not have the Holy Spirit helping them to avoid sin. Nonbelievers do not know what behaviors are sin. They often do not believe that sinful behaviors are wrong or a serious problem for their life and the lives of others. This reason is why God does not want you to have a lot of non-believing friends, non-believing acquaintances, and non-believing relationships.

When you are around born-again believers, even though they may have some sin in their lives, at least they know what sinful behavior is. Most believers are actively working to remove sin from their lives. When you spend most of your time with born-again believers, you will sin less. You will not sin as much as you might when you are around nonbelievers. Born-again believers also help show each other how to have good behavior. They can encourage one another and be kind to help when one of their own is struggling with sin.

An interesting story in the Bible, that tells about what happens when God's people are mixed amongst nonbelievers, is the story of Moses, the Israelites, and the Egyptians. The Israelites had been in captivity for about 400 years in Egypt. During this time period, they were influenced by the Egyptians, their pagan beliefs, and their pagan gods. When the Israelites were released from captivity, they showed many times how far they had wandered from God into sin. The most notable incident occurred at Mt. Sinai. When Moses did not return down the mountain for forty days, the Israelites returned to the pagan sins they had learned in Egypt when they made pagan gods to worship. They did not obey the voice of God and they sinned greatly. Their sins were so bad that God decided not to let the nation of Israel enter the promised land until all of the generation who had sinned against Him had died.

The holiday of Passover celebrates God's deliverance of His people from captivity. He bought His people out from nonbelievers and wanted His people to live set-apart lives in the promised land. God wants His people to live apart from nonbelievers to help them sin less. How would you apply the verses you looked up and the story of Moses to your life?

In America, there is no city, state, or geographic region where born-again Christians can live completely set-apart. Some denominations of Christians try to live near one another, or have started towns to help their believers have a place to live amongst other believers. What can you do when you don't have this type of living situation? How do you live a set-apart life according to God?

There are many things that you can do. First, you can choose most of your friends to be born-again believers. These friends you can find in many places. They may be at church, at school, at an activity, or in your neighborhood. You can also pray for Christian families to move into your neighborhood. Born-again Christian friends and born-again neighbors do not have to belong to the same denomination that you do to be good friends and good neighbors. Try to remember that churches may have some rules that differ, but if you focus on Jesus and a Bible, you will have many things in common.

Another way you can obey God is to choose Christian activities over non-Christian activities. These activities could include a sports team, a job, a concert, a party, or other types of activities. You can also select Christian workers to take care of you, such as your doctor, nurse, or dentist. Choosing a Christian education over a non-Christian education is a very important thing you can do. When you listen to Christian music, you obey God by keeping your music choices set-apart.

The important goal towards which to work is to make sure that you limit the amount of time you spend around non-Christians. This limitation doesn't mean that you will not be able to witness to others. For instance, if you have relatives that are not believers, instead of spending a lot of time with them, see them only occasionally. When you do see them, either share your beliefs or just behave well so that you will be a good example of a Christian.

When you have mainly Christian relationships, support other Christians, and exhibit the Christian way of living, your life will become a better beacon of light to draw others to Christianity. This result is because you will sin less, and others will see your goodness and the goodness of your life. Many will be drawn to Jesus by your qualities because they will also want goodness in their life.

When you live a set-apart life, you can write about your experiences and that writing will be interesting to others, as well as being a good witness.

CHAPTER 11

ACTION: WRITING SKILLS

11.1 An Outdoor Event

There are many social functions that you might attend or in which you might participate that are a vital part of life. These types of functions may include a party, wedding, picnic, sports event, church luncheon, youth group activity, etc. These functions are so natural to society that they are important places where a story or part of a story may occur. Because these types of functions are frequent occurrences in life, an important goal is that you learn how to write about them. When these functions are Christian, they will have different types of activities and behaviors; reading about them can not only be interesting, but also be models of good behavior from which others might learn. Therefore, Christian functions are good social functions about which to write.

The first writing assignment for this unit will be to write about an outdoor event. This event will contain a scene, people, and action. To make your writing realistic and comfortable, you paper should be about an event that you have attended and remember.

To begin jogging your memory of a social event you might like to describe, ponder your answers to the following questions. Have you ever played an outdoor sport? Do you have a brother, sister, or friend who plays an outdoor sport? Do you like to go skiing, boating, swimming, or ice-skating outside? Have you ever eaten at an outdoor picnic, at the beach, or in a park? Can you think of any other outdoor events in which you have participated?

Have these questions brought to mind a particular outdoor event that you enjoyed? Can you remember enough of that event to write about it for your writing assignment? If not, take a few minutes to try and think of an event that you can remember. On page 78, write a name for that event in the box under the words **WRITING CHART #7**.

You have completed six writing assignments which have included descriptions. You have no doubt become very good at describing. Because of this skill, you will not be guided through the steps to choose the words to describe the scene of your outdoor event. You are going to choose those words yourself.

To choose your description words, think about how the scene of your outdoor event looked. Take several minutes for this task. As you are thinking about your scene, write the main objects in the three boxes below the **DESCRIPTION WORDS** box on the writing chart. Add the colors and sizes of those objects to the appropriate columns. Next, decide on what objects are related to your main objects, just like a leaf is related to a tree. Write the names of those related objects in the columns under the main objects. Identify colors and sizes of the related objects in the columns next to their names.

11.2 The Characters

Describing an outdoor event involves describing both scenery and people. On the writing chart, you have recorded information about the scene of your outdoor event and about the objects in that scene. Now is the time to decide about the people or the characters that will be in your scene. If you went to a large event, there were probably a lot of people in attendance. For your paper, you can't write about each individual person at a large event; that task would take too long. However, you can write about a lot of people if you group them into categories, such as the crowd, the spectators, the audience, the skaters, etc. For example, if you describe a sports event, you can have spectators as well as players--or just the players. If you were at a picnic, you could have friends, guests, or family.

If you plan to write about a group of people in your event, identify them with a group name and then write that name on the writing chart in one of the **CHARACTER** boxes on page 78.

To think about individual people to include in your writing, try to think about something important that might have happened at the outdoor event you attended. What interesting activity occurred, like a boat ride on a lake or sackcloth races at a picnic? Was there any important behavior that was memorable, like a kindness extended to someone or unusually fair play in a game? Did someone help you to learn something, like how to ice-skate or how to ice fish? Pick one important happening or behavior from the event and then think about the people that were involved. Try to limit the amount of persons involved to two or three. You can use a person's proper name, such as Daniel, or a common name for someone, such as the goalie at a soccer match. Write the names for those people in the **CHARACTER** boxes.

You have learned that a character can be described in many ways. You can tell what nationality they are or how tall they are. You can describe their eyes, hair, or skin. Telling what clothes and accessories they are wearing is also helpful when describing your characters in your writing. These descriptions will help a reader become familiar with your characters.

The paper you will write for this writing assignment will not be long. To use every description for your characters in a short story is not possible. Yet, the best method is always to make notes about them anyway. When you make enough notes about your characters, you will have enough descriptions from which to pick and choose for your writing. For this reason, take several minutes to fill out the columns on the writing chart under the **CHARACTERS** and **CLOTHES AND ACCESSORIES** boxes.

11.3 The Action

An outdoor event is where something is happening; action is taking place. The action that you will write about is the action of the people at the event. Action is described by using action verbs in your sentences. To determine what action you will describe, ask yourself some questions. What kind of action might be happening at an outdoor event? Are people participating in a sport, playing a game, or eating food? Are they walking, running, hopping, or skipping? If there are spectators, what are they doing? What are the players of a game doing? How is a boat crossing a lake?

There are many types of action you could imagine about which to write. You must think carefully about what action you want to describe so that your reader can form a good picture of the scene or the event in his/her mind. Take some time to think of the action you want to be in your outdoor event. On page 78, write your thoughts under the **ACTION AND BEHAVIOR** box on the writing chart.

Behavior is an important part of your Christian walk. How you behave, how others behave, and how you respond to their behavior can show whether someone has Christian values or not. When composing stories, writing about good Christian value is important. This type of writing will help others see their own good behavior or try to improve their behavior. Sometimes, however, you may have to mention a bad behavior in a story. In these situations, always tell how the bad behavior is corrected in a way that shows wisdom from Heaven.

Think about the behavior of the characters you have selected who were involved at your event. How did they behave? Was their behavior good or bad? Was their behavior corrected if it was bad? How was it corrected? Write the answers to these questions under the **ACTION AND BEHAVIOR** box on the writing chart.

Your writing assignment is to write four paragraphs describing an outdoor scene with action. Use lots of description words so that a reader can see not only your scene in his/her mind, but also the people and action as it happens. Make the action come to life in your outdoor scene by giving enough description. For instance, if someone is kicking a ball, tell how hard he is kicking it and whether it goes down the field or out of bounds. Describe whether the kick made the ball soar through the air or roll on the ground. These extra details bring the action of your scene to life for the reader.

You will not be able to describe every single person, action, or piece of scenery in your paper, so you must choose which ones you think would be most interesting to a reader or which ones you find most interesting to describe. From the writing chart, choose the description words that will help a reader see your outdoor scene, people, and action as you do; then write your paper.

Here are two examples of outdoor events with descriptions of the scenery, the people involved, and the action.

1. The day of the soccer game was great! The sky was deep blue with not a single cloud. The air was still, warm, and sweet with the fragrance of fresh-cut, green grass. I was so excited to watch my brother play his last game of the season that I ran all the way from our car to the field. I got there before anyone in my family and staked out a little square of grass where we could sit.

Soon many people came and sat on both sides of the field. Some brought lawn chairs. Others brought towels or blankets to spread out on the ground. Parents, grandparents, brothers, and sisters all came to watch this game. Everyone was happy and cheerful. Some were talking just amongst themselves, and others were talking to the people sitting nearby.

My brother's team is named 'Big Green' because they wear green shirts. The team practiced while everyone else found their places to sit on the lawn. First, the players were wall-passing; then they did a lay-up and ran down the field to the goal. When the time came to play the game, everyone calmed down, and the spectators stopped talking. The time had come to turn their attention to the two teams on the field. Finally, the referee blew the whistle and started the game.

2. The Saturday race was an interesting event. There was no prize for winning but plenty of cheering each runner past the distance goals. The runners had even started at different spots so that no one could tell who was going the fastest!

Twenty runners charged past us one by one, some neck and neck, as my family stood by the roped-off track. Each runner was pushing a baby stroller with a sack of sand in the seat. Moms, dads, kids, and grandparents all ran past on their journey around the track. Some were laughing, and some looked worried as their strollers teetered on the verge of going out of control. Once in a while, runners forgot to keep their arms out straight as they ran, and their strollers quickly lost momentum.

The race was not easy work! Although the sky was cloudy, and the day slightly cool, many of the runners had developed a shiny sweat on their faces as they raced past the three-minute mark. When the race was over, everyone cheered and laughed heartily.

You see, the event was not really so much a race as a fun-hearted test to see how well each stroller held up under the pretend duress of a mother running to catch a bus, with her baby in a stroller. While the race was a bit of an exaggerated situation, the baby stroller manufacturing company wanted to carefully assess the maximum durability of each stroller. What a day, and what a lot of fun was had that year at my father's company picnic!

 Turn to the writing assignment and read it. If you have any questions, please ask your teacher. From here on, the papers you write will be longer. For this reason, this textbook will no longer include a page to prepare your sentences and paragraphs.

You will prepare your sentences and paragraphs on your own separate pieces of writing paper.

WRITING CHART #7

DESCRIPTION WORDS

	COLOR	SIZE			COLOR	SIZE			COLOR	SIZE
OBJECT	COLOR	SIZE		OBJECT	COLOR	SIZE		OBJECT	COLOR	SIZE

CHARACTERS

	NATION	SIZE			NATION	SIZE			NATION	SIZE
HAIR	EYES	SKIN		HAIR	EYES	SKIN		HAIR	EYES	SKIN

CLOTHES AND ACCESSORIES

OBJECT	COLOR	SIZE	OBJECT	COLOR	SIZE	OBJECT	COLOR	SIZE

ACTION AND BEHAVIOR

WRITING ASSIGNMENT #7

Your assignment is to write a description of an **outdoor scene with people and action**. Write your descriptions, using features, clothes and/or accessories, behavior, and action. Use lots of words that help a reader see a picture of your event in his/her mind when he/she reads your writing. Prepare your sentences and paragraphs on your own separate pieces of writing paper.

1. Format
- [ ] Write the name of your outdoor event in capital letters at the top of the page.
- [ ] Write your name under the title.
- [ ] Begin the first paragraph on the **second** line below your name.

2. Construction
- [ ] Write **four** paragraphs describing your outdoor scene with people and action.
- [ ] Each paragraph must have **seven** or more sentences.
- [ ] Each paragraph must have more than **thirty-five** words.
- [ ] Choose the features that are the most interesting.
- [ ] Choose the clothes and accessories that are memorable.
- [ ] Choose behavior, action words, and phrases that are accurate.

3. Grammar
- [ ] Capitalize your words properly.
- [ ] Use periods, exclamation points, question marks, and commas properly.
    Multiple comma rules:
    1. **One** describing word: no commas
    2. **Two** describing words: one comma if the describing words can be joined by the word **and**
    3. **Three** or more describing words: commas after all but the last describing word
- [ ] Indent the beginning of each paragraph.
- [ ] Each paragraph must contain unity, flow logically, and relate to one another.
- [ ] Make some of your sentences long and some short.
- [ ] Be careful to use proper word tenses.

4. Polish
- [ ] You may have to write your description several times.
- [ ] Only turn in a final copy of each paper if it has been written neatly.
- [ ] Make sure you have spelled all of your words correctly.
- [ ] Use the dictionary and the thesaurus to find better words.

5. Ethics
- [ ] Work on your own and make your descriptions original.
- [ ] Do not copy a description from any other writing.
- [ ] Do not write what you would not want a family member to write about you.
- [ ] Make sure the language of your paper conforms to Philippians 4:8.

6. Creativity
- [ ] Write your composition to create an interesting mental picture for your reader.

WRITING PREPARATION

You have written a paper about an outdoor event; now you will describe a celebration. Have you ever been to a wedding or a birthday party? Do you remember what kinds of activities you did? Can you describe how the guests and hosts of the celebration looked? What did the guests and hosts do at that celebration? Do you remember where the party was and how the scene looked? Were there any decorations that you can remember? Did anyone wear special clothes that you could describe? Were there any special emotions on that day?

Describing a celebration involves scenery, people, action, and emotions. In order to describe these elements of a celebration, you need to ask yourself questions about these elements. When you ask yourself questions, focus and think back to the specific event. At first you may not remember everything, but as you continue to ask yourself questions, you will begin to remember more things. Also, since you will not be writing an exact eyewitness account of the celebration, you must decide how to handle what you don't remember.

There are two kinds of writing that you need to consider in this situation. The first is nonfiction writing. **Nonfiction** writing is not a made-up story, but the **actual truth**. This type of writing should contain only truth in its entirety unless you specify that what is being written at a particular point is speculation. When writing nonfiction, you must do a lot of careful research to make your writing very accurate.

The second type of writing is named fiction. **Fiction** is writing ideas that you **create**. Fictional writing may contain true facts, but the main story and people are often created. When you cannot remember all the facts about an event, but it is interesting to use in your writing, you can write the ideas as a fictional story.

If you are writing about a nonfiction event after it has happened, but you cannot remember all of the details, the best policy is to leave out what you do not remember. A helpful procedure is to talk to others who attended the event, like your parents, brothers, or sisters, to see if they remember something that you do not. You can also pray for help in remembering, but if nothing new comes to mind, the best choice is not to invent anything. This decision exhibits the values of truth and honesty, where you only relate what you can truly remember.

For this writing assignment, you will be writing about a celebration that you truly remember. Therefore, the necessary guideline is for you to be as accurate as possible. Do not fill in your paper with any created material just to make the celebration sound good. To help your accuracy, you may have to think very hard and even pray hard, especially if the event was a long time ago.

About what kind of a celebration do you want to write for this lesson? On page 88, write a name for that event in the box below the **WRITING CHART #8** box. The four elements of a celebration are scenery, people, action, and emotions. Take some time to think of your celebration. Ask yourself questions that will help you remember the scenery, people, action, and emotions. Take whatever description words come to mind and write them in the correct boxes and columns on the writing chart. Don't forget to use your dictionary and thesaurus to help you find good and accurate description words

For this paper, since you will be describing several things, you will not be able to go into a lot of detail about your people. Remember to describe only the most important attributes of each person so that a reader can get a basic picture of those persons. Make the celebration come to life by choosing action words and explaining those actions with more than one or two words. What emotions did the people at your celebration display with their actions, voices, or features? Include those emotions in your writing, also.

Do you have a lot of description words on the writing chart? Decide on the best words you want to use in your writing; circle those words. Read **WRITING ASSIGNMENT #8** on page 89. Complete the grammar lessons and prepare your composition on clean writing paper.

CHAPTER 12

ACTION: GRAMMAR SKILLS

12.1 Grammar Rules

English grammar teaches you how to arrange your thoughts into words, sentences, and paragraphs so that your writing may be understood. There are many rules of grammar to learn. In this chapter, you will review rules about how nouns and pronouns must agree with their verb pairs. When verbs are converted into the past tense, they often change their spelling. These spelling changes are special and take some practice to remember.

Writing good sentences also takes practice. In this unit, you can no longer just write whatever you please and hope to get a good grade on your papers. You must think carefully about how your sentences are written and how they relate to one another. This chapter of grammar will review how to combine sentences in different ways to add variety to your papers and how to reduce repeated words and phrases in your sentences.

Read each grammar rule and do the **PRACTICE** exercises. When working on your writing assignments, remember to follow these rules. Part of your grade will be determined by how well you follow **all** of the rules you learn.

12.2 Subject/Verb Agreement in the Past Tense

In Chapter 9, you learned that paired subjects and verbs must agree in every sentence. The rule you learned was for verbs used in the present tense. Now you will learn about sentences that are written using verbs in the past tense.

> **RULE #1**
> In every sentence written in the **past tense**, any **subject** and **verb** that are paired must **agree** with one another.

This correct sentence has a **SUBJECT (boy)** and a **VERB (wanted)** that agree.
EXAMPLE: The **boy wanted** some new sports equipment.

When they follow rule #2, a subject and verb pair in the past tense agree no matter whether a subject is singular or plural.

> **RULE #2**
> When writing a sentence in the **past tense**, use the **past tense** form of the **verb**.

EXAMPLES:
She **enjoyed** the harp's beautiful sound.
We **went** to our cousin Mark's cabin.

Most verbs may be formed into the past tense by adding the two letters **ed** to the end of the verb. Look at the following verbs to see how this change occurs.

VERB

Present Tense	Past Tense
back	back**ed**
call	call**ed**
pick	pick**ed**
talk	talk**ed**
want	want**ed**

PRACTICE: Write the following verbs in their **past tense** form by adding the **correct ending**.

A. row_____ E. test_____ I. align_____
B. water_____ F. sew_____ J. touch_____
C. clean_____ G. back_____ K. click_____
D. cook_____ H. smooth_____ L. stay_____

    Being verbs tell what the subject is being. When using **being** verbs or the verb **have**, the past tense is spelled differently than the present tense. The correct spelling of these verbs must be memorized because they do not follow any rules. The following lists show the correct spelling of the past tense forms of these two verbs. Study them carefully.

VERB (to be)

Present Tense	Past Tense
am	was
is	was
are	were

VERB (have)

Present Tense	Past Tense
have	had
has	had

PRACTICE: In the following sentences, rewrite each **verb** in the **past tense**.

A. I **am** _____ making some lemonade.
B. She **has** _____ her friend on the telephone.
C. You **are** _____ picking the cucumbers.
D. They **have** _____ a quiet class.
E. We **are** _____ climbing the tree.

    Take a look at your celebration composition. Since this event occurred in the past, your paper should be written in the past tense. Check your sentences to make sure that all of the verbs that are forms of **to be** and **have** are spelled correctly. Most other verbs should end with the letters **ed**.

12.3 Past Tense Verb with Spelling Changes

    When some verbs are formed in the past tense, they must have a spelling change before the letters **ed** are added. There are three rules to help you with these verbs.

> **RULE #1**
> When forming the **past tense** of a verb that ends with the letter **e after a consonant**, **drop the e** before adding the letters **ed**.

    EXAMPLE: bike becomes bik**ed**

PRACTICE: On the lines provided, rewrite each of the following **verbs** in the **past tense**.

A. bounce_____ D. stake_____

B. heave_____ E. please_____
C. shame_____ F. seize_____

RULE #2
When forming the **past tense** of a one-syllable verb that ends with one consonant after a short vowel, **double the last consonant** before adding the letters **ed**.

EXAMPLE: top   becomes   top**ped**

PRACTICE: On the lines provided, rewrite each of the following **verbs** in the **past tense**.

A. pit_____ D. pet_____ G. stop_____
B. tip_____ E. step_____ H. blur_____
C. zip_____ F. plot_____ I. chat_____

RULE #3
When forming the **past tense** of a verb that ends with a **y** after a consonant, change the **y** to an **i** before adding the letters **ed**.

EXAMPLE: tarry   becomes   tarr**ied**

PRACTICE: On the lines provided, rewrite each of the following **verbs** in the **past tense**.

A. testify_____ D. vary_____
B. curry_____ E. classify_____
C. ally_____ F. clarify_____

Review the verbs in your celebration composition. Are they all written correctly in the past tense? If not, rewrite them at this time, making sure they follow the three rules for spelling changes that you learned in this lesson.

12.4 Irregular Verbs in the Past Tense

Some verbs do not add the letters **ed** in the past tense. These verbs are named **irregular** verbs. The past tense form of an irregular verb may not change its spelling at all or may change its spelling. Use a dictionary to spell the past tense of any word about which you are unsure. The following are examples of irregular verbs.

IRREGULAR VERBS

Present Tense	Past Tense
break	broke
sleep	slept
speak	spoke
take	took
teach	taught
write	wrote

Review the verbs in your celebration composition. Are they spelled correctly in the past tense? If you are unsure, look up their past tense spelling in a dictionary and rewrite them correctly at this time.

12.5 Similar Sentences

Writing good sentences takes practice. You must think carefully about how your sentences are written and how they relate to one another. When a writer writes well, he/she **rarely** uses the same words to start or end two sentences in a row. To begin writing better sentences, you will need to learn how to **vary** the **beginnings** and **endings** of your sentences.

Have you ever read a paper where all of the sentences started or ended with the same words? Did you begin to feel bored or agitated after reading the second or third sentence? Read the following sentences that all begin with the same words.

Her eyes were blue. **Her eyes were** big. **Her eyes were** sparkly.

These sentences are not interesting because they all start with the same words! To rewrite these sentences into better ones, they must be changed so that the beginnings do not all start with the same words. When sentences are varied in this way, they show your reader that you worked hard on your writing to present something interesting to read.

Do you know when you need to vary your sentences? If, when you read your writing, more than one or two sentences in a row begin or end with the same word or words, you need to rewrite those sentences. The following example shows how sentences that all **begin** with the same words can be rewritten differently.

EXAMPLE:
Her eyes were blue. **Her eyes were** big. **Her eyes were** sparkly.

REWRITTEN EXAMPLE:
Her eyes were blue and big. They also had a sparkly quality to them.

PRACTICE: Rewrite these sentences using **different words** at the **beginning** of each sentence.

A. She was wearing a dress. She was wearing a hat. She was wearing a coat.
_____
_____

B. The wedding was fun. The wedding was happy. The wedding was outside.
_____
_____
_____

C. The cake was three tiers tall. The cake was chocolate. The cake tasted good.
_____
_____
_____

D. The presents were big. The presents were wrapped with pretty paper and bows.
_____
_____

The following example shows how sentences that all **end** the with the same words can be rewritten differently.

EXAMPLE:
The party was **inside the house**. The people were **inside the house**. The music floated from **inside the house**.

REWRITTEN EXAMPLE:
The party was on a special day. All of the people had gone into the house. Lovely music floated to the street outside.

PRACTICE: Rewrite these sentences by using **different words** at the **end** of each sentence.

A. The pool party was a lot of fun. Splashing around was a lot of fun. Sunning on the deck was a lot of fun.

_____
_____

B. The birthday party was a cowboy theme. The decorations were a cowboy theme. The gifts were all supposed to be a cowboy theme.

_____
_____

C. The retirement party was on the boat. The guests were all on the boat. The food was all on the boat.

_____
_____

D. The day was very wet because of the rain. The picnic was canceled because of the rain. The roads were closed because of the rain.

_____
_____

Take a few moments to review the sentences you have written for your celebration composition. Have you written any sentences that begin or end with the same words? If so, rewrite them!

12.6 Compound Subjects and Predicates

Good writing has a **variety of sentences**. When a writer writes well, he/she rarely uses the same words to start or end two or more sentences in a row. Now you will learn how to **combine sentences** that have the **same subjects or predicates**. A predicate is the being or action verb together with its supporting words.

Instead of rewriting the same subjects or same predicates of two sentences, you can often combine them to make a new sentence. Sentences that begin or end the same way may have the same subject, subject-noun/pronoun, verb, or predicate. When you combine sentences, the words that are the same are used only once in the new sentence. Often the word **and** is also used to combine these sentence parts.

When two or more sentences that originally had some parts the same are combined, the new sentence is more interesting with a compound subject or predicate. The word **compound** means **combined or mixed together**. A sentence with a **compound** subject or predicate is a mixture of more than one of your original sentences. The following examples show how similar sentences may be combined to form better sentences. The words that are the same in each sentence are shown in bold.

EXAMPLE:
The basketball was orange. **The basketball** was round.

REWRITTEN EXAMPLE:
The basketball was orange and round.

EXAMPLE:
The mangoes **were sweet**. The bananas **were sweet**.

REWRITTEN EXAMPLE:
The mangoes and the bananas were sweet.

PRACTICE: Rewrite each pair of sentences below into **one** new **combined** sentence using the word **and** to combine them.

A. The policeman waited at the stoplight. The policeman stayed in his car.
_____
_____

B. The carpenters were working on the house. The roofers were working on the house.
_____
_____

C. The scientist mixed the solids. The scientist stirred the liquids.
_____
_____

D. The accountant counted the money. The banker counted the money.
_____
_____

12.7 Sentence Conjunctions

You have learned how to rewrite similar sentences and how to combine sentences that have the same subjects or predicates. Sometimes you might want to vary your sentence lengths by joining together two short sentences without changing any of the words in the original sentences. In this situation, you would create a new longer sentence from the two short sentences.

In order to join two sentences and create a new sentence that is grammatically correct, a grammatical "bridge" must be used. The bridge that is used in grammar consists of a **comma** and a **joining word**. Joining words are named **conjunctions**. Three popular conjunctions used today are the words **and**, **or**, and **but**. The following examples show how a comma and conjunction are used to join two short sentences into one new sentence without changing the original words.

EXAMPLE:
The teacher was grading papers. The students were doing their classwork.

REWRITTEN EXAMPLE:
The teacher was grading papers, **and** the students were doing their classwork.

EXAMPLE:
Should the doctor see the patient? Should the nurse see the patient first?

REWRITTEN EXAMPLE:
Should the doctor see the patient, **or** should the nurse see the patient first?

EXAMPLE:
The manager organized his schedule. The day's work was canceled by rain.

REWRITTEN EXAMPLE:
The manager organized his schedule, **but** the day's work was canceled by rain.

PRACTICE: Rewrite the following sentences into new sentences. Use a **comma** and one **conjunction** (and, or, but) to join the sentences without changing the original words.

A. The salesclerk completed the sale. The customer went home happy.
_____
_____

B. Is the milking machine clean? Does it need to be sterilized?
_____
_____

C. The baker made the bread. The pastry chef baked the cake.
_____
_____

Review the sentences you have written for your celebration composition. Have you written any sentences that have the same subjects or predicates? Would two of your sentence be more interesting if they were combined? If so, rewrite them!

12.8 Concise Sentences

Writing good sentences is hard work, but the result is well worth the effort. After you have written the sentences for your composition, review them to make sure they are **concise**. A **concise sentence** is a sentence that is clear and to the point. To make sure your sentences are concise, read them carefully. See if they **go on too long, sound too wordy**, or **contain too many repeated words**.

If one or more of your sentences has one of these problems, do the following.

TIPS
◆**TOO LONG:** Break up extra long sentences into two or more smaller sentences.
◆**TOO WORDY:** Rewrite sentences that are too wordy, making them shorter by removing unnecessary information or repeated information.
◆**TOO MANY REPEATED WORDS:** Remove repeated words or replace them with different words.

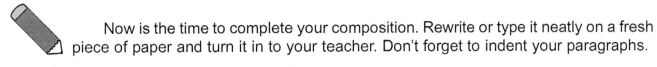
Now is the time to complete your composition. Rewrite or type it neatly on a fresh piece of paper and turn it in to your teacher. Don't forget to indent your paragraphs.

WRITING CHART #8

DESCRIPTION WORDS

SCENERY

	COLOR	SIZE		COLOR	SIZE		COLOR	SIZE
OBJECT	COLOR	SIZE	OBJECT	COLOR	SIZE	OBJECT	COLOR	SIZE

CHARACTERS

	NATION	SIZE		NATION	SIZE		NATION	SIZE
HAIR	EYES	SKIN	HAIR	EYES	SKIN	HAIR	EYES	SKIN

CLOTHES AND ACCESSORIES

OBJECT	COLOR	SIZE	OBJECT	COLOR	SIZE	OBJECT	COLOR	SIZE

ACTION AND BEHAVIOR

EMOTIONS

WRITING ASSIGNMENT #8

Your assignment is to write a description of a **real celebration.** Please include the scenery, people, action, and emotions at the celebration. Use lots of words that help a reader see a picture of the celebration in his/her mind when he/she reads your writing. Prepare your sentences and paragraphs on your own separate pieces of writing paper.

1. Format
- [ ] Write the name of the celebration in capital letters at the top of the page.
- [ ] Write your name under the title.
- [ ] Begin the first paragraph on the **second** line below your name.

2. Construction
- [ ] Write **four** paragraphs describing the celebration with people and action.
- [ ] Each paragraph must have **three to six** sentences.
- [ ] Each paragraph must have more than **twenty-five** words.
- [ ] Choose the features that are the most interesting.
- [ ] Choose the clothes and accessories that are memorable.
- [ ] Choose behavior, action, and emotion words and phrases that are accurate.

3. Grammar
- [ ] Capitalize your words properly.
- [ ] Use periods, exclamation points, question marks, and commas properly.
    Multiple comma rules:
    1. **One** describing word: no commas
    2. **Two** describing words: one comma if the describing words can be joined by the word **and**
    3. **Three** or more describing words: commas after all but the last describing word
- [ ] Indent the beginning of each paragraph.
- [ ] Each paragraph must contain unity, flow logically, and relate to one another.
- [ ] Make some of your sentences long and some short.
- [ ] Be careful to use proper word tenses.

4. Polish
- [ ] You may have to write your description several times.
- [ ] Only turn in a final copy of each paper if it has been written neatly.
- [ ] Make sure you have spelled all of your words correctly.
- [ ] Use the dictionary and the thesaurus to find better words.

5. Ethics
- [ ] Work on your own and make your descriptions original.
- [ ] Do not copy a description from any other writing.
- [ ] Do not write what you would not want a family member to write about you.
- [ ] Make sure the language of your paper conforms to Philippians 4:8.

6. Creativity
- [ ] Write your composition to create an interesting mental picture for your reader.

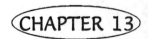

DIALOGUE: ETHICS SKILLS

13.1 Scriptural Ethics

UNIT 5 SUPPLIES
BIBLE
COLORED PENCIL
red
DICTIONARY
PENCIL
THESAURUS
WRITING PAPER

Conversation is one of the most frequent activities in which you engage each day. You have conversations at home, in your neighborhood, during school, at church, at social events, on shopping trips, in prayer, etc. In fact, most people speak more than they will ever write, and yet most English classes spend too little time teaching you how to converse properly.

There are proper ways to converse and inappropriate ways to converse. Similarly, there are also wise ways to speak and foolish ways to speak. Most people must learn about these ways through trial and error. However, Christians have a very good source of information to consult about how to converse. That good source of information is the Bible. The Bible actually contains a large amount of information about speaking which you could study for quite some time. If you combine that studying with practice, you will learn how to converse in ways that will honor Heaven and assure you that you have spoken wisely.

Scripture Study

Find the following verses in the Bible to find out what they teach about the words you speak. Write the verses on these lines.

YOUR WRITING AND LIFE SHOULD **PROMOTE** THESE TYPES OF BEHAVIORS.

Mishle/Proverbs 10:19 _____
_____

Mishle/Proverbs 17:27 _____
_____

Tehillim/Psalms 19:14 _____
_____
_____

These verses teach you about not talking too much and about making your conversation pleasing. We live in a world where people are in a hurry. This hurried lifestyle can lead to inadequate communications and even impatience with those who communicate. Oral communications are very important and cannot often occur quickly without rudeness, mistakes in understanding, or incomplete information being shared. These behaviors or attitudes are not good for you to develop, no matter how busy your lifestyle.

One of the mistakes of this lifestyle is to dominate a conversation because you think that you will not have enough time to say everything you want to say. When you talk too much, you are not being fair and letting others participate in communicating their thoughts and activities. In all conversation you should speak in moderation. This guideline means that you should not talk **too much** and not talk **too fast**. This practice also means that you should choose your time for conversation so that there will be enough time for everyone involved to speak adequately and thoroughly.

Everyone has something interesting to say. In group situations, let others have a chance to speak. You might find that you really enjoy what they have to say. If others are shy, help them to share in the conversation by asking them a question that you know they can answer. Try to pay attention to who has had a chance to speak; make sure that everyone has an opportunity to say something before the conversation ends or moves on to a new topic. Always look at the person who is speaking. Try to look that person in the eyes or at his/her face when he/she is speaking and when you are speaking.

When in a group conversation, listen to what others are saying before you answer or add to the conversation. If you want to ask a question, ask **only one** question at a time; then stop speaking to wait for the answer. If more than one person answers, listen to each answer before speaking again. Do not talk while another person is answering. Do not say "uh-huh." Simply nod your head up and down if you agree. If you do not agree, politely hold your head still and consider if you should voice your difference of opinion when the speaker has finished.

Make sure you stay with the current conversation until it shifts smoothly. Think about what you are going to say before you speak and don't interrupt others when they are speaking. Wait until they stop and then insert your conversation. If the group you are in does not stop long enough to let you speak, leave the group. A group of people that does not conduct their conversations fairly is a group in which you should not participate. This type of group will waste your time and lead you to develop bad communication habits.

Your words should always be kind and edify or build up others. Make sure your words are also necessary and helpful. Don't share with others things they do not have a need to know. Keep private things private. Talking about things that would be considered private or should not be shared with others, only leads to gossip. Gossip is a sin that you will study about in the next unit.

If you must talk about something that is disagreeable, choose your words in the most careful way you can to avoid gossiping or hurting others feelings. Speaking the truth can hurt if not done carefully. Consider how you would want someone else to tell you the truth about something you may have done wrong or about what another person has done wrong.

Good communications aren't just about having the most interesting things to say; they are also about manners, fairness, and carefulness in what you say. Even if you are shy or slow to speak, you can be a worthy communicator who is just and wise. If you follow this advice and really practice it, you will learn how to communicate better.

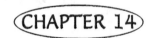

DIALOGUE: WRITING SKILLS

14.1 Dialogue in a Story

Just as conversations are an important part of your daily life, conversations are an important part of story writing. Every day you speak in conversations and hear others in conversation. Have you ever listened to a conversation for the purpose of writing spoken words on paper? Think back to the last conversation you heard today or yesterday. Can you remember what the people were saying who were involved in the conversation? How many people were involved in the conversation? Did those people talk about more than one subject? What did each person say? Could you write that conversation down on paper without the help of a tape recorder? Would you be able to write the conversation with correct grammar?

The conversations in a story are named **dialogue**. Writing a dialogue involves careful thinking about the way the characters might talk to each other. What will they say? How will they speak? When will they speak? Who might begin the dialogue? Who will end the dialogue? These are all questions you must ponder because a good dialogue must flow smoothly, be believable, and be grammatically correct.

For this writing assignment, you will write an indoor dialogue. First, you will have to think about where that dialogue will take place. Will it be in a restaurant, a kitchen, a museum, a school, or where? Take a minute or two to think about where an interesting dialogue might take place. A helpful idea is to think about a place you have had a memorable conversation. You could use that place as your location. When you have chosen a location, write it in the empty box below the **WRITING CHART #9** box on page 93.

In order to have a dialogue, you must have characters. For this assignment, you will need to write a dialogue between two characters. First, you must decide who those two characters are and what their names are. Will they be friends, your parents, a boy and girl, two boys, or two girls? What are their names? Take a minute to decide. Then write the names of your two characters in the two boxes below the name of your location.

Now you have a scene for a conversation and two characters who will engage in that dialogue. Tonight, think about what your characters might say in their dialogue. Tomorrow, you will work on that dialogue.

14.2 Creation of a Dialogue

In a story, the conversation between two or more characters is named the **dialogue**. Did you think about what your characters might say in the location you chose? Take a few more minutes now to think about their dialogue. They might talk about something in which they are interested, like a hobby or sports. They might talk about something they are about to do or have done, like an activity. Might they talk about something in the room where they are or something related to the room somehow?

In a story, the words that your characters speak to one another are named direct quotations. A **direct quotation** is the exact words of the speaker in a dialogue. The direct quotations may include more than one sentence of spoken words by each character and may take more than a single line of space on your paper. Think of what you want your characters to say to one another. Create four direct quotations that occur between your two characters. (Each character will talk two times.) Then write those four direct quotations on the lines on page 93.

Does the dialogue you have written make sense? Take a moment to read your dialogue out loud to see if it makes sense. When your four direct quotations make sense, get a clean sheet of lined writing paper. Take a careful look at that writing paper. Notice how it has many blue, horizontal lines and one red, vertical line near the left edge of the paper.

Put your finger on the top left corner of the paper. Now count down four lines with your finger, but keep it on the **left** side of the red, vertical line. Stop on line four. This line is where you will write the **name** of the first character speaking in your dialogue. Please write that name now.

Write your first character's words on the blue line, by beginning the first word on the **right** side of the red, vertical line after that character's name. If your character's conversation takes more than one line, make sure that you continue on the next line, but only write to the right of the red, vertical line.

When you have finished with your first character, immediately on the next line, write the second character's name and words as you were instructed to do for the first character. Continue writing this way until you have all four direct quotations to the right of the red, vertical line, with the names of the characters to the left of the vertical line. Remember to capitalize all names and the beginnings of sentences.

Use this dialogue to complete **WRITING ASSIGNMENT #9** on page 93.

WRITING CHART #9

DIRECT QUOTATIONS

1. _____
2. _____
3. _____
4. _____

WRITING ASSIGNMENT #9

Your assignment is to write an **indoor dialogue between two characters**. The dialogue must contain **eight** direct quotations. Remember that a direct quotation may contain more than one sentence and may take up more than a single line on your paper.

1. Format
- ☐ Write the location of the indoor dialogue at the top of the page.
- ☐ Write your name under the title.
- ☐ Begin the first line of dialogue on the **second** line below your name.

2. Construction
- ☐ Write **eight** lines of direct quotations between **two** characters.
- ☐ Each sentence must have **three or more** words.
- ☐ Each direct quotation must have a name to the left of the red, vertical line; this name will identify who is speaking.

3. Grammar
- ☐ Capitalize all names and the beginnings of sentences.
- ☐ Use periods, exclamation points, question marks, and commas properly.
- ☐ Make some of your sentences long and some short.
- ☐ Be careful to use proper word tenses.

4. Polish
- ☐ Only turn in a final copy of your paper if it has been written neatly.
- ☐ Use the dictionary and the thesaurus to find extra words.
- ☐ Make sure the conversation flows logically.

5. Ethics
- ☐ Work on your own and make the dialogue original.
- ☐ Do not write what you would not want someone to say about you.
- ☐ Make the language of your paper conform to Philippians 4:8.
- ☐ Your characters must be honest, believable, kind, and considerate.

6. Creativity
- ☐ Make the dialogue interesting.

WRITING PREPARATION

Was your first attempt to write a dialogue between two characters a success? In this lesson, you are going to write an outdoor dialogue. This dialogue will be longer and require more grammar. Try very hard to make the conversation even better than your last dialogue.

There are many places where an outdoor dialogue might occur, such as at a park, on a walk, in a row boat, on a campout, etc. Try to think about where a good dialogue could take place. If you remember a place you have had a memorable dialogue before, you could use that location for this assignment. When you have chosen a location, write that location in the empty box below the **WRITING CHART #10** box on page 98.

In order to have a dialogue, you must have characters. For this assignment, you will need to write a dialogue between three characters. First, you must decide who those three characters are and what their names are. Will they be friends, your family, or relatives? Take a minute to decide. Then write the names of your three characters in the three boxes under the name of your location.

What kind of dialogue might your characters have in the outdoors? Could they talk about something that they might see or some activity that they might be doing or watching? Might they talk about one topic or about more than one topic? For instance, if they were at a lake, would they talk only about the children swimming and playing on the beach or also about the boats on the lake, the birds flying around, and/or some fishermen?

Usually the length of the conversation can help you make this decision. If the conversation is short, staying focused on one topic is best; but if the conversation is long enough, you may have your characters talk about more than one topic.

Take a few minutes to decide what topic or topics your characters will be discussing in their outdoor dialogue. Make sure the topics you choose are about something outdoors. Write these topics in the **TOPICS** box on page 98.

You have selected the location of an outdoor dialogue, the names of your characters, and the topics about which they will speak. The next thing you need to decide is what each character's interests might be and consequently how he/she will talk. For instance, if four characters are going to talk about fishing, maybe one does not like fishing, but two do; maybe the fourth character likes only certain kinds of fishing.

Knowing these interests will affect how each character speaks about fishing. Think about what interest each of your three characters might have in the topic or topics about which you have chosen to write. In the **INTERESTS** box under each character's name, write what their interests concerning these topics are.

Writing a conversation requires a smooth flow of dialogue that is believable and grammatically correct. For this assignment, you will have to make up a dialogue between three characters, without listening to and recording a live dialogue first. Remember that the dialogue you create must be pleasant. Your characters must share their honest feelings and opinions, but be kind and considerate of others' feelings. They must not talk about any topic that is rude, mean, or not appropriate for their age.

Another important practice is to read the dialogue out loud several times while you are writing, to see if it makes sense. Make sure you ask yourself these questions. Would real people talk just like the characters do in the dialogue I am writing? Is this dialogue too choppy? Does it have too many ideas? When you are satisfied with the dialogue you have created, write it carefully on your final draft paper. Remember to write the names of the characters to the left of the red, margin line and the words they speak to the right of the red, margin line.

Read **WRITING ASSIGNMENT #10** on page 99. Complete the grammar lessons 15.1-15.4 and prepare your composition on clean writing paper.

CHAPTER 15

DIALOGUE: GRAMMAR SKILLS

15.1 Grammar Rules

Writing good dialogue takes practice because you must think carefully about what the characters of a story might say to one another. In this chapter, you will learn rules about how to punctuate dialogue with quotation marks and commas. You will learn about names of direct address and interjections. Read each grammar rule and apply it to your writing.

15.2 Quotation Marks

In a story, when two or more characters converse with one another, their conversation is named the **dialogue**. Writing dialogue is very different than writing descriptions. The exact words that a character speaks are named **direct quotations**. Direct quotations have their own special set of punctuation rules. **Quotation marks** are a type of punctuation mark that is used to identify the words in a direct quotation that a character is speaking.

Quotation marks always appear as pairs. They are placed at the beginning and at the end of a direct quotation. To understand how quotation marks are used, an example of a character and the words that she said is shown below. Notice that the name of the character is placed to the left of a black line. To the right of the line are the words the character speaks in the direct quotation. Where do you think the quotation marks should be placed?

Mary | I am looking for my red ball.

To punctuate this dialogue, quotation marks are drawn at both the beginning and the end of the spoken words. Quotation marks look like pairs of flying commas (" "). Each quotation mark contains two of these commas. The flying commas at the beginning of a direct quotation are drawn both upside down and backwards. At the end of the direct quotation, the flying commas are drawn right side up. The following direct quotation shows the correct placement of quotation marks.

Mary | "I am looking for my red ball."

The quotation marks have been drawn before the first word that Mary speaks and after the last punctuation at the end of the words that she speaks. What if Mary says more than one sentence? Where do you think the quotation marks should appear in this type of dialogue?

Mary | I am looking for my red ball. Do you know where it is?

The first quotation marks must be placed at the beginning of the first word that Mary speaks, but now the end of the direct quotation is **after** the second sentence. In this case, the last quotation marks are placed after the last punctuation at the end of the words that Mary speaks, which is after the second sentence. Here you see the correct placement of a pair of quotation marks.

Mary | "I am looking for my red ball. Do you know where it is?"

No matter how many sentences Mary speaks, the quotation marks will always be placed at the beginning of the first word that she speaks and after the last punctuation of the last word that she speaks.

PRACTICE: Add quotation marks to these direct quotations.

A. Sue | I need more exercise. Will you go for a walk with me?

B. John | I would like some more milk, please.

C. Blake | If you finish your project today, it will be completed before the May 1 deadline.

D. Terrance | The windows need to be shut. May I have a volunteer?

Look at your outdoor dialogue. Draw quotation marks around the direct quotations for each of your characters. Place the first quotation marks before the first words of dialogue and the last quotation marks after the punctuation which follows the last words.

15.3 Names of Direct Address

Now that you understand quotation marks, you will learn how to use commas with specific words in a direct quotation. These specific words are the names of the characters. In a direct quotation, if a character directly addresses the name of another character, either at the beginning of a sentence or the end of a sentence, a comma is used. The name of the character to whom the speaker is speaking is named the **name of direct address**.

A comma is drawn **after** the name of direct address if it occurs at the beginning of a sentence. If the name occurs at the end of the sentence, a comma is drawn **before** the name of direct address. The following sentence is an example of the name of direct address occurring as the first word of a sentence. In this sentence, a comma is drawn after the name Mary, but before the rest of the dialogue.

"**Mary,** have you found your red ball?"

In the next sentence, the name of direct address is Tom. Notice how the name Tom occurs at the end of the sentence. When the name of direct address is in this position, a comma must be drawn after the word that comes right before Tom's name.

"I would like to play ball**, Tom**."

PRACTICE: Add commas to these direct quotations.

A. "Sally I really care about your safety."
B. "I will pray for you Luke."
C. "Molly that was a delicious meal."
D. "I hope you come visit soon Annie."

Look at your outdoor conversation. Place a name of direct address in each of your direct quotations. Put one name at the beginning of a quotation and one at the end of another quotation. Draw a comma at the proper place in each quotation.

15.4 Interjections

When writing conversation, you might want to add extra emotion, feeling, or expression by using a little word at the beginning or end of a sentence in a direct quotation. There are many such little words, like **yes**, **no**, **oh**, **ow**, **ah**, **whew**, or **well**. These words are named interjections. An **interjection** is a little word that tells the reader that the character is speaking more expressively. An interjection may be either strong or mild. When a strong interjection is used in a sentence, an exclamation point is drawn after the interjection appears. The following example shows how an interjection and an exclamation point are added to the beginning of a direct quotation.

"**Whew!** It sure is a hot day."

Whew is a little word at the beginning of this direct quotation. An exclamation point is drawn **after** the word **whew**. If one of the words **yes**, **no**, **oh**, **ow**, **ah**, or **well** was used in the place of **whew**, you would also draw an exclamation point after that word.

When a mild interjection is used at the beginning of a direct quotation, a comma is drawn after the interjection appears. The following example shows how an interjection and a comma are added to the beginning of a direct quotation.

"**Ah,** I love the sound of harp music"

Ah is a little word at the beginning of this direct quotation. A comma is drawn **after** the word **ah**. If one of the words **yes**, **no**, **oh**, **ow**, **whew**, or **well** was used in the place of **ah**, you would also draw a comma after that word.

PRACTICE: Add an exclamation point to each of these strong interjections.

A. "No I refuse to tell a lie."
B. "Oh How did you surprise me and arrive so quickly?"
C. "Ow I stubbed my toe on the door!"

PRACTICE: Add a comma to each of these mild interjections.

A. "Oh I think I'll just rest for an hour."
B. "Yes the game starts at six o'clock."
C. "Well let's think of a better solution."

Look at your outdoor conversation. Add an interjection at the beginning of one of your direct quotations. Draw a comma or an exclamation point in the proper place.

WRITING CHART #10

TOPICS

INTERESTS

DIRECT QUOTATIONS

1. _____
2. _____
3. _____
4. _____
5. _____
6. _____
7. _____
8. _____
9. _____
10. _____
11. _____
12. _____

WRITING ASSIGNMENT #10

Your assignment is to write an **outdoor dialogue between three characters** that contains **twelve** lines of direct quotations.

1. **Format**
   - [ ] Write the location of the outdoor dialogue at the top of the page.
   - [ ] Write your name under the title.
   - [ ] Begin the first line of dialogue on the **second** line below your name.
2. **Construction**
   - [ ] Write **twelve** direct quotations between **three** characters.
   - [ ] Each sentence must have **four or more** words.
   - [ ] Each direct quotation must have a name to the left of the red, vertical line on your paper. This name will identify who is speaking.
   - [ ] Use a variety of action words.
3. **Grammar**
   - [ ] Use periods, exclamation points, question marks, and commas properly.
   - [ ] Remember to put commas before or after the names of direct address.
   - [ ] Draw an exclamation point or comma after the little words **yes**, **no**, **oh**, **ah**, or **well** at the beginning of a sentence in a direct quotation.
   - [ ] Draw quotation marks at the beginning and end of all direct quotations.
   - [ ] Capitalize all names and the beginnings of sentences.
   - [ ] Make some of your sentences long and some short.
   - [ ] Be careful to use proper word tenses.
4. **Polish**
   - [ ] You may have to write the dialogue several times.
   - [ ] Only turn in a final copy of your paper that has been written neatly.
   - [ ] Make sure you have spelled all of your words correctly.
   - [ ] Use the dictionary and the thesaurus to find extra words.
   - [ ] Make sure your conversation flows logically.
5. **Ethics**
   - [ ] Work on your own and make the dialogue original.
   - [ ] Do not write about anything that is an inappropriate subject of conversation.
   - [ ] Your characters must be honest, believable, kind, and considerate.
   - [ ] Make the language of your paper conform to Philippians 4:8.
6. **Creativity**
   - [ ] Make the dialogue interesting.

EXPLANATORY WORDS: ETHICS SKILLS

CHAPTER 16

> **UNIT 6**
> **SUPPLIES**
>
> BIBLE
> DICTIONARY
> PENCIL
> THESAURUS
> WRITING PAPER

16.1 Scriptural Ethics

You have been conversing for a good portion of your life. Perhaps you have been taught some good ethical skills on how to converse in a wise manner. In the last unit, you learned that the Bible contains a good amount of information about speaking in ways that are wise and scripturally honoring.

Speaking wisely means that you do not talk too much and that you take your time or find the time to communicate carefully. When you take your time, you can reduce misunderstandings and mistakes in communication. You should also never dominate a conversation when in a group; letting others have a chance to speak is important. To share and be fair, you may even have to help another person give verbal input to a conversation by asking them a question.

Good communication means looking at the other person to whom you are speaking. Think about what you are going to say before communicating so that you can try to make your words as kind and edifying as possible. Don't speak too fast and don't interrupt when others are speaking. When listening to another speaker, show understanding of what that person says by simply nodding your head up or down, but not by making sounds.

In the Bible, there were times when Jesus/Yahshua and God/Yahweh had to say things that were true but did not sound kind. To think that all speaking will be full of fun and sweetness is to not know God. Sometimes you must talk about difficult things. Some topics of conversation may require you to sound firm in your voice. If you have to correct something this experience is not always easy; but when you pray to God to find out how to speak wisely, He will give you His wisdom.

Not all speaking situations are worthy of your time, either. If you find yourself in a situation where the conversation is unfair or wrong, leave the conversation by excusing yourself. Do not just walk away, or that might cause an offense. A wise person does not commit an offense to be free of an offensive situation. You show poise when you can excuse yourself from a bad situation without offending or adding to the perverseness of the situation.

Good communications aren't just about having the most interesting thing to say. They aren't always about having fun either. Good communication is a serous matter that one must practice to learn how to do well.

Scripture Study

Idle talk often leads to sin. Bad and sinful communications are defined by the Bible to include the sin of gossiping which can often include the sin of slander. Find the following verses in a Bible and read what they teach about these sins. Write the verses on these lines.

YOUR WRITING AND LIFE SHOULD **NOT** PROMOTE THESE TYPES OF BEHAVIORS.

1 Timothy 5:13 _____

_____

Wayyiqra/Leviticus 19:16 _____

_____

Mishle/Proverbs 11:13 _____

_____

Mishle/Proverbs 20:19 _____

Tehillim/Psalms 101:5 _____

These scripture verses tell you about gossip and slander. Gossip is a sin. **A person who gossips** is someone who talks about the private affairs of others with people who do not need to know about those private things. **A person who gossips** also shares or spreads rumors. Do not engage in talk that is gossip. If someone who is gossiping to you, tell them to stop as nice as you can or try to change the topic of the conversation. If you ask a person to stop gossiping and he/she does not stop gossiping, excuse yourself from the conversation.

Do not let another person cause you to gossip by asking a question about someone or something that is none of his/her business. Answer the question by saying you do not want to gossip. This will end the probing and inform the other person that he/she is potentially initiating a conversation that is gossip.

It is not good to speak gossip and it is not good to listen to gossip because it can cause you to sin. You may sin by sharing that gossip with another person or you may sin by having bad thoughts in your head concerning the person about whom the gossip was shared. To make sure you do not gossip, always ask yourself whether a person has a need to know what you are thinking of sharing with him/her. Don't share with others things they do not have a need to know. Keep private things private. Talking about things that are unnecessary, private, or not to be shared with others may also cause others to sin by their continuing your gossip.

When someone makes up a false statement about another person or even repeats a false statement that they have heard, they commit a sin named slander. **Slander** is a type of talk that causes damage to another peron's character or reputation. Slander is unkind and malicious because a person decides to say untrue things on purpose.

Imagine how you would feel if someone spread a false story about you. Could you find all of the people that had heard that false story and correct what they had heard? Probably not. That is why it is important to never tell another person about something you heard unless you have verified yourself that it is the truth. Even then, you should not share unless the person to whom you are talking really has a need to know, like when a person's safety is at risk.

Both slander and gossip are sins. God does not like these sins at all. If you have committed these sins before, it is a good idea to ask Jesus for forgiveness. You might even need to go and correct any untruths you told. Remember that there are always consequences for sin if you do not repent and make amends. For most people, it is easier to correct a wrong than to take a punishment.

One way to avoid both gossip and slander in conversation is to avoid talking about other people. This does not mean that you cannot mention what you are going to take to someone's birthday party, that your Aunt Sue will be getting married on a certain date, or that you played baseball with Jeff and John last week. You can also make or share a compliment about another person; but be careful that the conversation does not go in a negative direction or go on to long,or you could fall into gossiping. If you try to limit your conversation to intellectual things, like work, hobbies, or vacations you will avoid most gossip. If you like politics, education, gardening, cooking, reading books, or other activities, talk about them instead of talking about other people.

Not all conversation is gossip, however. If person's sin is hurting you or someone else, you need to tell an adult who can help. If someone is in danger because of a sinful person, you need to warn the person in danger. If you are asked to tell the truth about someone's sinful behavior, tell the truth. If you have to talk to someone about a sinful person for one of these reasons, do not let the sinner, the person you talk to, or anyone else tell you that you are a gossip. These types of conversation are not gossip because sinful behavior must be uncovered and corrected. When a sinner has his/her sin exposed, it is not gossip.

Be wise about your conversations by being careful. You should also be careful about your story writing. Make sure that it does not contain or promote gossip or slanderous talk.

CHAPTER 17
EXPLANATORY WORDS: WRITING SKILLS

17.1 Creation of a Dialogue

In previous units, you learned how to write descriptions of characters, scenes, and action. You also had two good practices writing believable dialogue. In this unit, you will learn how to combine all of these elements together. This will help to make your conversations more interesting and help you to be ready to write your first story.

In a composition, whether you describe the scene of story or not, it is good to know the place where a dialogue occurs. For instance, if you decide that a character will mention something that is in the scene or particular to the scene, its location will be important to creating that dialogue. It is also important to decide how many characters will be involved in the dialogue.

To begin writing this paper, think about where the scene of the dialogue will occur. Think about whether the scene will be mentioned in the dialogue. Write the name of the scene in the box under the **WRITING CHART #11** box on page 105. Next, decide whether you will have two or three characters in the dialogue. Decide on the names for each of your characters, and write those names in the boxes under the name of the scene.

The dialogue that you create between your characters must be believable. The overall subject your characters talk about is the main topic of the dialogue. Think about what you want the topic of the dialogue to be for your characters. Will they talk about an activity, like sports or going to a play, an interest, like nature or astronomy, a hobby, like building a bird house or sewing a quilt, or what? It is important to pick only one topic for this dialogue. This will make it easier and less confusing to create a believable conversation between your characters.

After you choose a topic, you must think about any subtopics that your characters may discuss. For instance, suppose the topic for the characters' dialogue is an afternoon of fishing. Your characters might talk about many subtopics such as the boat ride, the types of fish caught, the type of fishing gear used, or the weather and water conditions that affected the fishing, etc.

Take some time to decide on the main topic and the subtopics of your character's dialogue. To help you with this, think about other conversations that you have had with friends or family. What kinds of things did you talk about that might be a good topic or subtopic? Remember that your subtopics must be related to the main topic. When you have decided on a main topic and two or three subtopics, write them in the **TOPIC AND SUBTOPICS** box on page 105.

You have chosen your scene, your characters, the main topic, and two or three possible subtopics for the dialogue. Now it is time to create that dialogue. On the **WRITING CHART**, there are four sets of lines for you to write four lines of conversation between your characters. You will write one direct quotation on each set of lines. For each direct quotation, start by writing the name of the character on the left of the vertical line but to the right of the letter A.

Then write the words of that character's direct quotation on the right side of the vertical line. You will write four short direct quotations. Make the words of each direct quotation fit on only the "A" line of each set of lines, leaving the next four lines blank. Draw quotation marks around each direct quotation. When you have completed the four direct quotations, read them several times to make sure that the conversation makes sense and is written grammatically correct. Make any corrections before completing today's work.

17.2 Explanatory Words

When you listen to an oral conversation there are no explanatory words in the dialogue. However, when you write a dialogue on paper, it is most helpful to include explanatory words for the reader. This is because **explanatory words** give information about the character who is speaking. The explanatory words tell how a character speaks the words of the direct quotation and give descriptions of that character.

The explanatory word that tells how a character speaks his/her words is generally the word **said**. The word **said** is the most frequently used explanatory word telling that a character has spoken. For this paper, use this word for all of your direct quotations. The word **said** may be placed before or after the direct quotation. For this paper, the word **said** will be written before the words of the direct quotation.

A list of the names of the characters in the left hand column followed by the direct quotation, looks like a script for a play. In a story for a book, the dialogue is not written this way. The dialogue in a story is written in a certain grammatical pattern. To learn this pattern, return to **WRITING CHART #11** on page 105. On line B, rewrite each of you four direct quotations by following these instructions. First, write the name of the character, followed by the word **said** and a comma. After the comma, leave a space before drawing the first quotation marks. Start the direct quotation by capitalizing the first word; and then, write the entire quotation with proper end of sentence punctuation. Finally, draw the closing quotation marks. By following this pattern, a simple line of dialogue would look like the following.

John said, "I like fishing."

In this dialog, first the name of the character was written. Next, the word **said** was added followed by a comma. A space was made before drawing the first quotation marks. The first word of the direct quotation was capitalized. The entire direct quotation was written with proper punctuation at the end of the sentence as though it were an independent sentence. Finally, the last quotation marks were draw. When following this pattern, a line of dialogue is complete and grammatically correct. When your four sentences of dialogue are correctly written in this manner then you may proceed on with this lesson.

In order to add the descriptive explanatory words to a direct quotation, you must first decide what they will be. To do this, you must determine the descriptions of what your characters look like. This involves thinking about what your characters are wearing as well as the color of their eyes, hair, and skin. Ask yourself questions. What nationality is the character? How tall is each character? Does a character have freckles on his/her face? Is one of the characters skinny? What other features can you think of to describe each character?

On **WRITING CHART #11**, write the names of each of your characters in the boxes under the **DESCRIPTION WORDS** box. Decide on the descriptions of your characters by filling in the columns just as you have done for prior papers. Remember the **OBJECT** column is where you record the information about how the character is dressed and more about what he/she looks like.

You now have enough information to write some of the explanatory words that will go with each character's direct quotation. The first sentence that you write will describe the character who is speaking. For instance, if one of your characters is named Sally, you could write the following sentences about her.

Sally has green eyes and brown hair. Her face is always friendly. She is wearing a blue dress with a white collar.

For each of your characters, look at the description words you have written on the writing chart. Next, look at the dialogue you created. On lines C and D, use your description words to write a sentence or two about the character who is speaking. Some of what you write will become part of the explanatory words for the dialogue.

Adding description words about the character to the explanatory words of a dialogue helps your reader to see a picture of that character while the character is speaking. This is done to approximate a real life situation where you would be looking directly at a person who is speaking to you. In a real life situation, you would be able to see how a person talking to you is dressed, what his/her facial features look like, etc. In a story, those things cannot be seen unless they are described to a reader.

Adding description words to the explanatory words is easy once you have determined what your characters will look like. Remember John who said he liked fishing at the beginning of this lesson? If John is a person who is tall and lanky, with black hair and blue eyes, some of this description could be used in the explanatory words. Using the dialogue on page 103, a new sentence could be written that gives a reader a mental picture of John as he is speaking.

The tall and lanky John said, "I like fishing."

The words tall and lanky tell you about John. These description words were placed in the explanatory words **before** the direct quotation. When the explanatory words, which contain words descriptive of the character, are placed in this manner before the quotation, a reader is able to see a picture of John before he speaks. Light travels faster than sound which causes the eye to see before the ear hears. Arranging descriptive character words before a direct quotation, therefore, most closely approximates a real life conversation.

If John was in a dialogue with another person named Susan, she would speak next. Suppose Susan had green eyes, blonde hair, and laughed a lot. Some of this description could be used in the explanatory words when she responds to John's comment about fishing.

The tall and lanky John said, "I like fishing."
Susan's green eyes sparkled with laughter as she said, "Wouldn't you love to go fishing on such a fine day as today?"

When Susan spoke, could you see her green eyes sparkling with laughter? Did the description words not only help you to see her but also how the two friends were relating to one another? Didn't they seem to be happy? Description words can add more than a picture to your writing, they can also add the emotions of the dialogue.

Take the time to finish the four direct quotations on **WRITING CHART #11** by adding descriptions of the characters in the explanatory words **before** the words each character speaks. Write your final dialogue for each character on line E.

Read **WRITING ASSIGNMENT #11**. If you have any questions please ask your teacher.

WRITING CHART #11

TOPIC and SUBTOPICS

DIRECT QUOTATIONS

1A. _____
B. _____
C. _____
D. _____
E. _____

2A. _____
B. _____
C. _____
D. _____
E. _____

3A. _____
B. _____
C. _____
D. _____
E. _____

4A. _____
B. _____
C. _____
D. _____
E. _____

DESCRIPTION WORDS

NATION	SIZE	NATION	SIZE	NATION	SIZE
HAIR	EYES	SKIN	HAIR	EYES	SKIN	HAIR	EYES	SKIN
OBJECT	COLOR	SIZE	OBJECT	COLOR	SIZE	OBJECT	COLOR	SIZE

WRITING ASSIGNMENT #11

Your assignment is to create **thirteen direct quotations between two or three characters**. In the explanatory words before each direct quotation, you must include the character's name and some description about him/her.

1. Format
- [ ] Write a title at the top of the page.
- [ ] Write your name under the title.
- [ ] Begin your first direct quotation on the second line below your name.

2. Construction
- [ ] Write **thirteen** lines of direct quotations between **two or three** characters.
- [ ] Each sentence must have **four or more** words.
- [ ] The explanatory words must occur **before** the direct quotation.
- [ ] Each direct quotation must contain a name in the explanatory words to identify who is speaking.
- [ ] A description of each character must also be presented in the explanatory words.

3. Grammar
- [ ] Use periods, exclamation points, question marks, and commas properly.
- [ ] Draw quotation marks at the beginning and end of all direct quotations.
- [ ] Capitalize all names and the beginnings of sentences.
- [ ] In the explanatory words, be careful that your names and your descriptions have the correct punctuation.
- [ ] Make some of your sentences long and some short.
- [ ] Be careful to use proper word tenses.

4. Polish
- [ ] You may have to write the dialogue several times.
- [ ] Only turn in a final copy of your paper that has been written neatly.
- [ ] Make sure you have spelled all of your words correctly.
- [ ] Use the dictionary and the thesaurus to find extra words.
- [ ] Make sure the dialogue flows logically.

5. Ethics
- [ ] Work on your own and make the dialogue original.
- [ ] Do not write about anything that is an inappropriate subject of dialogue.
- [ ] Your characters must be honest, believable, kind, and considerate.
- [ ] Make the language of your paper conform to Philippians 4:8.

TAKE YOUR TIME, AND YOU WILL CREATE AN INTERESTING CONVERSATION THAT IS PLEASANT AND KIND!

WRITING PREPARATION

You have written a dialogue with descriptions of the characters. For this writing assignment, you will add descriptions of the character's actions. You will also write the explanatory words at the end of the direct quotation, instead of the beginning.

To begin, first determine what kind of dialogue you would like to write and where it will occur. How many characters will speak in this dialogue? You may choose from two to three characters and then decide on their names. Record all of this information on **WRITING CHART #12** on page 117. Underneath these words, write the main topic and subtopics about which your characters will speak. Then consider how each of your characters might think or feel about the main topic and subtopics and write some notes.

You have chosen your scene, your characters, the main topic, and two or three possible subtopics for the dialogue. Now it is time to create that dialogue. On the **WRITING CHART**, there are four sets of lines for you to write four lines of dialogue between your characters. You will write one direct quotation on each "A" line. For each direct quotation, start by writing the name of the character that will speak on the left of the vertical line but to the right of the letter A.

Next, write the words of that character's direct quotation on the right side of the vertical line. You will write four short direct quotations. Make the words of each direct quotation fit on the "A" line, leaving the next four lines blank. When you have completed the four direct quotations, read them several times to make sure that the dialogue makes sense and is written grammatically correct.

The dialogue in a story is written in a certain grammatical pattern. To learn this pattern, return to **WRITING CHART #12**. On line B, rewrite each of you four direct quotations placing the explanatory words **after** the direct quotation by following these instructions. Draw the first set of quotation marks; then, write the direct quotation. At the end of the direct quotation, draw a comma followed by the final quotation marks. Finally, write the word **said**, the name of the character who is speaking, and draw a period after the name. By following this pattern, a simple line of dialogue would look like the following.

"Hi, Molly," said Marsha.

Did you notice that the first word after the final quotation marks, the word **said**, is **not** capitalized? This is because it is not the beginning of a sentence or a proper name. The word **said** occurs inside the sentence and thus is not capitalized.

There is another way that this dialogue can be written. The name **Marsha** could be placed before the word **said**. In this case, the name **Marsha** would be capitalized, because it is a proper name. All proper names are always capitalized no matter where they occur in a sentence. Here is how this would look.

"Hi, Molly," Marsha said.

There are many other words that could be used in the explanatory words to take the place of the word **said**. Words such as **questioned, replied, responded, asked, commented, shouted, whispered, yelled, exclaimed**, and others could be used. The important thing to remember when using another word besides the word **said** is that you must be sure your punctuation is correct. For instance, if you use the word **exclaimed**, you must draw an exclamation point at the end of the words of the direct quotation as shown in these sentences.

"Hi, Molly!" Marsha exclaimed.

"Hi, Molly!" exclaimed Marsha.

If Marsha had asked a question, a question mark would have been drawn in place of the exclamation mark. Inside a direct quotation, the appropriate punctuation must always be used, such as a comma after a statement, a question mark after a question, or an exclamation mark after an exclamation. These punctuation marks, however, are not the end of a sentence when explanatory words follow them.

Writing dialogue with a description of what the characters look like and are doing, involves carefully thinking about each character. What they will say as well as what they look like and do must be included in the dialogue. The easiest way to develop this type of dialogue is to write the direct quotation first. Then the descriptions and actions of a character can be added in a rewrite. When you concentrate on the dialogue separately from the description of your characters and their actions, you will be able to check that the dialogue flows correctly.

It's time to add some of the explanatory words that will go with each character's direct quotation. The first sentence that you will write will cover the action and descriptions of the character who is speaking. For instance, if the character Marsha has long, blonde hair, these explanatory words could be written into her dialogue.

"Hi, Molly," said Marsha as she pushed her long, blonde hair off her face.

Did the explanatory words mention an action of Marsha's? Did you get a little picture of what Marsha looks like from the explanatory words?

What will your characters look like in your dialogue? You can create different types of facial features and any other descriptive features that will help your reader to see what your characters look like. Write as many description words as you desire about what your characters look like on **WRITING CHART #12**. Then look at the dialogue you created. On lines C and D, use your description words to write a sentence or two about the character who is speaking. Finish the four direct quotations by adding descriptions of the characters and their actions in the explanatory words. Write this final dialogue for each character on line E.

You have learned a lot in this lesson. Here is an example of four lines of conversation that cover all you have just learned. Notice that each character's dialogue includes a description of what the he/she looks like and his/her actions."

"What a great day it is for a picnic!" Frank exclaimed as his strong hands reached for the picnic basket.
"Yes, I have been waiting all week for this day," said Sarah, his wife, removing the apron protecting her flowered dress.
"Will you be making an apple pie today, dear?" asked Frank--his dark, brown eyes widening in excitement at the thought of her delicious pies.
"I already have one made that you can remove from the refrigerator, if you like," Sarah replied as she pushed her medium length, brown hair behind her ears and reached for a loaf of bread.

Read **WRITING ASSIGNMENT #12** on page 118. Complete the grammar lessons and prepare your composition on clean writing paper.

CHAPTER 18
EXPLANATORY WORDS: GRAMMAR SKILLS

18.1 Grammar Rules

Writing good dialogue takes practice. Using good grammar in that dialogue is important. The apostrophe is a special punctuation mark. It may occur in words used in dialogue. Knowing when to use an apostrophe is very important to writing well.

Another part of speech that requires special grammar study is the verb. You have learned about the present and past tense forms of verbs. These verbs may be regular in their spelling or irregular when they take on their different forms. In this chapter, you will learn about a form of a verb named the past participle. Verbs that are difficult to understand in their different forms will also be studied. This grammar study will help you when writing your characters' dialogues.

18.2 Apostrophes

The apostrophe is important to correct grammar. The **apostrophe** looks like a flying comma ('). This **punctuation mark** is used in two types of grammatical situations. The first situation follows this rule.

> **RULE #1**
> An **apostrophe** is used when two words are put together to make one word. This word is named a **contraction**.

When two words are put together, an apostrophe (') is placed where a letter or letters are removed. Notice what happens to the underlined letter in the words below.

EXAMPLES:

was n<u>o</u>t	becomes	**wasn't**
did n<u>o</u>t	becomes	**didn't**
could n<u>o</u>t	becomes	**couldn't**

PRACTICE: Rewrite each pair of words as a **contraction**. Remember to put the two words together and remove the letter **o**. In its place draw an **apostrophe**.

A. were not_____   D. had not_____
B. was not_____   E. should not_____
C. would not_____   F. did not_____

When two words are put together, an apostrophe (') is placed where a letter or letters are removed. Notice what happens to the underlined letters in the helping words below.

EXAMPLES:

I h<u>a</u>ve	becomes	**I've**
he h<u>a</u>s	becomes	**he's**
he h<u>a</u>d	becomes	**he'd**

PRACTICE: Rewrite each pair of words as a **contraction**. Remember to put the two words together and remove the letters **ha**. In their places draw an **apostrophe**.

A. you have_____   E. they had_____
B. we have_____   F. she had_____

C. she has_____ G. we had _____
D. they have _____ H. it has _____

    The verb **have** is a special word. When it is used as a helping verb, it can be contracted with the subject (usually a pronoun) of the main verb. However, if **have** appears as the sentence's main verb, it cannot be contracted with the subject. The following examples will help you to understand this difference; study them carefully.

EXAMPLES:
MAIN VERB: **She has** a new dress for the party.
(Do not make the contraction **she's**.)
HELPING VERB: **She has** worn that new dress all day.
She's worn that new dress all day.

MAIN VERB: **They have** a badminton game in their yard.
(Do not make the contraction **they've**.)
HELPING VERB: **They have** played badminton all summer.
They've played badminton all summer.

MAIN VERB: **I had** a good time at the program.
(Do not make the contraction **I'd**.)
HELPING VERB: **I had** seen the program before.
I'd seen the program before.

PRACTICE: Rewrite the following sentences with contracted forms of the verb "have" **if** they can be contracted.

A. You have written an interesting book report.
_____

B. At her dentist appointment, she had no cavities.
_____

C. The exciting news is that we have a new baby in our family.
_____

D. Because of the job interview, he has hope for that promotion.
_____

E. I like that song, but it has played too many times on the radio today.
_____

F. I have a loose tooth in the front of my mouth.
_____

Note: If the word **not** is used with a form of the verb **have** which is being used as a helping verb, you may contract it with either the subject or the word **not**.

EXAMPLES:
We've not finished our homework.
or
We **haven't** finished our homework.

Check the dialogue you have created to see if it has words that can be formed as a contraction. If there are, form the words into contractions as learned in this study.

18.3 Apostrophes

The apostrophe is important to correct grammar. The **apostrophe** looks like a flying comma ('). This **punctuation mark** is used in two types of grammatical situations. The second situation follows this rule.

> **RULE #2**
> An **apostrophe** is used to show **possession**.

Possessive words show ownership of the word (noun) or words (nouns with adjectives) directly following them. There are three ways that possessive words are formed. In the next three days, you will learn about each one.

♦A **singular** word that names a person is made possessive by adding **'s** after the last letter of that word. In the following sentences, the kite belongs to Tom, and the sewing belongs to Jenna. Tom and Jenna own these things. To show ownership, the apostrophe (') and an **s** are added after each person's name, but before the things that are owned.

EXAMPLES:

Tom kite soared high above the trees.	becomes	**Tom's** kite soared high above the trees.
Jenna sewing was very good.	becomes	**Jenna's** sewing was very good.

PRACTICE: Rewrite the following sentences. In each sentence, first find the **person** who owns something. Then change that **singular** word to show ownership of the word that follows.

A. Todd hat was on his head._____
B. Tricia blue doll was lost._____
C. Phil home was across town._____
D. Stacy coat was in the closet._____
E. Bill umbrella had a hole in it._____

18.4 Apostrophes

Now you will learn more about the apostrophe! This important punctuation mark looks like a flying comma ('). Apostrophes are used to form contractions and possessive words. **Possessive words** show ownership of the word (noun) or words (nouns with adjectives) that directly follow. There are three ways that possessive words are formed. You learned how to change a singular word that names a person into a possessive word. The second way to show possession is similar.

♦**Plural** words that **do not** end in an **s** are formed by adding **'s** after the final letter of the word. This rule is only for nouns that name **animals** and **people**.

EXAMPLES:
To make the word **children** possessive, it is written like this: **children's**.

The **children's** bikes were lined up in a neat row.
The **men's** meeting was a success.

PRACTICE: Rewrite the following sentences. Change each **plural** word to show ownership of the word that follows.

A. The sheep wool was very thick._____

B. The deer families were nearby._____

C. The geese babies were quite large._____

D. The women party was a fun event._____

Check the dialogue you have created. Can you make the names of some of the characters possessive? Can you write the word or words after a name to belong to that character? If so, make the person's name possessive by adding an **'s**, just like you did in this lesson.

Can you add any plural words that can be made possessive? Do these plural words not have an **s** at the end of them already? If so, make that plural word possessive by adding an **'s** just like you did in this lesson.

18.5 Apostrophes

Today you will learn the last rule about the important grammar mark named the **apostrophe**. This punctuation mark looks like a flying comma ('). Apostrophes are used to form contractions and possessive words. **Possessive words** show ownership of the word (noun) or words (nouns with adjectives) that directly follow. There are three ways that possessive words are formed. So far, you have learned how to change two kinds of words into possessive words: (1) a singular word that names a person, and (2) one type of plural word that names animals or people. The third way to show possession is different from what you learned in Lesson 18.4.

♦**Plural** words that already end in **s** are formed by adding **only** an apostrophe after the **s**, which is the final letter of the word.

EXAMPLES:
To make the word **boats** possessive, it is written like this: **boats'**.

The **boats'** flags were waving in the breeze.
The **stores'** windows lined main street.

PRACTICE: Rewrite the following sentences. Change each **plural** word to show ownership of the word that follows.

A. The twins lunches were ready to eat._____

B. The five boys party hats were on the table._____

C. All of our players parents attended the game._____

D. The three families camping equipment was loaded into the bus._____

_____

Check the dialogue you have created. Are there any plural words that need to be made possessive? Do these plural words you wrote have an **s** at the end of them already? If so, make that word possessive by adding only an **apostrophe** as you did in this lesson.

18.6 Verb Forms

The **verb** of a sentence tells what a subject or character is **doing** or **being**. An **action verb** uses an **action** (doing) word. A **being verb** usually is some form of the verb "to be." Tense is about time. The time in a sentence may be past, present, or future. The verb or verbs in each sentence are the words that show the reader what tense the writer is using when writing that sentence. Since tense is also about time, the tense of a verb can also be past, present, or future. You learned about these verb tenses in previous grammar chapters. This chapter is about a new verb tense named the **past participle**. The past participle form of a verb indicates that something has occurred and **is finished**; whereas, the past tense only tells that something has occurred, but may not be finished.

A past participle verb is a verb that is written in the past tense but it has an additional "part." The word **participle** means **to partake or participate**. A past participle verb has another part that participates with a past tense verb. This extra "part" is named a **helping verb**. A past participle verb, therefore has two parts: the past tense verb itself and a helping verb. Because a part participle verb has two parts, it may also be named a **verb phrase**. The helping verb that is used in a past participle verb phrase is **have** (**has, had**).

For regular verbs, the past participle form includes a helping verb and the past tense verb (formed by adding **ed**). In Chapter 12, you learned how to change different types of regular verbs into the past tense. Here are several examples of those verbs.

REGULAR VERBS

PAST	PAST PARTICIPLE	PRESENT	FUTURE
liked	**have** liked	like	will like
jumped	**have** jumped	jump	will jump
stepped	**have** stepped	step	will step
chatted	**have** chatted	chat	will chat
testified	**have** testified	testify	will testify
clarified	**have** clarified	clarify	will clarify

PRACTICE: In the following sentences, write the regular verb in its past participle form. Remember to use either have, has, or had as the helping verb.

A. Yesterday, the grasshoppers _____ all over the grass. (jump)
B. They _____ playing for the day. (stop)
C. The butter _____ in the cooking process. (clarify)
D. The two sisters decided they _____ enough. (chat)

When an irregular verb is formed in the past participle it does not have **ed** added to the end of its spelling. An irregular verb may have the same spelling for the past participle form as the past form or there may be a spelling change. Still other irregular verbs have the letters **en** added in the past participle form with or without a verb spelling change. Here are several examples of irregular verbs. Study the list to see which verbs change.

IRREGULAR VERBS

PAST	PAST PARTICIPLE	PRESENT	FUTURE
slept	**have** slept	sleep	will sleep
taught	**have** taught	teach	will teach
broke	**have** broken	break	will break
spoke	**have** spoken	speak	will speak
took	**have** taken	take	will take
wrote	**have** written	write	will write
did	**have** done	do	will do
went	**have** gone	go	will go
laid	**have** laid	lay	will lay
lay	**have** lain	lie	will lie
set	**have** set	set	will set
sat	**have** sat	sit	will sit

PRACTICE: In the following sentences, write the irregular verb in its past participle form. Remember to use either have, has, or had as the helping verb.

A. The new kittens _____ until noon. (sleep)
B. Jerry _____ the dog out for a walk before dinner. (take)
C. All of the students _____ home from school. (go)
D. Early this afternoon the painters reviewed the work they _____. (do)

Check the dialogue you have created to see if it has any verbs that need to be formed in the past participle. If they do, spell them correctly by either consulting the lists on these two pages or a dictionary.

18.7 The Words "Lay" and "Lie"

Knowing when to use certain words can be confusing, especially when they are the words **lay** and **lie**. These two words are used in writing when you want to tell **what is placed or put somewhere** or when you want to tell that **someone/something** is **resting/reclining**. To know how to use these words correctly, you need to follow two rules. The first rule is about using the word **lay** in sentences.

> **RULE #1**
> The word **lay, lays (laid)** is used when you tell **what** you are **placing/putting** somewhere.

EXAMPLE: Lay the book on the table.

To decide if a sentence uses a form of **lay**, read the sentence and then ask yourself if the sentence is telling you **what** is being placed/put somewhere. If the sentence tells **what**, you will be able to insert the words **put** or **placed** for the word **lay**. (Don't get confused by the fact that **lay** is the past tense form of **lie**.)

EXAMPLE: He **laid** (put/placed) **the cup** on the counter.

PRACTICE: Read each sentence and decide if it is telling you **what** is being placed or put somewhere. Then write the correct form of **lay** on the blank line.
HINT: Try using the word **put** in the blank to see if **lay/lays/laid** is correct.

A. The banker _____ the coins on the counter.
B. They _____ blankets on their beds yesterday.
C. The children were going to _____ on their mats for a rest.
D. Dad and Mr. Harold _____ their tools on the floor.
E. Mom _____ the photo album in the hope chest last week.

How do you know when to use the word lie correctly in a sentence? The next rule is about using the word **lie** in sentences.

> ### RULE #2
> The word **lie, lies (lay, lain)** is used when you tell that **someone or something** is **resting or reclining**.

EXAMPLES:
Samuel, please **lie down**!
Mary **lay on the couch**.
That **book has lain on the counter** for three days.

To decide if a sentence uses a form of **lie**, read the sentence and then ask yourself if the sentence is telling you that **someone/something** is **resting/reclining**.

PRACTICE: Read these sentences and decide if the sentence is telling you that **someone/something** is **resting/reclining**. Then write the correct form of **lie** on the blank line.

A. The ribbon _____ on the sewing table.
B. Mrs. Trent instructed her son: "_____ down until you felt better."
C. Yesterday, the twins _____ their shoes inside the closet.
D. Those packages _____ on the porch all week long.
E. Those two bikes had _____ on the sidewalk since last night.

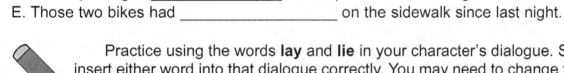

Practice using the words **lay** and **lie** in your character's dialogue. See if you can insert either word into that dialogue correctly. You may need to change the conversation a little so that it still makes sense.

18.8 The Words "Set" and "Sit"

Our conversation with others may include many types of words, some that are more difficult to know how to use correctly. The words **set** and **sit** are two difficult words. These two words are used in writing when you want to tell **what** is **placed or put somewhere** or when you want to tell that **someone/something** is **resting/seated**. To know how to use these words correctly, you need to follow two rules. The first rule is about using the word **set** in sentences.

> ### RULE #1
> The verb **set (set, have set)** is used when you tell **what** you are **placing/putting** somewhere. The noun or pronoun telling **what** must follow directly after the verb **set**.

EXAMPLES:
Timothy **sets the table** for dinner each night.
Tania **set the wooden spoon** on the counter.
The carpenter **has set the window** into its frame.

To decide if a sentence uses a form of **set**, read the sentence and then ask yourself if the sentence is telling you **what** is being placed/put somewhere. If the sentence tells **what**, you will be able to insert the words **put** or **placed** for the word **set**.

EXAMPLE: He **set** (put/placed) **the shoes** on the floor.

PRACTICE: Read each sentence and decide if it is telling you **what** is being placed or put somewhere. Then write the correct form of **set** on the blank line.
HINT: Try using the word **put** in the blank to see if **set** is correct.

A. The district attorney _____ the rules in his courtroom.
B. Mr. Homner _____ up the lunch tables before he arranges the chairs.
C. Crissy has _____ the picture into a frame.
D. The bread _____ on the table all night long.

How do you know when to use the word sit correctly in a sentence? The next rule is about using the word **sit** in sentences.

RULE #2
The word **sit** (sat, have sat) is used when you tell that
someone or something is **resting or sitting**.

EXAMPLES:
Three children **sit in the sandbox**
Mary **sat under a willow tree**.
That **milk carton has sat on the table** for two hours.

To decide if a sentence uses a form of **sit**, read the sentence and then ask yourself if the sentence is telling you that **someone/something** is **resting/sitting**. If the sentence tells you that **someone/something** is **resting/sitting**, you will be able to insert the words **resting** or **sitting** for the word **set**.

PRACTICE: Read these sentences and decide if the sentence is telling you that **someone/something** is **resting/sitting**. Then write the correct form of **sit** on the blank line.

A. The tzittzit _____ on the sewing machine table.
B. Mrs. Trent _____ up late last night.
C. The tiles have _____ on the floor since the repairman came last week.

Practice using the words **set** and **sit** in your character's dialogue. See if you can insert either word into that dialogue correctly. You may need to change the dialogue a little so that it still makes sense.
Complete the dialogue between the characters. Rewrite or type it neatly on a fresh piece of paper and turn it in to your teacher.

WRITING CHART #12

TOPIC and SUBTOPICS

DIRECT QUOTATIONS

1A. _____
B. _____
C. _____
D. _____
E. _____
2A. _____
B. _____
C. _____
D. _____
E. _____
3A. _____
B. _____
C. _____
D. _____
E. _____
4A. _____
B. _____
C. _____
D. _____
E. _____

DESCRIPTION WORDS

NATION	SIZE	NATION	SIZE	NATION	SIZE
HAIR	EYES	SKIN	HAIR	EYES	SKIN	HAIR	EYES	SKIN
OBJECT	COLOR	SIZE	OBJECT	COLOR	SIZE	OBJECT	COLOR	SIZE

117

WRITING ASSIGNMENT #12

Your assignment is to create **a dialogue that has fifteen direct quotations between two to three characters**. Write all the explanatory words after the direct quotations. Your explanatory words must include a description of each character and what he/she is doing as well as an appropriate word for **said**.

1. **Format**
   - ☐ Write a title at the top of the page.
   - ☐ Write your name under this title.
   - ☐ Begin the first direct quotation on the second line below your name.
2. **Construction**
   - ☐ Write **fifteen** direct quotations between **two or three** characters.
   - ☐ Each sentence must have **four or more** words.
   - ☐ The explanatory words must occur **after** the direct quotation.
   - ☐ Each direct quotation must contain a name in the explanatory words to identify who is speaking.
   - ☐ Descriptions of the characters and what they are doing must appear in the explanatory words.
3. **Grammar**
   - ☐ Use periods, exclamation points, question marks, and commas properly.
   - ☐ Draw quotation marks at the beginning and end of all direct quotations.
   - ☐ Capitalize all names and the beginnings of sentences.
   - ☐ Make some of your sentences long and some short.
   - ☐ In the explanatory words, be careful that your names and your descriptions have the correct punctuation.
   - ☐ Use the words **lie** or **lay**, **set** or **sit** in the dialogue.
   - ☐ Be careful to use proper word tenses.
4. **Polish**
   - ☐ You may have to write the dialogue several times.
   - ☐ Only turn in a final copy of your paper that has been written neatly.
   - ☐ Make sure you have spelled all of your words correctly.
   - ☐ Use the dictionary and the thesaurus to find extra words.
   - ☐ Make sure the dialogue flows logically.
5. **Ethics**
   - ☐ Work on your own and make the dialogue original.
   - ☐ Do not write about anything that is an inappropriate subject of dialogue.
   - ☐ Your characters must be honest, believable, kind, and considerate.
   - ☐ Make the language of the dialogue conform to Philippians 4:8.

BY NOW YOU ARE BECOMING A GOOD DIALOGUE WRITER!

PURPOSE: ETHICS SKILLS

UNIT 7 SUPPLIES

BIBLE
DICTIONARY
PENCIL
THESAURUS
WRITING PAPER

19.1 Scriptural Ethics

Why do people talk to one another? Some might answer to be friendly, to be helpful, to share knowledge, to become acquainted, to discuss important issues and ideas, or to warn of danger.

Where and how does a conversation begin? You have learned that life is full of events with opportunities for conversation. These events can occur almost anywhere: outside or inside. At any location, conversation begins because two or more people desire to speak with one another.

Is conversation best as a random event or should conversation have a purpose? In today's world, random talk occurs and is accepted as a method of communication by many, but is it scriptural?

In UNITS 5 and 6, you learned about conversing in a wise manner. Taking your time to communicate was one of the keys to this wisdom. Being fair in the exchange of conversation by looking at a person and not interrupting was also important to good communication. You learned that idle talk often leads to sin. Gossip and slander are two of the types of sin that can occur. Unplanned or random talk are much like idle talk. They are a type of communication that people use to fill in empty moments. This type of talk is more likely to lead to sin than a planned conversation that is grounded in ethical rules of communication.

Does this mean that random talk should be outlawed? Certainly a cheery hello to someone you don't know very well or an uplifting comment to someone can't hurt, or can it? The fact is that random talk, even when it is kind, can sometimes be the wrong thing to do. Talking to strangers is not a good idea. You should always be properly introduced to someone you don't know by a person whose judgement of others you can trust.

In today's world, as in the time of the Messiah, there are and were persons to whom you should not talk. Guarding your conversations and behavior in those conversations is important to not only good communication but your safety and God's purposes. Consider the person who has just been fired from his job for stealing. Should that person be consoled for unrepentant sin or rather given some time to think about that sin. Person's who sin without a conscience towards others are quick to grasp onto verbal kindness as a pardon for their wrongs even when they have never repented of them. These person's do not learn the lessons of their errors and often go on to perform more sin and even greater sins.

Random talk can interfere with God's plan to give a wrong doer time to think through his/her sins to repent of them and maybe even make amends for them. Don't let your random talk cause more trouble for the world than there already is; be wise and careful to plan as much of your communication as possible. To do this, you must remember several things you have learned.

1. Do not talk to strangers.
2. Do not engage in idle or random conversations.
3. Decide who are the people with whom you should communicate and those with whom you should not communicate.
4. Be careful and wise when you do speak.
5. Do not share secrets or information with those who do not have a need to know those secrets or information.
6. Get to know a person over a long period of time to determine if they are trustworthy of your confidences in conversation before you share with that person.

7. Keep the subjects you talk about in conversation limited to topics that are not personal, like hobbies, sports, education, etc.
8. Be accurate and truthful in your conversations with others.
9. Don't speak just to talk or be heard.
10. Don't babble, interrupt, tell jokes about others, or monopolize a conversation.

Conversation with others is really a serious matter involving many principles of ethical conduct. Being careful in your communications is important, but it is also wise to have something worthwhile to say. Therefore, to have good communications you must be a good student who listens well and desires to learn correctly. When you listen well, you will be able to **accurately** tell another person about the things you have learned from those oral communications. When you have a desire to learn, you will fill yourself with good information and knowledge that you may be able to share with others in your conversations with them.

Scripture Study

The Bible has much to teach about the wisdom and the knowledge you acquire and use in your communications with others. Read the following verses in a Bible to learn what they teach about this. Write the verses on these lines.

YOUR WRITING AND SPEECH SHOULD BE GUIDED BY THESE TRUTHS.

Mishle/Proverbs 10:13 _____
_____

Mishle/Proverbs 15:2 _____
_____
_____

Mishle/Proverbs 15:7 _____
_____

For several chapters, you have looked up verses from the book of Mishle/Proverbs. A **proverb** is a short saying that teaches a truth generally known or understood by the audience to whom it was given. A proverb is wisdom about how to correctly conduct one's life in ways that not only honor God but will also help you. The proverbs in the Bible were written to share wisdom with believers about practical ways to live everyday.

Sometimes these proverbs are a little hard to understand because they applied to people who lived so long ago (950-450 B.C.). However, the wisdom in scriptural proverbs is unchanging. To understand the harder ones, you must research the people, the language, and the customs of the time in which they were written.

For example, Proverb 10:13 uses two different words (understanding and heart) to convey and clarify a similar thought. A person who clearly understands a situation is able to speak wisely about that situation. The word heart is a word that was used long ago to also mean understanding, but it adds an additional clarity to the proverb because the heart also involved feelings. Thus, the first part of this proverb means that a person who has feelings and understanding speaks wisely, but a person who lacks feelings and understanding does not speak wisely. Furthermore, the unwise person should be struck with a rod on the back for his lack of compassion. This is because a person who lacks compassion will speak hurtful words into a situation involving feelings, instead of helpful words.

This proverb, therefore, warns that if you don't understand a problem and know how to solve that problem compassionately, don't offer a solution. You could really hurt the person having the problem and maybe even make the problem worse.

Proverb 15:2 teaches that a wise person shares knowledge carefully so that it is a blessing to others. Whereas, a foolish person randomly shares information whether it is not needed or helpful. This is like the first proverb but it covers more situations than just ones involved with a person's feelings.

Proverb 15:7 is the hardest of all to understand. However, once you understand its meaning it is very clear. Basically it means that wise people are full of wisdom that they freely share with other wise people who readily understand that shared wisdom. However, fools are not filled with wisdom so they cannot share wisdom or even understand wisdom.

What then is there to learn from these scriptures? First, be careful in all of your communications. Don't talk silly. Make your conversations count by sharing only the wisdom that you know is correct and that you clearly understand. Have compassion for another person's feelings when you talk. Don't randomly blurt out things you have heard just so you may sound knowledgeable. Trying to solve someone else's problems is not a good idea unless you truly have the right answer. Giving advise or making suggestions just for the sake of trying to sound wise can only lead to harm. However, when you do have good knowledge, share the knowledge you have learned in such a way that it blesses others.

Finally, learn to recognize the people in your life who are full of wisdom. Save your time for conversation with those people. Avoid conversations with those who are not wise because you will not learn anything useful from them.

CHAPTER 20

PURPOSE: WRITING SKILLS

20.1 Purpose in Dialogue

When writing a story, the conversations your characters have with one another should be guided by the same ethics the Bible teaches you to follow in your everyday conversations with others. Just as your conversations should not be random or silly, the dialogue of your characters should have a purpose.

When a story contains dialogue, that dialogue can be used to make the story either interesting and informative or boring and confusing. Have you ever read a story where the dialogue did not help the story? A dialogue that rambles on too long might cause you to grow bored when reading and make you decide to jump ahead in the story. If the dialogue is uninteresting you might want to close the book because you are not sure whether you want to continue reading anymore. Other dialogue, though funny and amusing, might have no purpose at all and make you forget the goal of the story.

Once you have read dialogue that rambles, is boring, or without purpose, you will realize how important good dialogue is to writing a good story. To create good dialog, not only do you need to follow scriptural ethics, but you must follow an important principle. The dialogue between characters must add something of **value to a story**, it must **have a purpose**. There are many types of dialogue you can create that will add value and purpose to a story. A dialogue that adds value and purpose might be written for one of the following reasons.

1. **To discuss or reveal something of importance to the story**
2. **To discuss or reveal something of importance to the characters**

Reason #1 states that a conversation in a story could add value and have purpose if it discusses something of importance to the story. What could be something that might be important to a story which would be best written into the dialogue rather than in the descriptions?

Consider the situation where a story is written that describes quite a bit of scenery for the reader. If those descriptions become too long and drawn-out a reader will become bored even when the descriptions are important to understanding the setting of the story. In this situation, the characters could dialogue about the scenery. They could walk around in the scenery discussing what it looks like. The characters could also mention aspects of the scene as they talk about something else. Even the explanatory words of the dialogue could contain descriptions of the scene.

The scenery is something that is important in most stories. Scenery may be described in the text of the story or it may be a part of the direct quotations of the characters. Descriptions of the scenery may also be added to the explanatory words of the dialogue.

Descriptions of the characters are also important to a story, but a long, continuous series of descriptions about the characters does not create an interesting story. While some descriptions can be made in the story narrative, the dialogue can also contain these descriptions. When the characters are talking with one another, they can discuss what each other is wearing. If they are talking about a new character that will soon appear in the story, they can describe the new character in their dialogue. Descriptions of the characters may also be placed in the explanatory words.

There is one more important subject that can be crucial to a story: an opinion of the time period in which the story is written. An opinion of the time period may be directly discussed by the characters or their conversation may be written to reveal their opinion. You may also write about that opinion in the explanatory words. A character's dialogue can be interesting and have purpose when it is used to discuss these things.

1. To discuss or reveal something of importance to the story
    a. Describing scenery
    b. Describing characters
    c. Describing an opinion of the time period of the story

The character's dialogue may also have value when it discusses **something of importance to the characters**.

Every character must have a personality. Their personality dictates how he/she will act and react in a story. The personality of a character can be revealed through dialogue or explained in the explanatory words.

If your characters were real, their personal opinions would also be important to them. In a story, the character's personal opinions are important because they help a reader get to know the characters better. The easiest place to reveal a character's opinion is the direct quotations, such as in a discussion about something, like politics, education, or vacations.

When characters discuss their opinions, they may also exhibit personality attitudes that reflect their opinions. These attitudes may be expressed by words, actions, or facial expressions that can be written about in the explanatory words.

Both a character's personality and opinion, as well as how he/she expresses that personality and opinion can add value to a story. Where a character is going can also be important to moving a story along. All of this information represent examples of the types of dialogue that discuss or reveal something of important to the characters.

2. To discuss or reveal something of importance about the characters
       a. Personality and opinions of the characters
       b. Attitudes that reflect personality and opinions
       c. Where characters are going

There are many types of dialogue that can add value to a story. In this chapter, you have learned about a few of the most common types of dialogue that you will find in a story. The complete list of what has been covered is shown here.

   1. To discuss or reveal something of importance to the story
       a. Describing scenery
       b. Describing characters
       c. Describing an opinion of the time period of the story
   2. To discuss or reveal something of importance about the characters
       a. Personality and opinions of the characters
       b. Attitudes that reflect personality and opinions
       c. Where characters are going

These types of dialogue are used in a story to convey information, keep a story interesting, give a story life, keep a story alive, and/or move a story along.

In prior units, you learned how to write conversation with the explanatory words either before or after the direct quotations. There is one more way to write conversation you must learn to be able to correctly write any type of conversation that contains a direct quotation with explanatory words. The final method of writing conversation has **imbedded** explanatory words. This means that a line of dialogue begins with part of a direct quotation, followed by the explanatory words, and then the remaining part of the direct quotation. An example of dialogue that has imbedded explanatory words is shown here.

"I went to the state fair on Saturday," **Mary said as she talked to her friend Sally,** "but I didn't see your mother's quilt there."

In this line of dialogue, the explanatory words occur in the middle of Mary's conversation with her friend Sally. Look carefully at the punctuation of this quotation. First, there is a full set of quotation marks before the explanatory words, then a second set of quotation marks was drawn after the explanatory words. Notice that there is also a comma after the word **Saturday**. The word **Mary** is capitalized because it is a proper noun. (Words that are not proper nouns are not capitalized at the beginning of imbedded explanatory words.) Next, the word Sally is followed by a comma **before** the direct quotation continues. The final quotation is punctuated with a full set of quotation marks. Make sure you follow this pattern of punctuation when writing a dialogue with embedded explanatory words.

Here are examples of the three ways to write dialogue with the correct punctuation.

    1. **Steve said,** "Can I get you a nice cold cup of water?"
    2. "I'm going to visit my cousin," **Jeff told his friend.**
    3. "The paper," **she said,** "is on the porch."

Turn to **WRITING ASSIGNMENT #13** and read it. If you have any questions please ask your teacher.

WRITING ASSIGNMENT #13

Your assignment is to write **two dialogues between two characters**. Write the first dialogue using reason #1 below. The dialogue must be about either 1a, 1b, or 1c. Write the second dialogue using reason #2 below. That dialogue must be about either 2a, 2b, or 2c.

1. To discuss or reveal something of importance to the story
   a. Describing scenery
   b. Describing characters
   c. Describing an opinion of the time period of the story
2. To discuss or reveal something of importance about the characters
   a. Personality and opinions of the characters
   b. Attitudes that reflect personality and opinions
   c. Where characters are going

1. **Format**
   - [ ] Write a title at the top of the page.
   - [ ] Write your name under this title.
   - [ ] Begin your first direct quotation on the second line below your name.
2. **Construction**
   - [ ] Write **eight** direct quotations between **two** characters for each dialogue.
   - [ ] Each sentence must have **six or more** words.
   - [ ] Each direct quotation must contain a name in the explanatory words to identify who is speaking.
   - [ ] Use a variety of action words and description words.
3. **Grammar**
   - [ ] Use periods, exclamation points, question marks, and commas properly.
   - [ ] Draw quotation marks at the beginning and end of all direct quotations.
   - [ ] Capitalize all names and the beginnings of sentences.
   - [ ] Make some of your sentences long and some short.
   - [ ] Be careful to use proper word tenses.
4. **Polish**
   - [ ] You may have to write the dialogues several times.
   - [ ] Only turn in a final copy of your paper that has been written neatly.
   - [ ] Make sure you have spelled all of your words correctly.
   - [ ] Use the dictionary and the thesaurus to find extra words.
   - [ ] Make sure the dialogue flows logically.
5. **Ethics**
   - [ ] Work on your own and make each dialogue original.
   - [ ] Do not write about anything that is an inappropriate subject of dialogue.
   - [ ] Your characters must be honest, believable, kind, and considerate.
   - [ ] Make sure the language of each dialogue conforms to Philippians 4:8.

WRITING PREPARATION

You have learned how to write descriptions of people, personalities, scenes, action, and dialogue as well as how to add purpose to dialogue. Now you will prepare your first story that reviews all of these elements by incorporating them into one paper. This paper will include people, places, and things that you might find in a bookstore.

To help you begin, you will ask yourself several questions that are listed below. You will decide on answers to each question that you might want to use in your paper. Use the **WRITING CHART #14** on page 133, to write those answers below each column heading. By example, you might answer question #1 below by writing the words parents, kids, and friends below the column heading titled **PEOPLE**. You might answer question #2 by writing about places in a bookstore, such as the checkout stand or a kid's corner. For question #3, things in a bookstore might include newspapers and periodicals.

1. Who might be shopping in a bookstore?
2. What kind of places are there inside a bookstore?
3. What type of things might you find in a bookstore.

There are many types of bookstores. There are new bookstores, used bookstores, Christian bookstores, secular bookstores, bookstores with just books, bookstores with books and music; bookstores with books, music, and toys, and even bookstores with cafes!

When was the last time you shopped in a bookstore? Do you remember how it looked? What did you do at the bookstore? What were the other people in the bookstore doing? Take a few minutes to think about these questions and write some notes on page 133, about what kind of store you were in, what the store looked like, and what the people were doing. You will need these descriptions to write your assigned paper.

The place where a story occurs is named the **scene**. Often knowing what the scene of a story is will help you to decide on the dialogue. Your scene in this paper is a bookstore or some place in a bookstore where a few people will have a conversation. Look at your list of places in a bookstore. Which place would you like to use in a story. Circle the name of that place. The place you circled will be the scene of your story.

A story must have characters. In the scene of the bookstore, imagine what type of people might be engaged in a dialogue in your story. Circle the type of characters in your list on the writing chart. Write two or three names for those characters on the writing chart.

In a story, a reader can learn about the scene in the descriptions, from the characters dialogue, or in the explanatory words. When you use one or more of these techniques a reader can imagine the scene or place more clearly in his/her mind.

To write the dialogue for this story, take some time to decide three things. First, will the characters talk about something related to the scene or unrelated? Second, what will the characters talk about or what will be the topic or topics of their dialogue? Third, will you only describe the scene, will the characters talk about the scene in their dialog, or will information about the scene appear in the explanatory words? To answer these questions, write some notes on the writing chart.

A story needs an introduction or opening paragraph to cause a reader to want to read what you have written. In a story, an opening paragraph can be very important. An opening paragraph can introduce or give important information about the characters, the scene, the time, the season, or an event. The opening paragraph can portray the mood of the story.

The opening paragraph of a story can be used to give a glimpse into the life of the characters in a particular situation. It may relate a feeling for what the characters are like in the story. The opening paragraph may also describe a situation of the scene that is helpful to the part of the story that is about to unfold. In the case of a bookstore, the opening paragraph may introduce the reader to the whole bookstore or a small section of the bookstore and one or two characters in that bookstore.

For this story, you must write an opening paragraph that describes the scene and mentions at least one character in that scene by name. To write the opening paragraph, decide what you will describe about the bookstore and what character will appear in this paragraph. Also think about what that character might look like and write some notes on how you would describe him/her. Write this information on the writing chart.

To turn your notes into a paragraph may be easy for you. If it is not, pray about how to do this. Always pray about everything you work on when you write. Jesus can guide you and help you to think straight about difficult issues. He will always help you to find the truth for your writing. Spending time with Him can even help you think of good ideas. When you pray to Jesus for help, you can ask these questions. What is a good idea for a paper? Which topics honor God? What do you think other people would enjoy reading? How should I write my paper?

When you pray about your writing, you honor Jesus with all of your work. You also learn to walk in communion with the Holy Spirit/Ruach Hakodesh.

Pray about how to begin your story in the opening paragraph. Write one or two versions on a separate piece of writing paper and your final version on **WRITING WORKSHEET #14**

Next, you must determine what will be the purpose of your paper. This will help you write about what will happen in your story as well as the dialogue. In order for a story to be interesting it must have a purpose. The purpose could be that one friend helps another friend find a good book to read. Another purpose could be that several friends meet at the bookstore to decide where to go on a vacation; they look at books about vacations and discuss them until they find one they want to buy. Maybe a husband and wife might need to go on a date to the bookstore to look at books, have a cup of hot chocolate, and talk about something important to them, like their children or what home school curriculum to use.

There are countless combinations of characters and reasons why they are at a bookstore. To help you think about the purpose your characters will be at the bookstore, first ask yourself some questions. How old are your characters? What things might be happening in their lives? What interests might they have separately or together? Why did they choose to go to a bookstore? Take some time to decide what will be the purpose of your story. Write the purpose of your story on the writing chart.

Next, you will work on the dialogue. Remember that when you are writing the dialogue you can add descriptions of the people and scenery in your explanatory words. For this story, you will write twelve lines of dialogue with explanatory words. By the end of the dialogue the purpose of your story must occur. Write a dialogue after your favorite opening paragraph on **WRITING WORKSHEET #14** .

Finally, write one concluding paragraph to your story that will finalize the purpose of the story and tell how the characters exited the bookstore. Write this paragraph after the dialogue on **WRITING WORKSHEET #14** .

Read **WRITING ASSIGNMENT #14** on page 134. Complete the grammar lessons as you work on your composition. When you are happy with your writing, prepare your composition on clean writing paper.

CHAPTER 21

PURPOSE: GRAMMAR SKILLS

21.1 Grammar Rules
Writing good dialogue takes practice. Punctuating your writing correctly is also important. In this chapter, you will learn about appositives and colons to help you recognize where to insert the correct punctuation in a sentence, around a phrase, or before or after a word.

Read each grammar rule and do the **PRACTICE** exercises. When working on your writing assignments, remember to follow these rules. Part of your grade will be determined by how well you follow **all** of the rules you learn.

21.2 Appositives
A very important part of grammar is proper punctuation because it helps to identify how different words or parts of a sentence relate to one another. Proper punctuation gives clarity to a sentence. Well-written sentences are easier to read and understand.

Nouns identify the "who" or "what" in a sentence. An **appositive** is a type of grammar situation where a noun is used in a special way. The word **appositive** means **two things that explain each other are positioned side by side**. In writing, this situation occurs when a noun or a pronoun **is followed by another noun that explains or further identifies** the first noun or the pronoun. An appositive may be a singular word or a phrase of words.

> **DEFINITION**
> An **appositive** is a noun (which may have other words describing that noun) **following a pronoun or another noun** and **explaining** or **further identifying** the first noun or pronoun.

EXAMPLES:
1. Levi Strauss, **a successful blue jeans company**, was started by a Jewish businessman during the California gold rush.
2. Lilacs, **pleasantly fragrant flowers**, make a nice bouquet.

In the first **EXAMPLE**, the noun **Levi Strauss** is followed by the noun **company** to explain that Levi Strauss is a company. The words **a successful blue jeans company** are an appositive phrase. In the second example, the noun **lilacs** is followed by the noun **flowers**. The words **pleasantly fragrant flowers** are an appositive phrase.

When writing an appositive or an appositive phrase, confusion may result if the correct use of punctuation is not chosen to clarify whether the explaining or identifying words are necessary or not to the meaning of the sentence. For this reason, two rules of grammar were made for appositives in order to show whether they are nonessential or essential. **Nonessential** appositives are not necessary to the meaning of the preceding noun/pronoun because they can be removed and the sentence will still make sense. Thus, they do not give essential, or necessary, information for the sentence's meaning. Therefore, a nonessential appositive uses two commas to be enclosed. Read this rule and then study the **EXAMPLES**.

> **RULE #1**
> Punctuate a **nonessential appositive** (the noun and extra words that explain or identify further the first noun or pronoun) by placing **a comma before and after it**. If the appositive is at the end of the sentence, place a comma only before the appositive.

EXAMPLES:
1. A cheerful employee at the entrance of Wal-Mart, **a large retail store,** greets customers.

2. My mom will make my favorite dessert, **a German chocolate cake**.

 In the first **EXAMPLE**, the noun **Wal-Mart** is followed by an appositive which tells what type of business it is. The type of business is an appositive because it explains the business further. Notice how a comma was placed both before and after the words, **a large retail store**. If the words **a large retail store** were removed from the sentence, the sentence would still make sense. This is why the appositive words in this sentence are nonessential.

 In the second example, the noun **dessert** is followed by an appositive which tells what type of cake it is. The type of cake is an appositive because it explains the dessert further. Notice how only one comma was placed before the appositive (German chocolate cake) but not at the end of the appositive. A comma was not placed after the word **cake** because the sentence ended, requiring an end of sentence punctuation mark which was a period. If the words **a German chocolate cake** were removed from the sentence, the sentence would still make sense. This is why the appositive words in this sentence are nonessential.

 Essential appositives are necessary to the meaning of the preceding noun/pronoun. They give essential, or necessary, information for the sentence's meaning. Therefore, an essential appositive does **not** need to be enclosed with commas.

> **RULE #2**
> Do **not** place a comma **before** or **after** an **essential appositive**.

EXAMPLES:
1. Have you seen the biographical movie <u>**The Sound of Music**</u> about a family in Austria?
2. At the history museum, my brother is taking the class **Early Minnesota Settlers**.

 In the first example, the title <u>**The Sound of Music**</u> tells essential information about the movie. Without the title, you would not know what biographical movie was about a family in Austria. The title of the movie is an essential appositive which does not require any commas. In the second example, the title **Early Minnesota Settlers** tells essential information about the class. Without the title, you would not know what class the brother was taking. The title of the class is an essential appositive which does not require any commas.

 Review this section one more time before trying to complete the following **PRACTICE** exercises.

PRACTICE: Read each sentence and find the **nonessential appositive**. Draw a **comma before** and **after** all of the words of those nonessential appositives.

A. My math teacher Mr. Gun likes for us to recite the multiplication tables.
B. That fabric piece the calico print is very colorful.
C. The new gas station Gas-n-Go is very large and clean.
D. My only cousin Nathan Bosch is fun to visit.
E. The tulip a member of the lily family blooms in the early spring.
F. Everyone boys and girls alike went for a sled ride down the hill.

PRACTICE: In the following sentences, you will find six nonessential appositives and two essential appositives. Draw commas where they belong.

A. Yahweh's Son Yahshua worked as a carpenter in Nazareth/Natsareth.
B. Their team the fastest runners won the trophy.

C. We boys are going to shoot some baskets.
D. A cocoon holds a caterpillar a future butterfly.
E. In science we learned about tarantulas part of the spider family.
F. The Psalms/Tehillim are written mostly by David/Dawid a man after Yahweh's own heart.
G. I treasure my new book bag a gift from my grandmother.
H. My favorite story is in the book <u>Little Women</u>.

PRACTICE: In the following sentences, add an appositive phrase to the blank space. Draw commas where they belong.

A. George Bush _____ gave his State of the Union speech last night.
B. The ice cream store _____ was closed on Saturday.
C. The book _____ was very helpful to read.
D. Our state _____ is a pleasant place to live.

Review the story you have written. Can you create a sentence that contains an appositive? Be careful to punctuate that sentence correctly.

21.3 Colons

A colon is another special punctuation mark. A **colon** consists of two dots placed one above the other (**:**). A colon is used in three types of sentences.

> **RULE #1**
> A **colon** is used to **introduce a list** (that doesn't follow a verb or preposition), a statement, or a formal quotation.

EXAMPLES:

A colon (**:**) is used in a sentence that **introduces a list**. The colon is placed **after** the word that is **before** the list of items.

She picked some **flowers:** roses, dahlias, and daisies.

When words such as "the following" or "as follows" appear in a sentence just before a list, a colon is also placed after these words, but before the list.

She picked **the following:** roses, dahlias, and daisies.

Sometimes a sentence will have a list where **no colon** is used. These sentences have a verb or preposition introducing a list. When a verb or preposition introduces a list, a colon is **not** used. The following examples will help you to understand this rule about lists and colons.

VERB-**NO** COLON
She **liked** roses, dahlias, and daisies.

> The **verb** "to be" is a **state of being verb**; it may appear in forms, such as **is, are, was, were, have, has,** etc. **Action verbs** express action, such as the verbs: **jump, run, get, take, eat,** etc.

PREPOSITION-**NO** COLON
She liked all flowers **except** roses, dahlias, and daisies.

> Common **prepositions** are words like **aboard, about, across, after, along, around, before, below, behind, by, down, except, in, like, off, on, over, to, through, under, until, up, upon, with**, etc.

PRACTICE: The following sentences each **introduce a list** of items. Some of the sentences require a colon. Add a **colon** where it belongs in each sentence.

A. On top of the table sat three books a dictionary, a thesaurus, and a biography.
B. We could not go to the party until two people were ready mom and dad.
C. Tomorrow we will go shopping for food milk, potatoes, and lettuce.
D. Each student was given a pencil, pen, and pad of paper.
E. The store sold several types of clothes pants, dresses, and coats.
F. The camping trip needed many supplies a tent, sleeping bags, pillows.
G. He wanted some new clothes like a shirt, a pair of shoes, and a tie.

PRACTICE: Complete the following sentence by adding **several events** that might occur at a park. Use a **colon** to introduce your list.

The park had these events_____
_____

PRACTICE: Complete the following sentence by adding **several names** that might be fun. Use a **colon** to introduce your list.

The dialogue was between several characters_____
_____

 Review your story. Create a list of items that require a colon in the opening paragraph, dialogue, or closing paragraph. Punctuate that sentence correctly.

21.4 Colons

A **colon** is another important punctuation mark that consists of two dots placed one above the other (:). A colon is inserted into three types of sentences. The first type of sentence you learned was one that introduced a list. Now you will learn about sentences that contain special statements.

> **RULE #1**
> A **colon** is used to **introduce** a list, **a statement** (that doesn't follow a verb or preposition), or a formal quotation.

EXAMPLE:
Two statement sentences may be joined together with a colon when **a statement is used to introduce another statement.** The statement that is being introduced must give more information about the first statement. Place the colon (:) **after** the last word of the first statement which is **before** the word or words of the second statement.

The girl showed her gymnastics skills: she turned three cartwheels.

PRACTICE: Each of these sentences **introduces a statement**. The second statement gives more information about the first statement. Some of these sentences are missing a colon. Insert a **colon** where it should be.

A. The light was very bright it illuminated the whole room.
B. The street outside was wet it was raining.
C. The bead was rising as it was baking in the oven.
D. They took the bike to the repair shop it was broken.
E. The muffins were almost done they needed five more minutes to brown.
F. The car crossed over the bridge after the bridge toll was paid.

PRACTICE: Complete each sentence by **adding a statement** that makes sense. Use a **colon** to introduce each statement.

A. The basket did not hold fruit_____
B. The sunset was beautiful_____
C. The dinner was very tasty_____
D. The corner store was not far away_____

PRACTICE: Make up a sentence that contains **two statements** separated by a **colon**. Write about something that you could use in your story.

_____
_____

Review the story you have written. Add the sentence you created on the above line to your story. Make sure you have punctuated that sentence correctly.

21.5 Colons

A **colon** is a punctuation mark that consists of two dots placed one above the other (:). A colon is inserted into three types of sentences. The first type of sentence was one that introduced a list. The second type of sentence contained two statements where the first statement was used to introduce another statement. The statement that was being introduced gave more information about the first statement. The third type of sentence contains a formal quotation.

> **RULE #1**
> A **colon** is used to **introduce** a list, a statement, or **a formal quotation** (that doesn't follow a verb or preposition).

EXAMPLE:

A colon (:) is used to introduce **a formal quotation** in a sentence that gives an **extra important saying** such as by a character in a book. To follow this rule, place the colon after the **last** word **before** the quotation.

In the story, John often **said:** "Be blessed!" (**FORMAL QUOTATION**)

PRACTICE: Each of the following sentences **introduces a formal quotation**. Some sentences are missing a colon. Add a **colon** where it belongs.

A. The main character liked to shout "I am free!"

B. My teacher always said "Cleanliness is next to Godliness."
C. Those daylilies are "Red flowers which are swaying in the wind."
C. In the bookstore many people asked the same thing "Where are the Bibles?"
D. The gardener was happy spring had come, he said "Yahoo!"
E. I like to follow behind "The lead runner."

PRACTICE: Complete each sentence by adding **a formal quotation** that makes sense. Use a **colon** to introduce your formal quotation. The first one is done for you.

A. My mother gave this advice_____
B. The main character frequently said this phrase_____
C. The children often sang this song_____
D. Every night we pray this prayer_____

_____

PRACTICE: Make up a sentence that contains **a formal quotation** with an extra important saying. Separate that saying from the rest of the sentence by a **colon**. Write about something that might happen in a bookstore.

_____
_____

  Review the story you have written. Add the sentence you created on the above line to your story. Make sure you have punctuated that sentence correctly.

21.6 Colons

A **colon** is a special punctuation mark that consists of two dots placed one above the other (:). A sentence is not the only place that a colon is used in grammar.

> **RULE #2**
> A **colon** is used to **separate numbers** when writing the time or writing a Scripture chapter and verse.

EXAMPLES:

Mark 13 4	becomes	Mark 13:4
12 30 P.M.	becomes	12:30 P.M.

PRACTICE: The following numbers need to be **separated**. Each one is missing a colon. Add a **colon** where it belongs.

A. 7 00 A.M.   C. Ibrim/Hebrews 14 3   E. 2 15 A.M.
B. 12 00 P.M.   D. Shemoth/Exodus 7 10   F. Mark 2 8

Complete your story. Rewrite or type it neatly on a fresh piece of paper and turn it in to your teacher.

WRITING CHART #14

BOOKSTORE

PEOPLE **PLACES** **THINGS**

NOTES ABOUT THE BOOKSTORE

NOTES ABOUT THE DIALOGUE

NOTES ABOUT THE OPENING PARAGRAPH

PURPOSE OF THE STORY

WRITING ASSIGNMENT #14

Your assignment is to write **a story about a bookstore**.

1. Format
- [ ] Write a title at the top of the page.
- [ ] Write your name under this title.
- [ ] Begin the opening paragraph on the second line below your name.

2. Construction
- [ ] Write at least a **one page** paper.
- [ ] The opening paragraph must contain a description of some part of the bookstore and **one** of your speakers.
- [ ] Write **twelve** lines of dialogue.
- [ ] Each direct quotation must have a name in the explanatory words that identifies who is speaking.
- [ ] Include descriptions of the characters and scenery.
- [ ] Use a variety of action words.
- [ ] Write **one** closing paragraph that finalizes the purpose of the story and tells how the characters exited the bookstore.

3. Grammar
- [ ] Use proper punctuation, indentation, and capitalization.
- [ ] Draw quotation marks at the beginning and end of all direct quotations.
- [ ] In the explanatory words, be careful that your names and your descriptions have the correct punctuation.
- [ ] Use proper word tenses and a variety of description words.
- [ ] Write a variety of paragraph sentences that are related to one another.
- [ ] Indent your paragraphs.
- [ ] Each paragraph must contain unity, flow logically, and relate to one another.

4. Polish
- [ ] Only turn in a final copy of your paper that has been written neatly.
- [ ] Make sure you have spelled all of your words correctly.
- [ ] Use the dictionary to check spelling and the Thesaurus to find extra words.

5. Ethics
- [ ] Work on your own and make the dialogue original.
- [ ] Do not write about anything that is an inappropriate subject of a dialogue.
- [ ] Make sure the language of your paper conforms to Philippians 4:8.
- [ ] Could your paper be of help to someone who may read it?

WRITING WORKSHEET #14
COMPOSE YOUR OPENING PARAGRAPH ON THE FOLLOWING LINES.

_____
_____
_____
_____
_____
_____
_____

COMPOSE YOUR DIRECT QUOTATIONS ON THE FOLLOWING LINES.

1. _____
2. _____
3. _____
4. _____
5. _____
6. _____
7. _____
8. _____
9. _____
10. _____
11. _____
12. _____

COMPOSE YOUR CLOSING PARAGRAPH ON THE FOLLOWING LINES.

_____
_____
_____
_____
_____

CHAPTER 22
PLOT: ETHICS SKILLS

UNIT 8 SUPPLIES

BIBLE
DICTIONARY
PENCIL
THESAURUS
WRITING PAPER

22.1 Scriptural Ethics

Have you ever read a story that was about the author or someone the author knows? Have you ever read a story where one of the characters was telling the story? In either of these types of stories was an opinion or point of view purposely conveyed to you?

Some stories are told by the person who experienced them, by a friend, or by a relative. While other stories are written by complete strangers. These stories may contain an opinion or point of view that the author purposely wants you to understand. That point of view or opinion may belong to the author or someone else. You may have read some of these stories, they fall under the categories of biography, autobiography, fiction, and news.

In this lesson, you will study how and why an author uses a story to convey a point of view as well as how to do this ethically. When a story is written to convey an opinion or point of view, it may be written using one of three methods.

1. **A character tells the story**
2. **A non-character tells the story**
3. **The author uses the characters and action to unfold the story**

Most stories are written using method #3. With these methods, an author may write a story to convey an opinion or point of view for one or more of these reasons.

1. **To convince others that a certain opinion or point of view is right**
2. **To teach a scriptural truth**
3. **Because the author wants his/her readers to know what his/her opinion is**

Most people in this world have opinions and points of view, but they are not always correct. For an opinion or point of view to be correct, it must be scripturally sound. When you write a story with an opinion or point of view, you must make sure that what you are sharing is the correct scriptural truth so that you do not teach others incorrectly.

How do you tell a story with an opinion or point of view that is scripturally sound? With this type of a story, you can't just start writing and hope that somehow something correct will develop. For this type of story, you must have a goal in mind.

If your goal was to write a story to teach a truth that is scripturally sound, first, you must decide what truth you want to teach. Next, you must be careful that your understanding of that truth is correct by studying all of the scriptures in the Old and New Testaments that relate to that truth. You must also be careful to understand what is taught about your chosen truth when different passages of the Bible seem to contradict one another.

For instance, the New Testament teaches you to love your neighbor while the Old Testament tells you to stay away from certain sinful people. What do you do when those certain sinful people are your neighbors? What is the correct behavior towards a sinful neighbor? How would you teach the different aspects of this truth to others? Would you teach someone to love without cautioning them? Certainly not! If you did, then you would be teaching incorrectly and actually may cause another person to get hurt which you certainly would not want to do.

When you want to write a story with an opinion or a point of view that is scripturally sound, you need to understand all aspects of the scriptures that deal with that truth. Learning how to do this will help you to write story to convey a truth that is scripturally sound. To help you get started, you will learn from an author who wanted to write a story. She was concerned about people who were stingy, selfish, and sometimes just ignorant of other people. From this concern, she decided to write about the need of another helpless person and some responses to that need that were either good or not good, eternally. The author thought the verses in Matthew/Mattithyahu 25:31-46 covered the exact point of view she wanted to convey in her story. Here is what these verses taught.

"And when the Son of Adam comes in His esteem, and all the set-apart messengers with Him, then He shall sit on the throne of His esteem.

"And all the nations shall be gathered before Him, and He shall separate them one from another, as a shepherd separates his sheep from the goats.

"And He shall set the sheep on His right hand, but the goats on the left.

"Then the Sovereign shall say to those on His right hand, 'Come, you blessed of My Father, inherit the reign prepared for you from the foundation of the world - for I was hungry and you gave Me food, I was thirsty and you gave Me drink, I was a stranger and you took Me in, was naked and you clothed Me, I was sick and you visited Me, I was in prison and you came to Me.'

"Then the righteous shall answer Him, saying 'Master when did we see You hungry and we fed You, or thirsty and gave You to drink? And when did we see You a stranger and took You in, or naked, and clothed You? And when did we see You sick, or in prison, and we came to You?

"And the Sovereign shall answer and say to them, 'Truly, I say to you, in so far as you did it to one of the least of these My brothers, you did it to Me.'

"He shall then also say to those on the left hand, 'Go away from Me, accursed ones, into the everlasting fire prepared for the devil and his messengers - for I was hungry and you gave Me no food, I was thirsty and you gave Me no drink, I was a stranger and you did not take Me in, was naked and you did not clothe me, sick and in prison and you did not visit Me.'

"Then they also shall answer Him, saying, 'Master, when did we see You hungry or thirsty or a stranger or naked or sick or in prison, and did not serve You?'

"Then He shall answer them, saying, 'Truly, I say to you, in so far as you did not do it to one of the least of these, you did not do it to Me.'

"And these shall go away into everlasting punishment, but the righteous into everlasting life.

Using this scripture passage the author first wrote the following story.

Love One Another

A young child stood begging on the street. A group of teenagers skated past the beggar. They were going to fast to notice the young child's skinny body. Several men and women walked by on their way to a business lunch. Their conversation distracted them from noticing the young child's dirty clothes and uncombed hair. An older couple on their empty-nest vacation stopped right in front of the beggar to admire the historic landmark across the street. They never noticed the young child's lack of shoes.

Soon a family with two children approached the spot where the young child was begging. The family's daughter noticed the young child and her heart was moved to help. She asked her father for two dollars. He refused and admonished her not to be concerned for such as the likes of the street urchin. The daughter persisted even as the father began to growing angry. She pleaded with her father for the welfare of the child, and some proper food and clothing. He would not relent. Tears welled up in her eyes. The father walked away in a huff. The family's son ran after the father pleading with him to help. The father ignored the beseeching of his own son. He was angry that his children had embarrassed him.

The mother who had stopped as soon as she encountered the beggar stood looking at the young child. Tears welled up in her eyes; she had nothing to give. Wiping the tears away, she prayed to Yahshua. "Please Yahshua, I want to help but cannot. Help this little child. My heart is in such great sorrow. I wonder who would help my children if they were on the street just like this little one? Who would help my husband if he were on the street? Oh Yahshua, please find someone to help this child," the woman cried in her mind and heart-felt prayer. Then she walked on in sorrow, never forgetting the poor street child.

In an office building near the site were the child was begging, a woman brought a brown paper bag to work. She asked those around her if they could contribute canned goods to the poor and needy by placing them in the bag. Two people said they didn't have any canned goods. In truth, however, they had decided they didn't want to make a donation because if it was not their idea they could not receive glory for giving.

Four other people said they weren't sure they had enough money to buy their own weekly groceries, so they might not be able to give. At the end of that week, each one of the four people had over five canned goods sitting in their pantries uneaten. Two men said, "sure," thinking about how they would look good in the eyes of their fellow employees for being such generous givers. Yet, when they went home, they assigned the task to their wives to accomplish.

One man went home and looked into his pantry; he had two cans of corn sitting on a shelf. He decided to give both cans. Nobody remembered his name or ever heard why he gave the two cans. He cut his meals down to one per day to make his budget stretch until his next paycheck.

Many years later, there was a throng of people standing before the judgement seat of Yahshua. The angels were instructed by Yahshua to separate the people into two groups. One group contained all of the people who walked by the little child begging in the street. The other group contained those who were asked to give to the bag of food for the poor.

Next, Yahshua had the angels separate five people from these groups. From the first group a mother, daughter, and son were separated. They were the ones who had wanted to help the young child begging in the street. From the second group, the angels separated out the woman who had asked for the canned food and the man who had given the two cans of corn. The five people were given praise by Yahshua and sent on to their Heavenly homes.

The people remaining in the two groups began to grumble. "What about us? Where is our praise and reward? We worked hard, too!" they said.

Yahshua looked at them and answered, "When the child sat begging on the street did you help her? When the bag for the needy was brought to work did you help fill it selflessly?"

The crowd stood silent. They could not defend themselves. They could not say, "yes."

Then, Yahshua instructed the angels to direct the two groups back out of Heaven. As they passed through the entrance to Heaven, they looked one more time upon the young child who had died an early death. They also saw a multitude of mothers, children, men, and aged people who had spent hungry days, cold winter nights, and years of loneliness because such as were now leaving Heaven had only thought of themselves.

22.2 Scriptural Ethics

After writing the story, the author began to have experiences of giving and helping others that did not always work out so well. She learned that in the world today, their are people who beg or apply for help and money from neighbors, churches, and other organizations while lying and deceiving about their need. As the author became aware of this, she wondered about what she had written. Was her point of view wrong to teach to give to all no matter what? Was the child really needy or part of a scheme? Should she warn people about those who falsely pretend to have a need? Was the scripture the correct one to have considered the basis for her point of view?

She went back to the scripture and read it over and over again until she found something that gave her an answer. First, she realized that she had been incorrectly taught the scripture. Second, she realized that to teach scriptural truth, she must not teach her point of view or the world's point of view but God's point of view. Thirdly, to understand Heaven's point of view, she must have a correct translation, an understanding of the scriptures in the context of the time and culture to whom they were given or spoken, and she must conduct a thorough study of the entire chapter in which the verses were found.

After thinking about the time period, the culture, and studying the entire chapter, she noticed that Jesus had said something very important in the scripture. He said that when you do not help **My brothers** you do not help Me. This scripture reveals that the **reign of Heaven** is for those who help the brothers of Jesus. Who are the people that are the brothers of Jesus? Are the brothers of Jesus everyone on earth? No, they are **only** born-again believers, both male and female.

A **born-again believer** is a person who has accepted Jesus as his/her personal Savior, repented of his/her sins, and been filled with the Holy Spirit. When a person has truly become a born-again believer, he/she cares about the troubles of others. This scripture teaches that born-again believers are to care about the troubles of other born-again believers by helping them. Interestingly, in the scripture passage, Jesus did not stop speaking to just His own brothers. He also told the goats (nonbelievers) that **their disregard for the troubles of born-again believers** was why they were condemned to everlasting punishment.

This passage of scripture was given to born-again believers to not only instruct them in right behavior towards other believers but also to encourage them in more than one way. First, the passage shows that Jesus knows all of a born-again believer's needs and troubles. He knows who offers help for those troubles and who does not. Second, the passage comforts and encourages the born-again believer who has selflessly helped the brothers of Jesus. That the sheep did not even remember what they had done, implies that they helped their brothers without thought of reward for themselves. It also implies that those acts were so commonplace amongst the sheep standing before Jesus, that they occurred as naturally as breathing air--an act that one does not consciously remember doing.

This passage clearly shows that only true born-again believers correctly, selflessly, and automatically do the righteous works of Jesus. All others are not believers.

From studying this passage very carefully, the author realized that if she wanted to base a story on Mattithyahu/Matthew 25:31-46, to be scripturally correct her point of view must be about helping other born-again believers. To teach the correct truth, she had to think long and hard about her life and what she knew about helping others. After much thought, she decided to write about her own life and marriage, where two people (a sheep/believer and a goat/nonbeliever) learned how to help and serve Jesus' brothers. The story came from the truth of her life so that it could be told accurately, honestly, and realistically. When writing in this way, her story would mirror scriptural truth to which others might be able to relate. She began her writing by jotting down the following notes about her life.

1. I was quiet and shy when I was young. Even as a baby, I was considered the most well-

behaved and easy-to-care for of my six siblings. I didn't cause trouble or get into trouble. I learned by watching and by listening. I liked my parents and enjoyed my brothers and sisters. Though quiet and shy, I often enjoyed interacting with other people.

2. I remember walking home from kindergarten through the snow in the winter as well as past the lovely tulips blooming in neighbor's yards in the spring. I remember the smell of fresh spring air coming through a window my mother opened when she came into my room to wake me up in the morning. One of my fondest memories in the summer included sitting on the porch shelling peas with my mother. In the fall, I enjoyed sitting on a swing that hung from a sturdy branch of an old apple tree in the backyard. I loved to pump that swing as high as I could. Other times, I enjoyed pushing my brother as high as he wanted to go on the same swing. The wood pile by the fence was another great place to play with my brothers and sisters, so many games could be invented with a stack of firewood.

3. The field behind our house was not filled in and would not be until long after we moved. My father grew a vegetable garden there in the summer. He enjoyed that immensely. I enjoyed it with him. I also enjoyed how happy it made him. When I was older, my sister and I could walk across that overgrown field to explore its mysteries. We found a lovely creek flowing through it that seemed to begin somewhere near a home. There we discovered two new friends. They were twin girls who were closer to my sister's age, but I still enjoyed their friendship.

4. Most of all, I loved sitting in church looking up at the cross. There Jesus hung in silent pain and suffering just as He had done so many centuries ago. I always felt strangely drawn to Him in a warm, wondering way.

5. There were other memories, too. I remember my mother not being home for my third birthday and how upset I was. I didn't understand that she was at the hospital giving birth to my sister. It was not the only time my parents had kept a secret; yet, when my mother came home with that special little person, I was overjoyed!

6. The winter day my older sister gave me a glass of water with soap in it, I felt betrayed. She told me it was something tasty to drink. I think she told me it was lemonade. It was not the last of her betrayals; yet, I have been a faithful friend to her all of my life.

7. I remember the neighbors next door. Their house was gloomy; their yard was shady and dark. I was told not to speak to them or interact with them. They had older children which I never seemed to see. It as not the last time that I lived next to strange neighbors; yet, I have never failed to help a neighbor in need even to the point of taking on great heartache or danger in my life.

8. When I was in kindergarten, there was a day I was late for school because the snow was so high it was hard to walk. My lateness made me feel bad as did my sleeping a little too long through nap time. It was not the last time I ever regretted something; yet, I am rarely impatient with others who are late or make mistakes.

9. Sometimes I also felt sad when the older kids were at recess. I would look out the window of our schoolroom longing to be outside playing with them. It was not the last time time I couldn't go out to play; yet, I rarely refuse spending time with a friend or believer at church who needs a listening ear to whom he/she can talk.

10. My childhood was thusly filled with a mix of good and bad experiences whose net result was that I was still quiet and shy when I became a teenager. I was quiet and shy during junior high school and high school. I was even quiet and shy during college and afterwards, for a while. Without realizing it, however, those experiences for better or for worse were making me into the person I would later become.

11. When I was seven, I became a born-again Christian. My childhood experiences were now silently being worked together to eventually cause a once quiet, shy, lonely girl to blossom into

a chatty, friendly, much befriended person. When this occurred I was happy, I was an adult, and I had developed into a person who was good at serving others.

12. Jesus had done and was doing a good work in me. That good work came though circumstances of His design that molded and shaped me even when I did not recognize them. While I had not yet been taught to distinguish between the sheep and the goats, I would learn that later through experiences with the good and the bad of serving others.

13. I was a good servant in the rough, except for one thing. That one thing was to know the deeper service of love in marriage. Without completely recognizing the need to learn that type of service, I was a bit like someone looking into a smokey mirror. Something inside of me recognized the need without having a clear enough focus to determine the whole picture. So, I began to long for a husband and through God's great love for me, He answered my desperate prayers for a spouse. By divine arrangement, I met and married a man who was not yet a born-again believer. However, Jesus knew his heart was already turning towards Christianity, Christians, and serving Him.

14. Having come from a family who were not Christians, my husband at first had a different idea of who to serve. After becoming born-again, he learned of a different way to serve and of a people who were different than he had been led to believe. He learned Jesus' way to serve by watching me serve. He learned by my serving him and he in return serving me. We suffered much and learned especially to suffer together while serving each other in those sufferings. In serving one another, my husband stood by me through sickness and in health, for better or for poorer, in riches and in poverty. I also stood by him through these good and not so good life experiences.

15. Those experiences ran the range of having so frugal a budget that I had to wear shoes with holes in them, hand-me-down clothes, and men's pants because they were cheaper than women's pants. Other experiences included not having enough food to eat, sickness, and persecution for the sake of Jesus. Through all the trials and turmoils, my husband who took me in by marriage was there to comfort, feed, and clothe me. He tended to me in times of need, helped me in times of trouble, and especially sorrow, standing by me together in everything.

16. We also served others. Through the years we served hundreds of thousands. Though my husband started out as a goat from a non-Christian family, he recognized the better service to Jesus' brothers. Though I at first was unable to discern who to serve, together we learned the Heavenly perspective of serving the born-again believer. Now there is no place my husband (or I) would rather be than in the service of Jesus to Jesus' brothers. I had truly learned to serve from sheep to sheep. My husband who served as a goat to sheep, became a sheep because He came to know the true Messiah through those sheep.

17. Thus, it is next to my husband that I hope stand when Jesus gathers the nations unto Heaven and divides them into the goats and the sheep. Then I want raise my hand to catch the eye of the One who both my husband and I love so dearly. If He noticed me and let me speak, I would tell Jesus the wonderful things my husband had been to me and to Jesus' brothers. I would thank Jesus for my husband. I would especially and humbly ask that he be included in the reign of the Heavens.

19. My husband's journey with Jesus did not start as early as mine, nor with the same love for the brothers. Yet, I hope that as I stand in Heaven, next to my husband, Yahshua would smile lovingly at him and say, "I know what a wonderful man your husband is because every good thing he did for you, he did for me." For these words I would be eternally grateful.

22.3 Scriptural Ethics

After writing her notes, the author reviewed what she had. Her notes contained many things that would be good in a story. There were also many things that she would not use in her story. Next, she began to write from her notes. Here is that story.

Love One Another
by Megan Christian

Megan leaned over the sink and opened the window. The smell of fresh, spring air coming through the window reminded Megan of her childhood...Almost half a century ago, a quiet little girl was born. Such a good baby she was. Even as a child, she was well-behaved though shy. She didn't cause trouble or get into trouble. Megan learned by watching and listening.

Her family eventually became a big one, with three boys and four girls. Megan loved her parents, brothers, and sisters very much. They were her whole world. Before her school-age years, Megan had many fun memories.

On warm summer evenings, she loved to sit on the porch beside her mother shelling peas. As they worked, they watched father teaching Jenna to ride a bike. Jenna was Megan's oldest sister and the first born. On summer days, Megan could also be found in the backyard sitting on a swing that hung from a sturdy branch of the old apple tree. She loved to pump that swing as high as she could. Other times, she enjoyed pushing her brother Sam as high as he wanted to go on the same swing. In the fall, Jenna and Sam played with Megan in the wood pile by the neighbor's fence in the backyard. So many games could be invented with a stack of firewood!

Megan's thoughts returned to her kitchen sink. She turned the water on to fill it and looked out the window again. Behind their property was a large field much like the one behind the house of her youth...That long-ago field had not filled in until after her family outgrew their house and moved. Each summer, father grew a vegetable garden in the field. He enjoyed that immensely. Megan enjoyed it with him. It made father very happy and Megan was happy, too.

Sometimes Megan and Jenna walked across the overgrown field to explore its mysteries. One day when they had gone what seemed to be a very long way for two little girls, they found a lovely creek flowing through the field. Looking like it begin somewhere near a home, they followed the creek and eventually discovered two new friends. The new friends were twin girls who were closer to Jenna's age, but Megan still enjoyed their friendship.

Another special friend Megan loved to see was at church. Each week, while father helped with the collection of the tithes, Megan sat looking up at the cross above the altar. There Yahshua hung in silent pain and suffering. She always felt strangely drawn to Him in a warm, wondering way.

There were also times of other memories...On her third birthday, Megan was very sad and cried a lot because her mother was not at home. Mother was at the hospital where a new baby sister was born. Megan didn't understand why her parents had kept this secret from her; yet, when mother came home with that special little person, Megan was overjoyed to see both of them.

Megan reached for a cup to wash and remembered a cold and damp winter day...On that day, Jenna tricked her into drinking a glass of soapy water. Her sister had told her it was lemonade but it tasted horrible and made her sick. It was not the last of Jenna's betrayals; yet, Megan was a faithful friend to her sister throughout life.

Then there were the neighbors next door. Their house was gloomy; their yard was shady and dark. Megan was not allowed to speak to them or interact with them. They had older children who never seemed to come outside. It was not the last time Megan lived next to strange neighbors; yet, she never failed to help a neighbor in need even when it involved great heartache or real danger.

Megan finished rinsing the last dish and set it in the drainer. She pulled the plug in the sink and after rinsing all the soapy water away, she dried her hands and sat down at the kitchen table. A pile of papers from her children's school work sat next to their family Bible. Megan looked through the papers to decide which ones to grade first. She paused at the drawing of a snowman, reflecting on her first year of school in kindergarten...One day had stood out among all of the rest, the day she had been late for school because the snow was difficult to walk through it was so high. She had felt bad that day for her lateness; yet, the experience had helped her to be understanding of others.

Her eyes moistened with tears as she gazed upon the picture her son had chosen to draw. Megan set the pile of papers down, wiped her eyes with her apron, and looked at the Bible on the table. What funny ways You shaped me, she thought thinking of God and His Word. You even caused a shy girl to blossom into a chatty, friendly, much-befriended person, though it did take until I was out of college to be accomplished...That's when marriage came. Having come out of her shyness, Megan had developed the social skills to meet a very special person named Walter.

Walter was not yet a Christian, though Megan had been one for over 20 years by the time she met him. Megan met Walter through a lovely Christian friend. Yahshua knew it was a perfect match as Walter's heart was already turning towards Christianity and serving Him. Until this point, Megan had served others in various ways both in church and outside of church. Now she would learn of a different way to serve. She would serve as a wife and mother.

Walter would also learn of a different way to serve. Having come from a family that ridiculed Christians and Christianity, he would learn of a people who were different than he had been led to believe. He learned Yahshua's way to serve by Megan serving him and he in return serving Megan. As a couple, they had many times of suffering, but they learned to suffer together while serving each other in those sufferings. In serving one another, Megan and Walter stood by one another through sickness and in health, for better or for poorer, in riches and in poverty. Through the trials and turmoils, Megan and Walter were there to comfort, feed, clothe, and tend to each other in times of trouble and especially in times of sorrow.

Megan opened the Bible to Mattithyahu/Matthew 25:31-46, and reread the verses she had come to know very well over the years. Yahshua taught service to others in this parable but not just to anyone; that service was to be to one's born-again brothers and sisters. While she had hardly ever wanted to admit it, when she was first married Megan's husband had been one of the goats mentioned in the parable. Yet, through Megan's suffering and service, Walter had learned of the better service to Yahshua's own; until over the years, Walter and Megan had together served hundreds of thousands. Very early in their marriage because of this type of service, Walter had become a born-again sheep. Megan's husband who served as a goat to sheep, became a sheep because He came to know the true Messiah through those sheep.

Megan thought about Heaven and the rest of eternity. She thought about how wonderful it would be to spend all of that time with her best friends in Yahshua--her husband and children. She was thankful that although the suffering to change a goat into a sheep was hard, it had blessed her with the most precious fruit.

Megan thought when Yahshua gathers the nations unto Heaven and divides them into the goats and the sheep, she would raise her hand in hopes of catching the eye of the One who loved her so dearly. She would tell Yahshua of the wonderful service her husband, the former goat, had rendered Yahshua's brothers. She would thank Yahshua face-to-face for Walter and humbly ask that he be included in the reign of the Heavens.

Walter's journey with Yahshua had not started as early as Megan's, nor with the same love for the brothers as she was taught. Thus as Yahshua had spoken to the sheep in Mattithyahu/Matthew 25:31-46, Megan hoped He would smile lovingly at Walter and commend him by saying, "I know what a wonderful man you are because every good thing you did to one of the least of these My brothers, you did for me."

For these words Megan would be eternally grateful.

Megan's story was created from real life, though Megan and Walter are fictional. When the author decided to stick with the scripture she had found and change **her** point of view to Jesus', she wrote a story that revealed the true blessing of obeying the Word of God. She was able to clearly see how faithful Jesus had been in her life in His quiet, silent ways. While the second story is not as entertaining as the first, it was a true story about real people with remarkable positive results for everyone involved. It portrays true fruit as well as having a real emotional impact on its readers. This type of result can only occur when real life is truthfully shared with others in story form.

A story is a powerful vehicle to share truth, encourage others, and pave the way for fruit in other lives. That truth, however, must be ethically sound. A Christian's point of view is ethically sound when it is based on a correct understanding of scriptures.

Knowing how to correctly share the Word of God comes from careful study, having a correct translation, and understanding the scriptures in the context of the time and culture to whom there were given or spoken. Learning the truth of the scriptures from being a doer of the Word is also necessary. Deciding to fit current trends of behavior in the world into what the scriptures teach is a great mistake.

In the first story, the husband did not get saved. He did not learn to serve others. The wife and children ended up in heaven alone without a husband and a father. In the second story, the wife did not abandon or divorce her goat of a husband but continued to serve him and other born-again persons through all kind of sufferings. Great compassion, love, perseverance, faithfulness, repentance, and forgiveness were a part of the success of the marriage between Megan and Walter. There was no story-book romance where everything was sweet and perfect; however, the fruit of following Jesus and walking in His Word **produced perfect fruit**.

PLOT: WRITING SKILLS

23.1 Development of a Plot

Conversation is an important tool in a story. A conversation can have a purpose by conveying information in an interesting manner. Conversation can also give a story life, keep a story alive, and move the pace of a story along.

Just like conversation, action needs to have a purpose, too! To learn about action with a purpose, you need to learn about the plot of a story. The **plot** of a story has to do with how a story is arranged, the action, the series of events that lead to the story's end, and the purpose of the story. The following is a good definition for the plot of a story.

PLOT: the overall plan of action in a story that is carefully worked out

Every story must have an overall plan of action. This plan causes the action to flow from one event to another in a manner that is smooth and makes sense. In conversation, you learned that a character's words could be used to help a reader understand something that is important to the story or to the characters in the story. When developing the plot of a story, a writer can use the action to serve one of three purposes.

   1. **Action can be used to show the progress of events or encounters in a story.**
   2. **Action can be used to show how a character or characters encountered a problem and solved that problem.**
   3. **Action can be used to show how a character or characters discovered something.**

To develop a story, a writer first decides upon the type of story. Will the story be an action adventure, a life-revealing drama, or an inspirational story? Once a writer has chosen what type of story, then he/she must decide upon the purpose of the story. Will the story be about an opinion or a point of view? A story could also chronicle someone's life. Some stories are written to tell about learning something. Still other stories are written to portray the lifestyle of people living in a particular time period. Whatever the writer chooses, the action of a story will not make sense at all unless it is carefully developed around a purpose.

Next, the characters and the events of the story must be chosen. Once these two things are decided upon, the action of the story can be planned. The action can either be planned out in advance of writing or the action can be developed as work on the story progresses. In either case while the story is being written, the action may need to change and/or be adjusted until it flows well enough to make sense and be believable.

If the action of a story does not flow logically from one event to another, the story will have dead ends. Have you ever had someone talking to you when they lost their train of thought? Did their conversation come to an abrupt end? Did the sudden end to the conversation make you feel lost or confused? When a writer does not make the action in a story flow well, the reader becomes lost, confused, and cannot find a way to connect the dead ends together. Dead-end action in a story is not understandable.

   1. **All action must be related or connected in a story so that by the end of the story the reader does not feel lost or confused.**
   2. **When the action of a story is related or connected so that it flows well, it will make sense or be sensible to the reader's understanding.**

Once all of the action is written and the story told, an ending must be determined. A good ending is as important as a good story. If the ending falls flat, your reader will feel disappointed. Disappointment is not the way you want a reader to remember your story. Therefore, an ending must carefully bring the reader to a conclusion that resolves the story and satisfies the reader that the story is complete.

23.2 Realistic Action

Can a person fly through the air without the aid of an invention? A person can't jump ten feet high in their bare feet, can he/she? Have you ever seen a train merrily skip and jump down its track as though this behavior were its normal mode of operation? Of course you haven't. These types of action are nonsense and unbelievable in the reality of the universe.

To write fantasy types of action in a story is like telling a lie because a lie is something that is not true. So, be very careful when writing action in your stories that it is believable in the reality of the universe because a sensible person does not want to read foolishness.

The action of a story must be believable in the reality of the universe.

What kinds of action are appropriate for a Christian to include in his/her writing? The action in a story should line up with Christian values. The action should not be sinful. For example, stories about killing or violence should only be written when relating a true life story; they should never be made up just for fun. This is because the Bible teaches the value of human life. Murder is a sin, but peace is a fruit of the Holy Spirit.

There are other kinds of sin in The Scriptures that you should never write about in a story. Lying, stealing, greed, and jealousy are a few of the types of sin you should not write about in a story unless that sin is clearly corrected. The action of a story does not have to be a dangerous or a spectacular event either; offensive action is also not a good idea in a story.

Everyday life is interesting! Sometimes something unusual happens in everyday life that may also be interesting. Realistic, truthful, and even simple action in a story are all good types of action. Simple types of action draw your reader into your story. Simple action is entertaining, and interesting because most readers can relate to this kind of action. Excesses, extremes, ungodliness, lies, and action used for its shock value offends more than it entertains or adds interest to a story. A good way to remember what kind of action is best for the gentle Christian spirit is to remember these three words: **realistic, truthful, and simple**.

While a toddler may use his/her imagination during play or to have make believe play pals on a lonely day, the child usually pretends about something that is possible in reality. A healthy imagination is not a bad thing, but there is a fine line between imagination and unhealthy fantasy. Imagination deals with real, concrete possibilities; fantasy deals with the impossible, absurd, or sinful.

23.3 Development of the Action

Now that you understand the type of action you should focus on in a story, it's time to learn about the level of action for a story. Developing a story is like climbing a mountain. The beginning of a story is like starting at the bottom of a mountain. In the beginning, there is a long distance to climb. You may not be sure how to get to the top of the mountain. However, you at least know that if you persist you will reach the top of the mountain somehow. When a climber makes it to the top of a mountain, the hard climb is completed. The climber can then enjoy the view before returning down the mountain.

Writing a story is a process similar to mountain climbing. In the beginning, you may have a large or difficult project to write. You may not know what to write about or how to write the events your story. However, through perseverance your story will be developed and written. When the last sentence of your story is written, you can enjoy the story while rewriting and editing its contents.

A story that is like a mountain climb will contain action. That action must be developed in some meaningful way. Will there be a lot of action or only a little bit of action? When developing your story, you must think carefully about the type and amount of action. Try making notes about different types of action that could occur so that you have several ideas from which to choose. For instance, for a story about a mountain climb try to imagine how the main character might get to the top. Here are several possible ideas for stories one could write.

1. **The mountain is easy to traverse and gentle sloping. The main character simply walks straight up the mountain to the top.**

2. The mountain is slightly more rugged and steep. The main character must walk around the mountain in a spiral path until he/she reaches the top.
3. The mountain is steep, rough, and rocky with cliffs and plateaus. The main character must climb up the mountain in a zig-zag fashion using both hands and feet to climb.
4. The mountain is very steep. The main character must use special equipment and rock climbing techniques to get to the top.

Each one of these mountain climbs has a different type action even though the topic of the story is the same. In these examples, each type of solution to climbing the mountain involves a different amount of exertion or level of action in the story. Thus the action of a story depends upon the amount of conflict the writer wants to have his/her characters experience.

Suppose you want to write a story about a teenager who is traveling on a train to visit his aunt, but he really doesn't want to visit her. What kind of action might this type of story have? What events might happen to the teenager that could change his attitude to one of being content about visiting the aunt? Perhaps one or all of the following events might happen.

1. The teenager finds a magazine on the train and reads an article about how wonderful it is to have an aunt who loves her nephew.
2. The conductor or a passenger tells a story about the a delightful time visiting a relative.
3. The teenager has nightmares or worries a lot on the trip about not having a good time at the aunt's house but determines to persevere by obeying his parents who sent him.

The amount of action and conflict that could be written in this story depends upon whether the writer chooses to use one, two, or all three of these events. The action of these events will also help develop the plot of getting the teenager to the aunt's house with a changed attitude. Within this action the characters' dialogue can be developed. That dialogue may also link one type of action to another.

When writing the action and dialogue, remember to make both as realistic as possible. In real life no one lives from one action packed event to another. Life just doesn't happen that way. Sometimes people just stand around talking. This kind of stationary action is fine in a story. Whether the action is moving or stationary, when writing the dialogue concentrate on writing interesting dialogue. You can include descriptions of the scenery, characters, and other information that creates a visual picture in a reader's mind.

Once all of the action and dialogue are written, an ending must be determined. A good ending will carefully bring the narrative to a conclusion that resolves the story and satisfies the reader that the story is complete. Endings that resolve a story show how the events or drama of a story turns out or how the characters learned to deal with a challenging situation. These endings may solve a problem or reveal something which indicates the story is complete.

You have learned much about writing stories. There is still one more thing to know. In order to be a successful writer, you must write, write, write, and write some more! So, get started by reading **WRITING ASSIGNMENT #15** on page 148. As you write, complete the grammar lessons and prepare your composition on clean writing paper. If you have any questions please ask your teacher. When you begin to work on your story, think about the real life, scriptural lessons you have learned. Make lots of notes on what you know before writing your story. Those notes will help you to write a good story.

WRITING ASSIGNMENT #15

Your assignment is to write a **story of your choosing** where the main character has **a problem to solve**. For the plot of the story, include at least 2-3 events that try to help the main character solve his/her problem.

Make at least one of your events a conversation that helps the main character in some way to solve his/her problem. Use conversation as well as narrative to describe the people and scene. The story must be 3-5 pages. Remember to work on your own. Make your story, action, and conversation original but believable and realistic.

1. **Format**
   - [ ] Write a title at the top of the page and write your name under this title.
   - [ ] Begin the opening paragraph on the second line below your name.
2. **Construction**
   - [ ] Write a **three to five** page paper.
   - [ ] Your story must follow this outline.
       1. **Open story and introduce characters**
       2. **Character discovers problem and begins adventure**
       3. **Develop readers understanding of the problem and adventure through action and conversation**
       4. **Character tries to solve problem**
       5. **Character solves problem**
       6. **Story winds down and ends**
   - [ ] Each direct quotation must have a name in the explanatory words that identifies who is speaking.
   - [ ] Include descriptions of the characters, scenery and action.
   - [ ] Write **one** closing paragraph that ends the story.
3. **Grammar**
   - [ ] Use proper punctuation, indentation, and capitalization.
   - [ ] Draw quotation marks at the beginning and end of all direct quotations.
   - [ ] In the explanatory words, be careful that your names and your descriptions have the correct punctuation.
   - [ ] Use proper word tenses.
   - [ ] Write a variety of paragraph sentences that are related to one another.
   - [ ] Indent your paragraphs.
   - [ ] Each paragraph must contain unity, flow logically, and relate to one another.
4. **Polish**
   - [ ] Only turn in a final copy of your paper that has been written neatly.
   - [ ] Make sure you have spelled all of your words correctly.
   - [ ] Use the dictionary to check spelling and the Thesaurus to find extra words.
5. **Ethics**
   - [ ] Work on your own and make the dialogue original.
   - [ ] Do not write about anything that is an inappropriate subject of a dialogue.
   - [ ] Make sure the language of your paper conforms to Philippians 4:8.
   - [ ] Could your paper be of help to someone who may read it?

CHAPTER 24

PLOT: GRAMMAR SKILLS

24.1 Grammar Rules

Writing a good story takes practice. Punctuating your writing correctly is also important. In this chapter, you will learn about hyphens, semicolons, and paragraph margins. Read each grammar rule and do the **PRACTICE** exercises. When working on your writing assignments, remember to follow these rules.

24.2 Hyphens

The hyphen is a type of punctuation that is important to good communication. The **hyphen** is a short line (-) that is drawn between the two words of some compound words. Remember a compound word is one big word made up of two independent words, like jellyfish, bookmark, and textbook. There are several types of compound words that require a hyphen. The next three rules will teach you about the compound words that require hyphens. The first rule concerns the writing of compound words that represent the numbers 21-99.

> ### RULE #1
> When a number from 21-99 is written as a compound word,
> a **hyphen is drawn between** the **two individual number words**.

EXAMPLE:
twenty-one

PRACTICE: Write each of these **numbers** as a **compound word** with a **hyphen**.

A. 32 _____
B. 26 _____
C. 55 _____
D. 84 _____

E. 43 _____
F. 71 _____
G. 67 _____
H. 98 _____

24.3 Hyphens

The hyphen is a type of punctuation about which you are learning. Drawing a hyphen is easy, but you will not use it very often in writing. The **hyphen** is a short line (-) that is drawn between the two words of some compound words. Remember a compound word is one big word made up of two independent words, like outlook, workbook, and notebook.

There are several types of compound words, however, that require a hyphen. The first rule taught you to draw a hyphen between the two words for numbers 21-99 when they are written as words. The second rule has to do with compound words that contain the word **all**.

> ### RULE #2
> When the word **all** is used in **a compound word** so that the meaning of the compound word suggests **that it covers everything**, the compound word is **hyphenated**. For exceptions to this rule, check the dictionary.

EXAMPLE:
all-knowing

PRACTICE: On the next page, make **compound words** out of the following words. Write each compound word beginning with the word **all** and draw a **hyphen** where it belongs.

| powerful | inclusive | fired | right | clear | important |

A._____ D._____
B._____ E._____
C._____ F._____

When writing your story, try to use a few hyphenated words in your writing. This will help you to remember how to form hyphenated words and will also help you to be comfortable with using them in your writing.

24.4 Hyphens

The hyphen is a type of punctuation that is easy to draw, but not used very often in writing. The **hyphen** is a short line (-) that is drawn between the two words of some compound words. Remember a compound word is one big word made up of two independent words, like washroom, cookbook, fireplace, stovepipe, and popcorn.

There are several types of compound words that require a hyphen. The first rule taught you to place a hyphen between the two words for numbers 21-99 when they are written as words. Next, you learned about hyphenating some compound words that contain the word **all**. The third rule of hyphens covers compound words that are used to compare,

---
RULE #3
When a compound word contains **a comparison word** and the compound word is written before a **noun, the comparison word is hyphenated**.
Examples of comparison words include **better**, **best**, **lesser**, **little**, and **well**.

EXAMPLE:
well-mannered child

PRACTICE: Rewrite the following **phrases** drawing a **hyphen** where it is needed.

A. little liked clam_____
B. better known fact_____
C. best loved bicycle_____
D. lesser valued item_____
E. well done paper_____

When writing your story, try a few hyphenated words in your writing. This will help you to remember how to form hyphenated words and will also help you to be comfortable with using them in your writing.

24.5 Semicolons

The semicolon is a type of punctuation mark that is important. The **semicolon** has both a period and a comma, one on top of the other (;). There are three rules for the use of the semicolon. The first rule is about putting two sentences together.

RULE #1
Use a **semicolon** between **two parts of a sentence** that can stand alone as individual sentences.

EXAMPLES:
♦**Susan got the mail;** Jonathan opened each letter.
   (These can be two sentences.)
  Susan got the mail. Jonathan opened each letter.
♦**The president was in his office;** the vice-president was speaking to him.
   (These can be two sentences.)
  The president was in his office. The vice-president was speaking to him.

♦**The intern wanted a job;** the company was looking for an employee.
   (These can be two sentences.)
  The intern wanted a job. The company was looking for an employee.

Study these examples until you can complete the **PRACTICE** exercise yourself.

PRACTICE: In each of these sentences, draw a **semicolon** where it is needed.

A. The lake was iced over the skaters were having fun.
B. Malcolm was a cab driver Marcus was a cook.
C. The roof was under construction the frame of the house was complete.
D. The printer was printing steadily the books would be ready soon.
E. The park is for playing the school is for learning.

In your story, did you write a sentence with two parts that can stand alone as two sentences? Did you connect the two sentences with a semicolon?

24.7 Semicolons
Knowing how to use the semicolon is important. The **semicolon** has both a period and a comma, one on top of the other (;). There are three rules for the use of the semicolon. The third rule is about long sentences with at least two parts, where each part already contains a comma.

> **RULE #3**
> A **semicolon** is used to separate two independent **sentence parts that already contain commas**.

EXAMPLE:
♦**On the first day, Yahweh created day and night;** on the seventh day, Yahweh rested.

PRACTICE: In each of these sentences, draw a **semicolon** between the parts with **commas**.

A. In the airplane, the passengers were ready in the terminal, the passengers waited.
B. In the evening, we catch fireflies in the morning, we let them go.
C. In the morning, I study math in the afternoon, I study history.

In your story, did you write two sentences that already contain commas and could be connected with a semicolon? If so, insert a semicolon and transition word where they belong.

24.6 Semicolons

The semicolon is an important type of punctuation. The **semicolon** has both a period and a comma, one on top of the other (;). There are three rules for the use of the semicolon. The second rule is about **transition words**. When a long sentence contains two individual sentences, sometimes a **transition word** is used to cause a smooth flow from the first sentence to the second sentence.

> **RULE #2**
> If in a sentence you use a **transition word**, such as **therefore**, **however**, **likewise**, etc., you must still use a semicolon **between** the two parts of a sentence that can stand alone as individual sentences.

In each one of the following examples, there are two separate sentences that are connected together using a semicolon and a transition word. Notice how the semicolon is placed **before** the transition word in each example.

EXAMPLES:

♦**The five o'clock bell sounded; therefore,** I stopped working.
    (These can be two sentences.)
The five o'clock bell sounded. I stopped working.

♦**The farmer set out to hoe his garden; however,** the garden was not weedy.
    (These can be two sentences.)
The farmer set out to hoe his garden. The garden was not weedy.

♦**Daniel made his bed; likewise,** His little brother picked up his toys.
    (These can be two sentences.)
Daniel made his bed. His little brother picked up his toys.

Did you see where the semicolon and the transition word were added? Did you notice that the semicolon was added **before** the transition word? Study these examples until you can complete the **PRACTICE** exercise yourself.

PRACTICE: Add a **semicolon** to each of these sentences where it is needed.

A. Jessica was a mother moreover, she was a good mother.
B. Warren was a student indeed, he was home schooled.
C. The baby was fine however, she was not hungry.
D. The dinner was almost ready thus, the children set the table.
E. The lights were out therefore, the electrician replaced them.

 In your story, did you write two sentences that can be connected with a semicolon and a transition word? If so, insert a semicolon and transition word where they belong.

24.8 Paragraph Margins

All paragraphs must have **margins** that are as straight as possible on both the left and right sides of the page. When a book report is typed on the computer, this goal may be accomplished by using the **justify** button.

GLOSSARY

Characters: the people in a story
Creative writing: the art of using inventiveness in writing
Description: the use of words to draw a picture
Dialogue: the conversation in a story
Dictionary: a book containing an alphabetical listing of words, with definitions and other information about those words
Explanatory words: the words that tell information about the speaker of a conversation
Fiction: a made up story with made up characters and events
Name of direct address: the name of the person to whom a character is speaking that is contained within the words of the direct address
Nonfiction: a true story with real characters and events
Object: a person or material thing that can be seen or touched
Paragraph: a grouping of related sentences, usually about one topic
Personality: a person's unique patterns of habit as well as unique physical and mental types of behavior
Quotation marks: a set of punctuation marks used to enclose a direct quotation
Scene: the place of action or setting in a story; consists of depth as well as animate and inanimate objects
Sentence: a word or group of words that express a complete thought
Story: a true or made up compilation of related events, images, feelings, objects, and people that when combined together to create an informative or interesting tale
Style: the unique manner or way in which a writer uses words in writing
Synonym: a word with the same meaning or nearly the same meaning as another word
Thesaurus: a reference book in alphabetical order, containing many descriptive or useful words, synonyms, and antonyms
Topic: the subject of a paragraph or the subject for discussion or conversation; the one idea or object about which the rest of the sentences in the paragraph are written

INDEX

A

Action
    an outdoor event 74-77
    plot 144-145
    realistic 146
    in a scene 33-34
    words 19, 33, 62, 113
Action verbs 62, 113
Adjectives 60-62
And
    "and, or, but" 86-87
    too many 23-24
Apostrophes
    contractions 109-111
    possessive 111-113
Appositives 127-129

B

Behaviors 54, 76-77
But, and, or 86-87

C

Capitalization
    common and proper noun pairs 44-45
    the first word in a sentence 20
    nouns and pronouns of the Trinity 45-46
    a person's name 20
Characters
    accessories 54-55, 76
    behaviors 54, 76-77
    clothing 54-55, 76
    definition 52, 153
    description 53-55, 75-76
    features 53-54
    identifying 52-53
    names 52-53
    personalities 54
Creative writing 7, 153
Colons
    introducing a formal quotation 131-132
    introducing a list 129-130
    introducing a statement 130-131
    to separate numbers 132
Commas
    with adjectives 61-62
    with appositives 127-129
    with sentence conjunctions 86-87
    in a series 22-23
Common nouns 43-45
Compound subjects 85-86
Compound predicates 85-86
Concise sentences 87
Conjunctions 86-87
Contractions 109-111

D

Declarative sentences 21
Describing 8-15
Description 8-15, 153
Dialogue
    creating 92, 102-103
    definition 91, 153
    explanatory words 103-104
    purpose 121-123
    in a story 91-92
Dictionary 67, 153

E

Exclamation points 21-22
Exclamatory sentences 21-22
Explanatory words
    definition 103, 153
    in dialogue 103-104
    imbedded 123

F

Fiction 80, 153
Fragments, sentence 65-66
Future tense 24, 113-114

G

Grading charts 163-164
Grammar rules 20, 40, 60, 81, 95, 109, 127, 149

H

Have, has, had 82, 109-110
Helping Verbs 63-65, 113-114
Homonyms 66-67
Hyphens
    comparison words 150
    number words 149
    with the word "all" 149-150

I

Imperative sentences 21
Indention of paragraphs 26
Interjections 96-97
Irregular verbs
    future 113
    past participle 113-114
    past tense 83, 113
    present 83, 113

J

Joining words 86-87

L

Lay and lie 114-115

N

Names of direct address
    in dialogue 96
    definition 153
Nonfiction 80, 153
Nouns
    common 43-45
    definition 40
    idea 42-43
    pairs, common and proper 44-45
    person 40-41
    place 41
    proper 43-46
    thing 42

O

Object
    definition 153
    words 10-11, 42
Or, and, but 86-87

P

Paragraphs
    definition 153
    indention 26
    margins 152
Past participles 111-112
Past tense
    irregular verb 83, 113
    participles 113-114
    subject/verb agreement 81-82
    verb spelling changes 82-83
    use of 24
Periods
    declarative sentences 21
    imperative sentences 21
Personality
    definition 153
    describing 54
Plagiarism 6
Plots 144-145
Possessive nouns 111-113
Predicates 65-66, 85-86
Present tense
    subject/verb agreement 62-63, 81-82
    use of 24
Pronouns 45-46
Proper nouns 43-46

Q

Quotations
    definition 95, 153
    marks 95-96
    names of direct address 96

S

Scenes
    action in 33-34
    definition 153
    details 14-15
    development 32-33
    qualities 31-32
    of a story 13-14
Scriptural ethics 7-8, 30-31, 50-52, 71-74, 90-91,
    100-102, 119-121, 136-144
Semicolons
    connecting sentence parts with commas 152
    connecting stand-alone sentences 150-151
    with transition words 151-152
Sentences
    concise 87
    conjunctions 86-87
    combining 85-86
    complete, rules for 66
    declarative 21
    definition 153
    exclamatory 21-22
    fragments 65-66
    imperative 21
    length 24-25
    similar 84-85
    statements 21
    subject/predicate 65-66
    subject/verb agreement
        past tense 81-82
        present tense 62-63
Sentence variety 84-86
Set and sit 115-116
Statements 21
Stories 137-138, 142-144, 153
Styles
    definition 34, 153
    of writing 34-35
Subjects 62-63, 65-66, 81-82, 85-86
Subject/verb agreement
    past tense 81-82
    present tense 62-63
Synonyms 67, 153

T

Thesaurus 67, 153
Topic
    definition 6, 153
    of a paragraph 15
Trinity 45-46

V

Verbs
    action 62, 113
    agreement 62-63, 81-82
    being 62, 113
    "have" 82, 113-114
    helping 63-65, 113-114
    irregular verbs, past tense 83
    participles 113-114
    past tense verb spelling changes 82-83
    plural 63
    present tense 62-63
    present/past/future tense 24, 113-114
    singular 63
    tense 24
    "to be" 62, 82

W

Writing
    assignments 17, 28, 37, 48, 57, 69, 79, 89,
        93, 99, 106, 118, 124, 134, 148
    charts 16, 27, 36, 47, 56, 68, 78, 88, 93, 98,
        105, 117, 133
    choices 7
    creative 7, 153
    fiction 80, 153
    nonfiction 80, 153
    styles 34-35
    worksheets 18, 29, 38, 49, 58, 70, 135

RESURRECTION RESOURCES PRODUCTS

BIBLE

SCRIPTURES

ENGLISH

GRADESMART TEXTBOOKS

ENGLISH AND WRITING:
GRADE 5
GRADE 6
GRADE 7
GRADE 8

CHRISTIAN LITERATURE AND WRITING:
GRADE 9

PACESETTER TEXTBOOKS

BOOK REPORTS

CREATIVE WRITING

ESSAYS AND RESEARCH REPORTS:
LEVEL A
LEVEL B

HISTORY

PACESETTER BOOKS

THE SIGNERS OF THE
DECLARATION OF INDEPENDENCE

THE SIGNERS OF THE
UNITED STATES CONSTITUTION

MATH

GRADESMART TEXTBOOKS

MATH:
KINDERGARTEN
FIRST GRADE

SCIENCE

GRADESMART TEXTBOOKS

SCIENCE:
GRADE 7
GRADE 8

PACESETTER TEXTBOOKS

LAB REPORTS:
GRADES 3-12
COLLEGE

MORE LAB REPORTS:
LEVEL ONE
LEVEL TWO

SCIENCE SUPPLIES

LAB EQUIPMENT

LAB KITS

THE PERIODIC TABLE OF THE ELEMENTS

SCHOOL SUPPLIES

ART PACKS

ERASERS

HOME SCHOOL DAILY PLANNER

PENCILS

TO ORDER PRODUCTS ON-LINE:
www.thefathersbooks.com

ANSWER KEY
PRACTICE EXERCISES

UNIT 1

Page 20
PRACTICE
A. **T**hat flower is red.
B. **T**he tree is big.
C. **W**ater was everywhere.
D. **S**wimming is fun.
E. **S**ailing is swell.
F. **F**ishing requires patience.
PRACTICE
A. **R**alph   E. **J**enny
B. **A**lex   F. **P**eter
C. **M**ark   G. **S**arah
D. **C**indy   H. **M**oses

Page 21
PRACTICE
A. That seagull is big.
B. The barn is red.
E. There are two chairs on the patio.
F. Michael caught several fish.
PRACTICE
A. Help me put the pickles in the jars.
C. Ride your bike to the end of the street.
D. Drink all of the milk in the glass.
F. Please help me carry the packages.

Page 22
PRACTICE
A. That's the most beautiful color I've ever seen!
C. What a great surprise!
D. Last night's music concert was spectacular!
F. The stars are extremely bright tonight!
PRACTICE
A. Ellen, Rita, and Jeff went sledding with their fathers.
B. Jenna, Joleen, and Jasmine planned a party for their new friend.
C. I went to the play with Rebecca, Amy, and Joanna.
D. I sang in the choir with Arnold, Hal, and Kevin.
E. Sonia, Gerald, and Louise went to visit their grandparents across the street.
F. I will call Eric, Alice, and Tom to dinner.

Page 22-23
PRACTICE
A. My bike, skates, and sled are all blue.
B. A goose, duck, and frog were sitting beside the lake.
C. The coral reef was in shades of pink, orange, and yellow.
D. The new sweater was soft, white, and pretty.
E. Those bananas are long, yellow, and ripe.
F. His face was familiar, friendly, and kind.

Page 23-24
PRACTICE
Possible answers:
A. The grocery store was crowded. Many people were shopping. They all were buying food.
B. The sun was bright, making the desert air very dry. The sand under my feet was hot.
C. The hikers were walking uphill while they were talking to each other. They were telling funny stories.
D. For lunch I ate a hamburger with some french fries. I also drank a vanilla shake.

Page 25
PRACTICE
Examples:
A. We went camping in a tent for our vacation last year. Before that, we stayed in a hotel.
B. The night was dark. In the warm air, the birds were quiet.
C. Mosheh/Moses was a leading prophet. He was also a husband and a father.
D. Tommy played in the sand. He built a castle and dug a canal. When he was done, Tommy filled the canal with water.

Page 26
PRACTICE
    Joseph/Yoseph wanted to obey Yahweh. He wanted to protect his family and give his family a good life. When the angel of God told him to leave Bethlehem/Beth Lehem, he listened and did what he was told. Yoseph took his small family to Israel/Yisrael.
    The janitor at the Philpod's Company worked late at night after all of the employees had gone home. He liked the quiet of the evening hours because he could complete his work faster. Every night he remembered the employees of the day hours and how hard they had worked. Knowing that he personally could make their daytime hours more comfortable and pleasant, he tried earnestly to clean each employee's office as if it were his own.

Page 40
PRACTICE
PERSON: mom, dad, etc.
PLACE: park, ocean, etc.
THING: pen, book, etc.
IDEA: love, mercy, etc.
PRACTICE
car	skates	book
doctor	walnut	teacher
building	banana	

Page 40-41
PRACTICE
mother, daughter, baby, sister, etc.
father, son, brother, nephew, etc.

Page 41
PRACTICE
teacher, banker, barber, etc.
PRACTICE
| fellow | human | man or men |
PRACTICE
| **ocean** | lake | pool |
| **beach** | river | stream |
PRACTICE
| **desert** | valley | canyon |

PRACTICE
zoo   volcano   camp   theater   mountain or fountain

Page 42
PRACTICE
flower, weed, hose, snail, etc.
rake, hoe, wheelbarrow, grass, etc.

PRACTICE
Buildings: store, garage, house, etc.
Vehicles: car, truck, camper, etc.
Animals: cat, dog, mouse, etc.
Plants: tree, rose, weed, etc.
Tools: hammer, saw, wrench, etc.

PRACTICE
porch   river   tree   brook

PRACTICE
love, hate, sorrow, etc.
joy, content, pleased, etc.

Page 42-43
PRACTICE
goodness, kindness, gentleness, friendliness, helpfulness, etc.

Page 43
PRACTICE
tantrum   fit   kindness   charity

PRACTICE
Kim   Antarctica
Venus   Texas

Page 44
PRACTICE
The common nouns are identified in **bold** print.
1. The **postal route** was out of the way for Bob Stewart.
2. Flora pruned the **roses** in her **garden** in February.
3. My **sister** likes to look for **seashells** at the **beach** near Oceanside.
4. **Money** is not to waste but to use with care.
5. When **winter** is over, we will happily travel to Iowa and Minnesota to visit **friends**.

Page 45
PRACTICE
A. **M**ount **B**aldy   D. **M**issouri **R**iver
B. **S**uez **C**anal   E. **L**ake **E**rie
C. **O**hio **D**rive   F. **N**iagara **F**alls

Page 46
PRACTICE
A. Show me **Y**our ways, O **Y**ahweh; teach me **Y**our paths.
B. And **H**e said, "**A**bba, **F**ather, all is possible for **Y**ou. Make this cup pass from **M**e. Yet not what I desire, but what **Y**ou desire."
C. And turning around and seeing **H**is taught ones, **H**e rebuked Kepha/Steven, saying, "Get behind **M**e, Satan! For your thoughts are not those of **E**lohim, but those of men."

Page 60
PRACTICE
The adjectives are identified in **bold** print.
A. The **gold** medal was won by a **great** athlete.
B. She had a **big** umbrella.
C. The **slow** elephant walked down the road.
D. The sky turned **pink** and **purple** just before sunset.
E. Inside the building, a **round** fountain made a **musical** sound.
F. Bananas are **sweet** and **soft** when they are **ripe**.

Page 61-62
PRACTICE
A. The huge, brick house was built on a hill.
B. The soft, green grass was wet with dew.
C. The winter white paint was perfect for the kitchen pantry.
D. The tall, long fence surrounded a small garden house.
E. Father added a log to the hot, flamy fire.
F. The large Monday brunch started before all of the guests arrived.

Page 62
PRACTICE
The action verbs are identified in **bold** print.
A. My dog likes to **run** fast.
B. Jesse **closed** the window.
C. The ballerina **twirled** on her toes.
D. The band **marched** around the block.
E. Lisa **braided** her long hair.

PRACTICE
The being verbs are identified in **bold** print.
A. Tony **was** a basketball player.
B. The pasture **is** green.
C. I **am** very cold.
D. Doughnuts **are** yummy!
E. There **are** four grandparents with homes on my street.

Page 63
PRACTICE
A. likes   D. jumps
B. throws   E. sharpens
C. takes   F. buys

PRACTICE
A. give   D. help
B. pick   E. weed
C. sing

Page 65
PRACTICE
A. rolled   D. blinked
B. flew   E. watered
C. floated

PRACTICE
A. giggled, told   D. ate
B. is   E. hit, shouted
C. slept, played

PRACTICE
A. was
B. should

C. can
D. would
E. may
PRACTICE
A. would have
B. might have
C. had been
D. should have
E. have been

Page 66
PRACTICE
C. ~~King Shaul/Saul the first~~.
D. ~~Shall not want~~.
F. ~~Golyath/Goliath was taller than~~.

Page 67
PRACTICE
A. blue
B. four
C. here
D. in
E. know
F. pair
G. sew
H. their
I. Where
J. week

Page 82
PRACTICE
A. rowed
B. watered
C. cleaned
D. cooked
E. tested
F. sewed
G. backed
H. smoothed
I. aligned
J. touched
K. clicked
L. stayed

PRACTICE
A. was
B. had
C. were
D. had
E. were

Page 82-83
PRACTICE
A. bounced
B. heaved
C. shamed
D. staked
E. pleased
F. seized

Page 83
PRACTICE
A. pitted
B. tipped
C. zipped
D. petted
E. stepped
F. plotted
G. stopped
H. blurred
I. chatted

PRACTICE
A. testified
B. curried
C. allied
D. varied
E. classified
F. clarified

Page 84
PRACTICE
Each sentence must begin with different words, such as in these examples.
A. A lady was wearing a pretty dress. When the weather became cold, she put on a hat. Then she slipped on a coat.
B. The wedding was fun. All of the guests were happy. The ceremony took place outside.
C. The wedding cake was three tiers tall. Inside, the cake was chocolate with white frosting. Everyone agreed that the cake tasted very good.
D. The biggest presents were from the cousins. They were wrapped with pretty paper and bows.

Page 85
PRACTICE
Each sentence must end with different words, such as in these examples.
A. The pool party was a lot of fun. Splashing around, I swam to the steps. Sunning on the deck gave me a nice tan.
B. The birthday party had a special theme. The decorations were covered with cowboys. The gifts were all supposed to contain cowboy toys.
C. The retirement party was about to begin. The guests were all on board the boat. The food was all ready to eat.
D. The day was very wet and rainy. The picnic was cancelled because of the rain. The roads were also closed because they were overflowing with rain water.

Page 86
PRACTICE
A. The policeman waited at the stoplight and stayed in his car.
B. The carpenters and the roofers were working on the house.
C. The scientist mixed the solids and stirred the liquids.
D. The accountant and the banker counted the money.

Page 87
PRACTICE
A. The salesclerk completed the sale, **and** the customer went home happy.
B. Is the milking machine clean, **or** does it need to be sterilized?
C. The baker made the bread, **but** the pastry chef baked the cake.

Page 96
PRACTICE
A. Sue   "I need more exercise. Will you go for a walk with me?"
B. John   "I would like some more milk, please."
C. Blake   "If you finish your project today, it will be completed before the May 1 deadline."
D. Terrance   "The windows need to be shut. May I have a volunteer?"

PRACTICE
A. "Sally, I really care about your safety."
B. "I will pray for you, Luke."
C. "Molly, that was a delicious meal."
D. "I hope you come visit soon, Annie."

Page 97
PRACTICE
A. "No! I refuse to tell a lie."
B. "Oh! How did you surprise me and arrived so quickly?"
C. "Ow! I stubbed my toe on the door!"

PRACTICE
A. "Oh, I think I'll just rest for an hour."
B. "Yes, the game starts at six o'clock."
C. "Well, let's think of a better solution."

Page 109
PRACTICE
A. weren't
B. wasn't
C. wouldn't
D hadn't
E. shouldn't
F. didn't

Page 109-110
PRACTICE
A. you've
B. we've
C. she's
D. they've
E. they'd
F. she'd
G. we'd
H. it's

Page 110
PRACTICE
A. You've
B. no contraction
C. we've
D no contraction
E. it's
F. no contraction

Page 111
PRACTICE
A. Todd's hat was on his head.
B. Tricia's blue doll was lost.
C. Phil's home was across town.
D. Stacy's coat was in the closet.
E. Bill's umbrella had a hole in it.

Page 112
PRACTICE
A. The sheep's wool was very thick.
B. The deer's families were nearby.
C. The geese's babies were quite large.
D. The women's party was a fun event.

Page 112-113
PRACTICE
A. The twins' lunches were ready to eat.
B. The five boys' party hats were on the table.
C. All of our players' parents attended the game.
D. The three families' camping equipment was loaded into the bus.

Page 113
PRACTICE
A. have or had jumped
B. have or had stopped
C. has or had clarified
D. had chatted

Page 114
PRACTICE
A. had slept
B. had taken
C. had gone
D. had done

Page 115
PRACTICE
A. lays or laid
B. laid
C. This sentence does not use a form of lay.
D. lay or laid
E. laid

PRACTICE
A. lies or lay
B. lie
C. This sentence does not use a form of lie.
D. lay
E. lain

Page 116
PRACTICE
A. set or sets
B. sets or set
C. set
D. This sentence does not use a form of set.

PRACTICE
A. sits or sat
B. sat
C. sat

Page 128
PRACTICE
A. My math teacher, **Mr. Gun**, likes for us to recite the multiplication tables.
B. That piece of fabric, **the calico print**, is very colorful.
C. The new gas station, **Gas-n-Go**, is very large and clean.
D. My only cousin, **Nathan Bosch**, is fun to visit.
E. The tulip, **a member of the lily family**, blooms in the early spring.
F. Everyone, **boys and girls alike**, went for a sled ride down the hill.

Page 128-129
PRACTICE
A. Yahweh's Son, **Yahshua**, worked as a carpenter in Nazareth/Natsareth.
B. Their team, **the fastest runners**, won the trophy.
C. We **boys** are going to shoot some baskets.
D. A cocoon holds a caterpillar, **a future butterfly**.
E. In science we learned about tarantulas, **part of the spider family**.
F. The Tehillim/Psalms are written mostly by Dawid/David, **a man after Yahweh's own heart**.
G. I treasure my new book bag, **a gift from my grandmother**.
H. My favorite story is in the book <u>Little Women</u>.

Page 129
PRACTICE
(Possible answers)
A. George Bush, **our president**, gave his State of the Union speech last night.
B. The ice cream store, **Cool and Yummy**, was closed on Saturday.
C. The book, **Beautiful Manners**, was very helpful to read.
D. Our state, **Ohio**, is a pleasant place to live.

Page 130
PRACTICE
A. On top of the table sat three books: a dictionary, a thesaurus, and a biography.
B. We could not go to the party until two people were ready: mom and dad.
C. Tomorrow we will go shopping for food: milk, potatoes, and lettuce.
D. This sentence does not require a colon.
E. The store sold several types of clothes: pants, dresses, and coats.
F. The camping trip needed many supplies: a tent,

sleeping bags, pillows.
G. This sentence does not require a colon.
PRACTICE
The park had these events: **(student must list several events here)**.
PRACTICE
The dialogue was between several characters: **(student must list several characters here)**.

Page 130-131
PRACTICE
A. The light was very bright: it illuminated the whole room.
B. The street outside was wet: it was raining.
C. This sentence does not require a colon.
D. They took the bike to the repair shop: it as broken.
E. The muffins were almost done: they needed five more minutes to brown.
F. This sentence does not require a colon.
PRACTICE
A. The basket did not hold fruit: **(student must add his/her own statement here)**.
B. The sunset was beautiful: **(student must add his/her own statement here)**.
C. The dinner was very tasty: **(student must add his/her own statement here)**.
D. The corner store was not far away: **(student must add his/her own statement here)**.

Page 131-132
PRACTICE
A. The main character liked to shout: "I am free!"
B. My teacher always said: "Cleanliness is next to Godliness."
C. This sentence does not require a colon.
D. In the bookstore many people asked the same thing: "Where are the Bibles?"
E. The gardener was happy spring had come, he said: "Yahoo!"
F. This sentence does not require a colon.

Page 132
PRACTICE
A. My mother gave this advice: **(student must add his/her own formal quotation here)**.
B. The main character frequently said this phrase: **(student must add his/her own formal quotation here)**.
C. The children often sang this song: **(student must add his/her own formal quotation here)**.
D. Every night we pray this prayer: **(student must add his/her own formal quotation here)**.
PRACTICE
The student must make up a sentence that contains **a formal quotation** separated from the rest of the sentence by a **colon**. The sentence must be written about something that happened in the book he/she read.
PRACTICE
A. 7:00 A.M.
B. 12:00 P.M.
C. Ibrim/Hebrews 14:3
D. Shemoth/Exodus 7:10
E. 2:15 A.M.
F. Mark 2:8

Page 149
PRACTICE
A. thirty-two
B. twenty-six
C. fifty-five
D. eighty-four
E. forty-three
F. seventy-one
G. sixty-seven
H. ninety-eight

Page 150
PRACTICE
A. all-powerful
B. all-inclusive
C. all-fired
D. all-right
E. all-clear
F. all-important
PRACTICE
A. little-liked clam
B. better-known fact
C. best-loved bicycle
D. lesser-valued item
E. well-done paper

Page 151
PRACTICE
A. In the airplane, the passengers were ready; in the terminal, the passengers waited.
B. In the evening, we catch fireflies; in the morning, we let them go.
C. In the morning, I study math; in the afternoon, I study history.
E. Look at that huge flower!

Page 151-152
PRACTICE
A. The lake was iced over; the skaters were having fun.
B. Malcolm was a cab driver; Marcus was a cook.
C. The rood was under construction; the frame of the house was complete.
D. The printer was printing steadily; the books would be ready soon.
E. The park is for playing; the school is for learning.

Page 152
PRACTICE
A. Jessica was a mother; **moreover**, she was a good mother.
B. Warren was a student; **indeed**, he was home schooled.
C. The baby was fine; **however**, she was not hungry.
D. The dinner was almost ready; **thus**, the children set the table.
E. The lights were out; **therefore**, the electrician replaced them.

ANSWER KEY
TESTS

TEST #1
1. B
2. C
3. C
4. D
5. C
6. A
7. D
8. B
9.
A. The robins ate the berries.
B. **F**rank took a long walk.
C. **T**he museum was closed.
D. Help me take the groceries inside.
E. Look at that huge flower!
10.
A. Sally, Sue, and Sarah sang a lovely song together.
B. They played hopscotch, tag, and leapfrog all afternoon.
C. The best stories were written by Phil, Tom, and John.
D. Green, yellow, and white ribbons decorated the flower baskets.

TEST #2
1. D
2. C
3. B
4. A
5. C
6. B
7. C
8. A
9. C
10. D

TEST #3
1. C
2. B
3. D
4. D
5. C
6. C
7. A
8. A
9. A
10. D

TEST #4
1. A
2. D
3. C
4. B
5.
A. jumped
B. raked
C. stepped
D. allied
6.
A. slept
B. took
C. wrote
D. broke
7. Possible sentences:
A. The hat was black. On top of the hat were two feathers.
B. The lake is very large. The entire body of the lake is on a reservation.
C. Each morning we go fishing. In the afternoon, we take another hike up the mountain.
D. It is almost two o'clock. The time for your nap is getting closer.
8. Possible sentences:
A. Sailing is fun. Fishing with my dad is may favorite outdoor activity.
B. The weather is very cold. The snowman is made of white snow.
C. The garden is full of flowers. The vase is large enough to fit one dozen flowers.
D. I like tomato juice. Jeremy does not like juice made with tomatoes.
9.
A. The sisters **and** the brothers were baking bread.
B. Passover is a scriptural holiday **and** is celebrated once a year.
C. The red clay was drying in the sun **and** cracked in many places.
D. The cantaloupe **and** apple were ripe.
10. B.

TEST #5
1. B
2. D
3. C
4. A
5. B
6. C
7. A
8. D
9. A
10. C

TEST #6
1. C
2. D
3. B
4. A
5. C
6. D
7. D
8. A
9. D
10. A

TEST #7
1. D
2. B
3. A
4. D
5. C
6. C
7. A
8. B
9. C
10. D

TEST #8
1. D
2. D
3. A
4. D
5. B
6.
A. twenty-three
B. forty-five
C. seventy-eight
D. ninety-nine
E. thirty-four
7. A
8. D
9. B
10. C

GRADING CHART

WRITING ASSIGNMENT

	1	2	3	4	5	6	7
Format							
♦Does the paper have the following:							
A title at the top of the page?							
Student's name under the title?							
One empty line before the first paragraph?							
Construction							
♦Does the paper have the required:							
Words and sentences?							
Paragraphs?							
Pages?	▓	▓	▓	▓	▓		
♦Is the paper written about the assigned subject?							
Grammar							
♦Is the paper punctuated correctly:	▓						
Commas?	▓						
Periods?	▓	▓					
Question and exclamation marks?	▓						
Quotation marks?	▓	▓					
♦Are words properly capitalized?							
♦Are paragraphs indented?	▓						
♦Are word tenses correct?							
♦Is there a variety of descriptive words?							
♦Is there good usage of action words?	▓	▓	▓	▓	▓	▓	
♦Is there sentence variety?							
♦Does each paragraph contain unity, flow logically, and relate to one another?							
Polish							
♦Is the paper neat (no smudge marks, readable handwriting, etc.)?							
♦Are all words spelled correctly?							
Ethics							
♦Is the paper original?							
♦Is the language kind, good, and lovely?							
♦Is the writing about a subject that is pleasing and honorable?							
Creativity							
♦Is the paper interesting and enjoyable?							
SUBTOTAL							
DIVIDE BY	80	100	105	110	110	115	120
NEW SUBTOTAL							
TOTAL (Multiply NEW SUBTOTAL by 100%)							
GRADE							

If the student has completed an item correctly, fill in its box with the number **5** or a number less than **5** for partially correct. Do not grade boxes shaded gray.
Assign a grade as follows: 90-100% = **A**, 80-89% = **B**, 70-79% = **C**.
A paper with a grade less than 70% should be rewritten!

GRADING CHART

WRITING ASSIGNMENT

	8	9	10	11	12	13	14	15
Format								
♦Does the paper have the following:								
A title at the top of the page?								
Student's name under the title?								
One empty line before the first paragraph?								
Construction								
♦Does the paper have the required:								
Words and sentences?								▓
Direct quotations								▓
Paragraphs?		▓	▓	▓	▓	▓		
Pages?	▓	▓	▓	▓	▓	▓		
♦Is the paper written about the assigned subject?								
Grammar								
♦Is the paper punctuated correctly:								
Commas and periods?								
Question and exclamation marks?								
Quotation marks?	▓	▓						
♦Are words properly capitalized?								
♦Are paragraphs indented?		▓	▓	▓	▓	▓		
♦Are word tenses correct?								
♦Is there a variety of descriptive words?		▓	▓					
♦Is there good usage of action words?		▓	▓	▓				
♦Is there sentence variety?								
♦Does each paragraph contain unity, flow logically, and relate to one another?		▓	▓	▓	▓	▓		
Polish								
♦Is the paper neat (no smudge marks, readable handwriting, etc.)?								
♦Are all words spelled correctly?								
Ethics								
♦Is the paper original?								
♦Is the language kind, good, and lovely?								
♦Is the writing about a subject that is pleasing and honorable?								
Creativity								
♦Is the paper interesting and enjoyable?								
SUBTOTAL								
DIVIDE BY	115	90	100	100	105	105	125	115
NEW SUBTOTAL								
TOTAL (Multiply NEW SUBTOTAL by 100%)								
GRADE								

If the student has completed an item correctly, fill in its box with the number **5** or a number less than **5** for partially correct. Do not grade boxes shaded gray.
Assign a grade as follows: 90-100% = **A**, 80-89% = **B**, 70-79% = **C**.
A paper with a grade less than 70% should be rewritten!

TEST #1
MULTIPLE CHOICE

CIRCLE THE CORRECT ANSWER FOR EACH QUESTION. (5 points each question)

1. What does the art of creative writing produce?

A. a pretty picture for hanging on a wall
B. something that is good to read
C. a collage of words
D. an article for a newspaper

2. Which of the following is a bad ethical choice for creative writing?

A. fiction
B. reality
C. fantasy
D. biography

3. Philippians 4:8 teaches you _____.

A. sin sells stories
B. bookstores sell what they want, not what the customer wants
C. to think about good things
D. what Philip did for Yahshua/Jesus

4. Description is very important to creative writing because you can_____.

A. draw a mental picture with words
B. identify the names of objects
C. use object words, color words, and size words
D. all of the above

5. What is the scene of a story?

A. a flat picture on a wall
B. the character who acts badly
C. the setting where the action takes place
D. none of the above

6. A sentence with more than _____ **and(s)** should probably be rewritten.

A. one
B. two
C. three
D. four

Copyright © 2007. This page may not be copied or reproduced.

7. Verb tense is about _____.

A. how close the letters in a word are to each other
B. how close the words in a sentence are to each other
C. stress
D. time

8. The sentences in a paragraph should _____.

A. all be of the same length
B. vary in length
C. have the same number of words in them
D. all be indented five spaces from one another

FOLLOW THE INSTRUCTIONS FOR EACH QUESTION.

9. Rewrite these sentences with correct grammar. (5 points)

A. The robins ate the berries_____
B. frank took a long walk._____
C. the museum was closed._____
D. Help me take the groceries inside_____
E. Look at that huge flower_____

10. Draw commas in the correct places in each of these sentences. (4 points)

A. Sally Sue and Sarah sang a lovely song together.
B. They played hopscotch tag and leapfrog all afternoon.
C. The best stories were written by Phil Tom and John.
D. Green yellow and white ribbons decorated the flower baskets.

Grade = # points correct = _____X 100% =   %
                  49

TEST #2
MULTIPLE CHOICE

CIRCLE THE CORRECT ANSWER FOR EACH QUESTION. (5 points each question)

1. What qualities represent good, ethical writing?

A. righteousness
B. goodness
C. kindness
D. all of the above

2. What do quality words impart to a scene?

A. color
B. vigor
C. personality
D. action

3. What type of words can be used to describe a scene?

A. articles
B. color words and size words
C. pronouns
D. contractions

4. What words describe what an object is doing?

A. action words
B. describing words
C. quality words
D. all of the above

5. What is the style of a story?

A. the way the characters are dressed
B. the type of action
C. the unique use of words, phrases, and sentences
D. the type of story

6. A noun is a word for _____.

A. an adverb
B. a person, place, thing, or idea
C. a sentence conjunction
D. use when transitioning a sentence

7. A common noun is a(n) _____.

A. adjective
B. adverb
C. general word or name for a person
D. specific name or word for a person

8. A proper noun is a _____.

A. specific name for a person
B. verb substitute
C. general word or name for a person
D. contraction

9. A common noun that is paired with a proper noun should be _____.

A. indented
B. plural
C. capitalized
D. singular

10. A noun or pronoun that refers to God/Yahweh, Jesus/Yahshua, or the Holy Spirit/Ruach Hakodesh is always _____.

A. common
B. plural
C. singular
D. capitalized

Grade = # points correct = _____ X 100% =   %
         50

TEST #3
MULTIPLE CHOICE

CIRCLE THE CORRECT ANSWER FOR EACH QUESTION. (5 points each question)

1. From where does the best wisdom come?

A. mankind
B. false religions
C. Heaven
D. all of the above

2. From what does the mouth speak?

A. the overflow of the heart
B. the wisdom of the mind
C. the intelligence of the ages
D. the inner parts of the stomach

3. The people in a story are named the _____.

A. reader
B. cohorts
C. audience
D. characters

4. What can you describe about a character?

A. hair, eyes, skin
B. head, torso, legs
C. size, shape, nationality
D. all of the above

5. The personality of a character is _____.

A. the patterns of habit of a person
B. physical or mental types of behavior
C. both A and B
D. A only

6. The clothing and accessories of a character should _____.

A. never be described
B. always be described
C. be described as necessary
D. both A and B

7. A word that describes a noun by giving more information is a(n) _____.

A. adjective
B. adverb
C. pronoun
D. verb

8. A verb is a(n) _____.

A. doing or being word
B. active word
C. container for flowers
D. sentence fragment

9. A homonym is a word that _____ another word.

A. sounds like
B. is different from
C. is the opposite of
D. has the same meaning as

10. A synonym is a word that _____ another word.

A. sounds like
B. is different from
C. is the opposite of
D. has the same meaning as

Grade = # points correct = _____ X 100% = _____ %
                  50

TEST #4
MULTIPLE CHOICE

CIRCLE THE CORRECT ANSWER FOR EACH QUESTION. (5 points each question)

1. From where does salvation come?

A. belief in Jesus/Yahshua
B. belief in God/Yahweh
C. acts of kindness
D. good works

2. How can you avoid sinning?

A. live set-apart from sinners
B. choose friends that are born-again
C. choose a Christian education
D. all of the above

3. What kind of functions are natural to society?

A. sporting events
B. outdoor events
C. both A and B
D. none of the above

4. Any subject and verb that are paired must _____ one another.

A. be next to
B. agree with
C. follow
D. all of the above

FOLLOW THE INSTRUCTIONS FOR EACH QUESTION. (4 points each question)

5. On the lines provided, rewrite each of the following verbs in the past tense.

A. jump_____
B. rake_____
C. step_____
D. ally_____

6. On the lines provided, rewrite each of the following irregular verbs in the past tense.

A. sleep_____
B. take_____
C. write_____
D. break_____

Copyright © 2007. This page may not be copied or reproduced.

7. Rewrite these sentences using different words at the beginning of each sentence.

A. The hat was black. The hat had two feathers.
_____

B. The lake is very large. The lake is on a reservation.
_____

C. Each day we go fishing. Each day we take another hike up the mountain.
_____
_____

D. It is almost two o'clock. It is almost time for your nap.
_____
_____

8. Rewrite these sentences using different words at the end of each sentence.

A. Sailing is fun. Fishing with my dad is fun.
_____

B. The weather is very cold. The snowman is very cold.
_____

C. The garden is full of flowers. The vase is full of flowers.
_____

D. I like tomato juice. Jeremy does not like tomato juice.
_____

9. Rewrite each sentence into one new combined sentence using the word **and**.

A. The sisters were baking bread. The brothers were baking bread.
_____

B. Passover is a scriptural holiday. Passover is celebrated once a year.
_____
_____

C. The red clay was drying in the sun. The red clay was cracked in many places.
_____
_____

D. The cantaloupe was ripe. The apple was ripe.
_____

10. A sentence conjunction requires a _____ and a _____.

A. contraction, comma
B. conjunction, comma
C. connecting word, comma
D. comma, transition word

Grade = # points correct = _____ X 100% =   %

TEST #5
MULTIPLE CHOICE

CIRCLE THE CORRECT ANSWER FOR EACH QUESTION. (5 points each question)

1. Good conversation means that you should _____.

A. talk briefly and quickly
B. not talk too much or too fast
C. always sit down
D. never let others speak

2. When you ask someone a question, what should you do?

A. answer the question yourself before letting the person answer
B. ask the question more than once before letting the person answer
C. make funny noises to encourage the person to answer the question
D. give the person time to answer the question

3. When the conversation is not fair in a group of people, what should you do?

A. stay and be silent
B. make noises to get the attention of the group members
C. politely excuse yourself from the group
D. interrupt the conversation whenever you can

4. What are the conversations is a story named?

A. dialogue
B. chat
C. communication
D. discussion

5. When the characters are speaking in a story, is it important to know where their conversations occur?

A. no
B. yes
C. sometimes
D. once in a while

6. The exact words of a character are named the _____.

A. chit chat
B. dialogue quotation
C. direct quotation
D. individual quotation

7. What type of punctuation marks are used when writing the conversation of a character?

A. quotation marks
B. semicolons
C. hyphens
D. apostrophes

8. The punctuation marks used in a character's conversation are placed around what type of words?

A. the describing words
B. the explanatory words
C. the name of direct address
D. the direct quotation

9. What is the name of direct address?

A. the name of the character who is speaking
B. the name of the character to whom one is speaking
C. the name of the main character of the story
D. the name of the director of a play

10. What does an interjection tell a reader about a character?

A. the character is speaking
B. the character is interrupting
C. the character is excited
D. the character has just entered the scene

Grade = # points correct = _____ X 100% =   %
              50

TEST #6
MULTIPLE CHOICE

CIRCLE THE CORRECT ANSWER FOR EACH QUESTION. (5 points each question)

1. A gossip is a person who _____.

A. spreads rumors
B. talks about the private affairs of others
C. both A and B
D. none of the above

2. Slander is a type of talk that causes _____.

A. damage to another person's reputation
B. damage to another person's character
C. damage to another person's bad behavior
D. both A and B

3. The explanatory words give _____.

A. an explanation of the story
B. information about the character who is speaking
C. an explanation about the story plot
D. information about the purpose of the story

4. Which of the following dialogues is punctuated correctly?

A. Sarah's blue eyes sparkled as she said, "What a lovely day!"
B. Sarah's blue eyes sparkled as she said, "What a lovely day"!
C. Sarah's blue eyes sparkled as she said, What a lovely day!
D. "Sarah's blue eyes sparkled as she said," What a lovely day!

5. Which one of the following words is a contraction?

A. well-done
B. cannot
C. don't
D. "new life"

6. Which one of the following phrases correctly shows possession?

A. she wants a dog
B. that boys ball
C. everyone needs a notebook
D. the teacher's manual

Copyright © 2007. This page may not be copied or reproduced.

7. Which one of the following phrases correctly shows possession?

A. the sheep's wool
B. the three captains' hats
C. he will buy a basketball
D. both A and B

8. What is the past participle of a verb?

A. a past tense verb and a helping verb
B. a past tense verb and an article
C. a past event and a helping verb
D. none of the above

9. In which of the following sentences is the word **lay** used correctly?

A. He lay the book on the table yesterday.
B. The children were told to lay down on their mats.
C. The packages had lay on the porch all night long.
D. Mother lay the dishes on the table.

10. In which of the following sentences is the word **set** used correctly?

A. The janitor set the chair on top of the table.
B. Grandpa set on the coach this morning.
C. The doughnuts have set on the counter all day long.
D. none of the above

Grade = # points correct = _____ X 100% =   %
             50

TEST #7
MULTIPLE CHOICE

CIRCLE THE CORRECT ANSWER FOR EACH QUESTION. (5 points each question)

1. Which of the following is true?

A. Random talk can interfere with God's/Yahweh's work.
B. You should guard your conversations and behavior.
C. You should be careful and wise when you speak.
D. all of the above

2. A person who has feelings and understanding will most likely speak _____.

A. foolishly
B. wisely
C. mysteriously
D. none of the above

3. A wise person who shares knowledge carefully makes that knowledge a _____.

A. blessing to others
B. proverb
C. not needed or helpful
D. all of the above

4. A fool is not filled with wisdom so he/she cannot _____.

A. share wisdom
B. understand wisdom
C. be a blessing to others
D. all of the above

5. A dialogue has purpose when it discusses or reveals something _____.

A. important to the story
B. important to the characters
C. both A and B
D. none of the above

6. Which of the following sentences contains an appositive?

A. The baker made bread; the chemist made plastics.
B. The farmer tilled his field; thus, the farmer's wife hoed her vegetable garden.
C. The summer festival, Celebrate Our Messiah, was on a lovely, warm day.
D. The tree, tall and majestic, was covered with snow.

7. Which of the following sentences uses a colon to properly introduce a list?

A. The three wise men brought these gifts: frankincense, gold, and myrrh.
B. The sailor's uniform was neat and clean: the fabric was white with blue stripes.
C. The announcer at the baseball game began the game with these words: "Play ball!"
D. none of the above

8. Which of the following sentences uses a colon to properly introduce a statement?

A. The three wise men brought these gifts: frankincense, gold, and myrrh.
B. The sailor's uniform was neat and clean: the fabric was white with blue stripes.
C. The announcer at the baseball game began the game with these words: "Play ball!"
D. none of the above

9. Which of the following sentences uses a colon to properly introduce a formal quotation?

A. The three wise men brought these gifts: frankincense, gold, and myrrh.
B. The sailor's uniform was neat and clean: the fabric was white with blue stripes.
C. The announcer at the baseball game began the game with these words: "Play ball!"
D. none of the above

10. Which of the following is punctuated correctly?

A. 2-30 P.M.
B. Ibrim/Hebrews 10;12
C. both A and B
D. Mark 2:13

Grade = # points correct = _____ X 100% =   %
              50

TEST #8
MULTIPLE CHOICE

CIRCLE THE CORRECT ANSWER FOR EACH QUESTION. (5 points each question)

1. A story may contain an opinion or point of view to _____.

A. convince others that a certain opinion or point of view is right
B. teach a scriptural truth
C. know what the opinion of the author is
D. all of the above

2. When writing a story containing a scriptural truth you must _____.

A. study the New Testament
B. study the Old Testament
C. understand how to deal with contradictory verses
D. all of the above

3. When teaching scriptural truth, whose point of view must you teach?

A. God's/Yahweh's
B. yours
C. the world's
D. all of the above

4. The plot of a story is _____.

A. how a story is arranged, the action, the series of events, and the purpose of the story
B. the overall plan of action in a story that is carefully worked out
C. a diagram of the story
D. both A and B

5. The action of a story must _____.

A. always thrill the reader
B. be believable in the reality of the universe
C. have a few dead-ends
D. always be spectacular

6. Correctly write each of these numbers as a compound word.

A. 23 _____
B. 45 _____
C. 78 _____
D. 99 _____
E. 34 _____

7. Which of the following is hyphenated correctly?

A. all-powerful
B. all-boys
C. all-night
D. all-done

8. Which of the following is punctuated properly?

A. well-done
B. well-kept secret
C. all-complete
D. both A and B

9. Which of the following sentences needs a semicolon?

A. The rabbit liked to eat carrots, lettuce, and hostas.
B. The sun was setting therefore, we stopped working.
C. In the morning I will get some fresh milk for breakfast.
D. The cattle were lowing as the baby slept.

10. Which of the following sentences needs a semicolon?

A. The airplane destinations were the following Dallas, Fort Worth, and San Antonio.
B. In the story the main character married a nice man.
C. In the ocean, we swim on the sand, we sunbathe.
D. none of the above

Grade = # points correct = _____ X 100% = _____ %
     50